Sociology: an Introductory Course

P. L. Selfe

NELSON

Thomas Nelson and Sons Ltd.
Lincoln Way Windmill Road
Sunbury-on-Thames Middlesex TW16 7HP
P.O. Box 73146 Nairobi Kenya

Thomas Nelson (Australia) Ltd.
19–39 Jeffcott Street West Melbourne Victoria 3003

Thomas Nelson and Sons (Canada) Ltd
81 Curlew Drive Don Mills Ontario

Thomas Nelson (Nigeria) Ltd.
8 Ilupeju Bypass PMB 1303 Ikeja Lagos

First published in 1975   ISBN 0 17 448100 4
Reprinted 1976 (twice), 1977
© P. L. Selfe 1975

Photoset in Malta
by St Paul's Press Ltd.
Printed in U.K.
by The Camelot Press Ltd,
Southampton

Contents

Preface

The purpose of this book is to provide a comprehensive introduction to the principles and methods of Sociology. Its format has been determined largely by the needs of students who are undertaking the subject for the G.C.E. Ordinary Level and equivalent examinations and who have little or no previous experience of its scope.

The book will enable the newcomer to Sociology to grasp the basic concepts and facts of the subject quickly and will help him to interpret relevant material in a scientific and sociological way. The areas in which the student will be examined are fully covered, the emphasis being mainly on the social structure of Britain.

To assist the newcomer, clear definitions of terminology are provided, together with suggested reading and a list of useful teaching resources, including films, filmstrips, and publications. Short extracts or summaries from research material appear throughout the book, so that the student can see how a sociologist endeavours to gain his information and interpret it, and how he builds his theories about the nature of society.

The book is aimed to meet the growing demand for a comprehensive text in Sociology as it becomes more popular as an examination subject. However, the areas which it covers will also provide a source of discussion and debate for others who wish to deepen their understanding and gain a sociological perspective on the society in which we live. The details and data with which the book deals should provide a greater insight for the school leaver into the nature of the social world that he is about to enter, and it will serve as a useful background book for students studying allied subjects.

The preparation of this book has been greatly facilitated by advice and guidance from Dr K. W. Watkins, to whom I am deeply grateful.

P.L.S.

Acknowledgements

Thanks are due to the following for permission to reproduce copyright material: The British Broadcasting Corporation: article by Lord Hill in the *Listener*; The Carfax Publishing Company and Professor S. John Eggleston: table 'Pupils Remaining after Minimum Leaving Age' from an article in *Comparative Education*; Rosica Colin Ltd: *Saturday Night and Sunday Morning* by Alan Sillitoe; The Daily Telegraph Ltd: news item on 'Population Study'; Peter Davies Ltd: *All our Future* by Douglas, Ross and Simpson; Guardian Newspapers Ltd: article on 'Comprehensive Schools' by Bryan Allen, interview with John Trevelyan; The Controller, H.M. Stationery Office: tables from *From 15–18* and *Social Trends* No. 3 (Crown copyright); The Hutchinson Publishing Group Ltd: *Film in English Teaching* by P. Knight; Michael Joseph Ltd: *The Shook-up Generation* by E. Harrison Salisbury; MacGibbon and Kee Ltd: *Folk Devils and Moral Panics* by Stanley Cohen; The New English Library: *Family and Class in a London Suburb* by Peter Willmott and Michael Young; The Observer Ltd: articles by Anna Coote and Gerald Leach; Penguin Books Ltd: *The Family and Marriage in Britain* by Ronald Fletcher (Penguin Special, pp. 27–8), *The Pre-School Years* by Willem van der Eyken (Penguin Education Special, p. 23), *The Sociology of Religion* ed. Ronald Robertson (p. 11), *Soviet Education* by Nigel Grant (Pelican, pp. 47–8); Laurence Pollinger Ltd and the Estate of Mrs Frieda Lawrence: poem by D. H. Lawrence; The Radio Times and London Express News and Features Services Ltd: facsimile reproduction of a page from the *Radio Times* including a cartoon from the *Evening Standard*; The Editorial Board of the *Sociological Review*: article 'Affluence and the British Class Structure' by David Lockwood and John H. Goldthorpe. Acknowledgements are also due to the following for illustrations reproduced on the pages listed: Associated British Cinemas Ltd, 123; Associated British-Pathe, 124 (from the film *Al Capone*); Australian News and Information Service, 24–5, 27 (upper), 214; British Aircraft Corporation Ltd, 161; British Broadcasting Corporation, 117, 171; British Leyland Motor Corporation Ltd, 163; Cadbury Ltd, 40; Camera Press Ltd, 43, 174, 179, 238 (lower); Campaign for Nuclear Disarmament, 139; J. Allan Cash Ltd, 175, 207, 238 (upper); Central Office of Information (Crown Copyright photographs), 158, 196 (by permission of the Home Office), 208; the Commissioner of Police of the Metropolis, 193; MGM-EMI Distributors Ltd, 130 (from the film *How the West was Won*); Ford Motor Co. Ltd, 148; Fox Photos Ltd, 150, 178; Henry Grant, A.I.I.P., 22, 71, 91, 92, 94, 95, 134, 189; Japan Information Centre, London, 153; Keystone Press Agency Ltd, 128, 137, 141, 157 (upper), 204, 248–9, 251; London Express News and Feature Services, 112 (upper), 171; Mansell Collection, 27 (lower), 30–1, 41, 48, 73, 98, 230, 243; Mary Evans Picture Library, 160; Novosty Press Agency, 99; Paul Popper Ltd, 55, 76, 86, 110, 241; Radio Times Hulton Picture Library, 245; Rank Leisure Services Ltd, 122; Shelter, 68, 197; Stevenage Corporation, 219; Syndication International, 59, 112 (lower); Topix, 113; United Society for the Propagation of the Gospel, 57; Volvo Concessionaires Ltd, 167 (lower); WHS Advertising Ltd, 106; Barnaby's Picture Library, 21, 182, 218; Simon Dray, 246.

1 What is Sociology?

Every day the mass media, the press and broadcasting in particular, bring us news of disasters, conflicts and new problems to be solved. Perhaps another sector of the work force is on strike, the fans at football matches have become more violent, the number of people obtaining divorces is increasing, students may be causing unrest in another university . . . .

Items like these are common daily events. Sometimes we may stop and ask, 'But why are privileged groups like students causing all this disruption?' 'Are football fans more violent now than in the past — if so why?' 'Why do more and more married couples find it impossible to live together?' Whenever we ask such questions, we are asking sociological questions. We are interested in the ways in which people behave in society, and the effects that particular things in society have on them: for example — religious belief, college or university life, support for a local football team. If we go further and attempt to answer the questions carefully and impartially with reference to relevant facts and other details, then we are giving a sociological analysis.

Sociology studies the behaviour of people in a careful and scientific way. Sociologists study the way in which a society is organized. They examine the facts about crime and deviant behaviour, and try to locate their causes; the way that the family system has developed and the consequences of divorce on the lives of family members; the influence and power of the mass media; the kinds of work available and how occupations are selected; the way population grows and the problems that result; how governments are elected and the changing attitudes of the electorate: the kinds of schools that are established, their functions and the way the pupils respond. Sociology shows us the extent to which the environment in which we live has a significant effect on our day-to-day behaviour.

For example, consider the general consequences of having been born in Britain. We are taught by parents and teachers to speak English, to dress in clothes which are western in style, to eat with a knife and fork, to think about getting a job similar to that of our father or friends, to play football and cricket, to listen to a style of music developed in

Europe or North America, to adopt a form of the Christian religion, and so on.

The concept or idea of 'society' is the most fundamental and basic one to sociology. It refers simply to the social arrangement whereby individuals and groups of people live a common way of life within an organized system — so that all are in a constant process of interaction with each other. The result is that the patterns of behaviour of human beings in a society are fairly predictable. This is because the social culture of the society (all the traditional and accepted ways of behaving) is transmitted from one generation to the next. Sociologists investigate the regularities and the irregularities in behaviour of people in their social context. They take into account the influences of the culture and the social institutions of the society on their behaviour. When some of the more important of the cultural ways of the society become customary and traditional they are called 'social institutions'. Sociologists are particularly interested in such institutions as the family and marriage, work, education, political system, religion, etc. They are interested to find out their influence and their function for individuals and for society as a whole. They may ask for example, what kind of education system do we have in Britain? Why do some children perform well in school and others badly? What functions or purposes does the education system serve?

It is only by living in a society and therefore having constant contact with others that we become fully integrated and socialized members of it. We learn to accept its traditions and customs and to behave in accordance with its norms and values. These are taught to each person by what sociologists call 'agencies of social control'. These include:

(*a*) The family unit, which guides and trains the child in its formative years in the ways in which it is expected to behave in most social situations (as well as providing a source of security and affection).

(*b*) The school, which not only provides detailed knowledge and the means of securing a livelihood for the individual, but also reinforces the need for particular kinds of social behaviour (for example, to be punctual, to attend, to accept particular principles of social organization — democracy, diligent work etc.).

(*c*) The Church, which lays down a particular moral code and provides a sense of unity and belonging. (We may not all be practising Christians, but a daily act of Assembly or Religious Instruction in school will no doubt have given us all a greater affinity for Christianity than any other religion.) In the same way the majority of those born in Ceylon are Buddhist, in Egypt Muslim, in Israel Jewish.

Individuals are also subject to the sanctions of the law of the land. But behaviour is also guided to some extent by the pressures of public opinion. People generally like to behave in ways acceptable to others for fear of what they will think of them if they do not. It is uncomfortable to be the 'odd man out'. Rather than become the subject of critical comment most of us prefer to conform to the accepted patterns of behaviour. (Consider what happens to the eager child in school who constantly hands in homework before the teacher has remembered to ask for it! What are the possible alternatives for (a) the child, (b) the remainder of the class? What is the most probable outcome of the situation if it occurs a number of times?)

Groups of all kinds — friendship groups, teams, classroom groups — quickly develop 'norms' of behaviour: that is, ways common and accept-able to all members, and with which all must conform if they are to be well-integrated members of the group. Can you suggest any norms which are common to any group of which you are a member?

It can be shown that without constant human interaction we should not be 'human' at all — in the sense that we should not be able to use the normal human capacities of speech, thought, self reliance, and so on. Some cases of children who have been reared in almost total isolation have been recorded which illustrate this. In America in 1938 two children, Anna and Isabelle, were about six years old when they were discovered and removed from their inadequate environment. In each case the child had been kept in isolation from all other human contact other than that of a mother who was herself unable to give proper care and attention to the child. They had been kept alive but had not received any kind of social training. The result was that both Anna and Isabelle were like young babies. They could do nothing for themselves. The mother of Anna was mentally retarded and the mother of Isabelle was a deaf mute. At the time of their discovery neither of the children could walk or talk or do anything that showed intelligence.

The society that we have been born into greatly affects our general ways of behaving in that we adopt its cultural standards and traditions. Other societies naturally have a different social culture — and it is not possible to say that one culture is 'better' than another, only that it is different: a point that is important when considering race relations. Immigrants are often criticized for not adapting themselves immediately to the ways of the host society; but it is clearly difficult to cast off traditional values and attitudes and adopt new ones.

Perhaps more significant, however, is the direct influence of our family background in determining our personality, our beliefs, our aims in life, and the degree of success that we attain.

Consider how the environment would shape much of the general behaviour of a growing child in China, India, or Lapland.

Sociology shows us the ways in which our attitudes, our ideas and beliefs are shaped by the fact that we were born into a particular society, into a particular family at a particular time.

If a baby is born into the already large family of an unskilled labourer in Birmingham who can barely make ends meet, that child will clearly grow up with a different attitude to life than one born into a small family of a very wealthy stockbroker who lives in a farmhouse in the Surrey countryside.

Draw up a chart like this and suggest some of the expected differences:

	Child of Birmingham labourer	Child of Surrey stockbroker
Age 0—5		
Age 6—11		
Age 12—16		
Age 17—21		
Age 22—30		
Age 31—65		

It is important for the sociologist to obtain facts to substantiate his statements.

What is the difference between fact and unsubstantiated opinion? Add some more examples to this table to illustrate your answer.

Fact	Opinion
In 1920 there were approximately 12,000 men in prison. Now there are more than 38,000.	There were millions of people in prison 50 years ago, and it's no different now.
The population of Britain was 10 million in 1801, 55 million in 1971, and if present trends continue it will reach 980 million in the year 2500.	We haven't got a population problem in Britain with only 55 million inhabitants. They have in America with 200 million and China with 750 million.
A study in 1966 showed that 500,000 families were living on or below the poverty line (the level of supplementary benefits).	I don't think that poverty exists in modern Britain.

4

Facts are open to proof. They are definite statements about a state of affairs. They can be agreed by all who investigate them. In sociology they are obtained by careful and methodical investigation. Opinions are often formed without reference to facts, but it is quite acceptable in sociology to form an opinion on the basis of facts that can be substantiated. It would be unwise to write: 'I think that crime is increasing at an alarming rate.' It would be better to write: 'The crime rate has increased from 600,000 offences in 1951 to 1,800,000 in 1971. This seems to be an alarming rate.'

You will notice that sociology has developed a specialized vocabulary. This is true of all disciplines which tackle their subject matter in a rigorous and scientific manner. Terms must be used in a sense which will be familiar to all who undertake the subject. It is important, therefore, to become familiar with the terminology and to use it as frequently as possible in discussion and in essay writing, so that it becomes a natural part of your thinking in the subject.

Sociology is also a subject which requires much statistical evidence to support findings. Familiarity with detailed facts and figures is greatly facilitated by recalling them in argument, debate, and discussion. Then they begin to spring readily to mind, and again become a natural part of your sociological thinking — rather than having to 'learn them by rote' for examination purposes.

Sociologists wish to make a scientific examination or analysis of aspects of social life. They work to obtain definite knowledge which will explain certain social phenomena. This knowledge must be subject to experiment and re-experiment or to observation and survey which is open to rigorous statistical test. It is not sufficient, therefore, for the sociologist to say: 'I should think it is likely that the child of a Surrey stockbroker will enjoy better educational facilities, obtain better qualifications, undertake a well paid and enjoyable job and generally live a happier and more fruitful life than the child of a Birmingham labourer.' If he wishes to compare the life styles of different occupational groups he must obtain definite facts from as many Surrey stockbrokers as he can and from a similar number of Birmingham labourers.

In this respect the sociologist is making use of the concept or idea of social class. He is, in effect, saying — let us take two extreme ends of the social scale, on the one hand the unskilled manual worker, and on the other the highly successful professional white collar worker, and see whether there are major differences in their attitudes, life styles, and life chances.

If, for example, he holds a theory that educational success is dependent mainly on the occupation of the father then he will devise a questionnaire or opinion poll to elicit the information he requires to test it, whilst also measuring the IQ (intelligence quotient) levels of the children in whom he is interested. He may then say, categorically, that as the result of diligent research methods he has found that children in Class 1 (Surrey stockbrokers included) display particular characteristics in educational terms, whereas children in Class 5 (whose fathers would include Birmingham labourers) display others. See research findings, page 7.

What is science?

Science is a systematic and methodical search to acquire knowledge and a deeper level of understanding. In order to obtain knowledge the scientist must be able to make accurate measurements of the quantities he is dealing with, and make logical deductions from his observations and experiments. In this way he may gain insights which lead him into deeper investigations. His findings should enable him to make accurate predictions about the way the subject matter of his study will behave in the future under specified conditions.

THE CHARACTERISTICS OF SCIENCE
1 It is methodical. It requires controlled and directed thinking, which, when successful, results in the organization of what were previously disconnected facts in a body of theory.
2 Its method is rational – obtained through reasoned study, with the possibility of testing and re-testing results to check their validity.
3 Its aim is to discover generalizations and also laws of nature, which add to man's knowledge by accurately describing the true nature of things around us.
4 The conclusions of scientific investigation are always provisional and subject to correction. (If they are not open to correction or disproof, they are not scientific theories, but mere speculation or else 'acts of faith'. For example, it is not possible to prove the existence of God, and so religion cannot be 'scientific' in its statements.)
5 Scientific statements should be predictive.

THE SCIENTIFIC METHOD
The steps that all scientists follow include:
1 The identification of a specific problem or phenomenon to be investigated.
2 The selection of a viable method to study the problem.
3 The careful observation and collection of relevant data.
4 The investigator formulates an hypothesis – a plausible guess or explanation to account for the phenomenon, which can be tested.
5 He designs an experiment or method of testing his hypothesis.
6 The results must then be analysed.
7 He may then formulate a theory based on the tested and validated hypothesis and the carefully interpreted data.
8 He reports his findings and conclusions, which must be open to further retesting by others who may be interested.

Study the research findings on page 16 to see how a sociologist observes these processes in his investigations.

Following the eight steps listed, outline the approach that you would adopt if you were to carry out the same investigation. Be sure, first of all, to state clearly what it is that you wish to find out.

The method and approach of sociology

Sociologists endeavour to understand how a society operates, how its various parts interact and function so that some harmony and stability is achieved, enabling social life to develop and progress. They are also interested in the causes of conflict and the effects and influences of the social pressures which are exerted on individuals who live in a society; and so they seek to establish testable hypotheses and theories to explain the phenomena that they observe. In order to do this they must build up a body of reliable knowledge. This may often be difficult in the social sciences, and particularly sociology, since there are areas which are difficult to measure or quantify. (It is difficult to measure how 'religious' people are, for example.)

Experimentation for the chemist is comparatively simple. If he wishes to establish a theory about the effect of mixing two chemicals, he can experiment with them in a laboratory as often as he wishes. For the sociologist it is generally more difficult. A sociologist who wishes to test a theory about the causes of revolution in a society cannot arrange for the conditions to occur for his benefit. Nor can a theory like that of Marx (who suggested that all societies pass through certain stages of development from primitive to communist) be easily tested. Thus sociologists tend to concentrate on areas of social life in which they can accumulate data, and so provide a description of the way a society has developed. Facts about the composition and changes in the population, about wealth and poverty, the nature of particular social problems, facts about work and leisure activities, about the system of education, the social class structure, and so on. They also try to discover new knowledge about social life to explain why particular social problems and other previously unexplained phenomena occur. (For example – why do some children become delinquent? to what extent are the mass media influential in forming or changing attitudes? what is 'social class'? etc.)

Examine the following two examples.
1   Suggest other lines of research which could be undertaken in the areas cited in the examples. What other facts could be discovered and by what means? To what use could the knowledge discovered be put by Government agencies?
2   Summarize the conclusions found in the first example.

RESEARCH FINDINGS 1
The chances of an unskilled manual worker's child (Social Class 5) being a poor reader at 7 years old are six times greater than those of a professional worker's child (Social Class 1). The chances of a Social Class 5 child being

a non-reader at this age are 15 times greater than those of a Social Class 1 child. One explanation for this is the home background of most middle class children; they arrive at school tuned in not only to the educational demands but also to the way they are expected to behave in school. More working class children, even by the age of 7 years, are showing hostility towards the teachers or, worse still, withdrawal, depression, and a writing off of adult standards.[1]

The possibility that an unskilled labourer has a shorter expectation of life than other members of the community is raised in the Registrar General's report on Occupational Mortality. This statistical study, which took ten years to compile, compares the health and mortality rate of the unskilled in 1961 with those of men who work in professional, semi-professional, skilled, and partly skilled jobs. The report comments that the most disturbing feature of the survey is the apparent deterioration among the unskilled social classes when their results are compared with those in earlier analyses. While the mortality rate of all men in 1961 fell at all ages (except 70 to 74) that for the unskilled men rose at all ages (except 25 to 34). It seems that the unskilled category has not benefited from the major social changes which have benefited the majority of their compatriots. The next decennial survey will, presumably show whether this trend has been continued.[2]

RESEARCH FINDINGS 2

The handicap of a poor start in life is illustrated by the findings of a survey carried out by sociologists and published in October 1971. The investigators found that the chances of a successful early life are heavily loaded against the illegitimate child. They are three times as likely as legitimates to be placed in day care while their mothers work. They are twice or more as likely to be of below average in general knowledge, oral ability, and reading ability as adopted children. By the age of seven they are seven times as likely as adopted children to receive insufficient maternal attention. The survey followed the development of 600 children born illegitimately from 3 to 9 March 1958 in England and Wales. It compared the fortunes of those who were kept by their mothers or adopted with the progress of the 16,000 born and raised legitimately from the same week onwards. The proportion of unmarried mothers and children who had moved house 3 or 4 times was three times as high as for families with legitimate children. The most outstanding feature was the privileged position of adopted children. Four times as many adopted children were in middle class homes. The only area of equality shared by all the children seven years later was their physical development. As a result of the disadvantages an at present unknown number will grow up into alienated adults or the inadequate parents of tomorrow. To minimize the inequalities the survey

[1] *From Birth to Seven*, Davie, Butler & Goldstein, 1972.
[2] *Occupational Mortality*, H.M.S.O., 1971.

recommends a national wage for one parent families 'in recognition that the children are our major resource and that motherhood is an important job that women do for society'.[1]

	Non Adopted	Adopted	Legitimate
Below average general knowledge	36.4%	15.1%	23.9%
Poor reading ability	48.7%	18.4%	28.1%
Low maternal interest	29.3%	4.3%	4.7%
Financial problems	20.8%	0%	7.4%
Housing problems	18.1%	1.6%	7.3%

Sociologists do not predict that all illegitimate children will be poor readers, live in financial hardship, or lack maternal care. What they suggest is that an illegitimate child is much more likely, according to accurately compiled statistical evidence and observational techniques, to suffer in these ways. There will always be exceptions, but in general a child from this particular background will fare less successfully than one from a legitimate middle class background in which the mother has herself had a comparatively happy and stable home life, has succeeded in her education, and has had few financial problems to contend with. Sociologists might wish to make further studies of the same children at the ages of 14 and 21 to see whether the differences remain.

Much sociological knowledge is acquired through survey and question-naire methods, by reference to published statistics (the Registrar General's Census details, for example) and to other official documents which may not normally be available to the general public (police files for example), and by direct observation and recording. In general the sociologist works to the rule that his data should be gathered in an objective manner, that is without any of his own personal feelings or prejudices influencing the facts that he records. This is why methods of direct observation and recording are not widely used, since it may be difficult for the observer to remain completely impartial and to record in a total objective manner. However, the method has been used successfully in an interesting study entitled *The Unattached*, by Mary Morse.

Examine the following examples and note the different methods by which the sociologists concerned have acquired their information.

Example 1: *The Unattached*, by Mary Morse
The book is a report of a three-year project carried out by the National Association of Youth Clubs. The project is an example of a mode of social study that owes little to the formal techniques of surveys by questionnaire, standardized interviewing, and other sampling methods. This mode of study relies a great deal for its success on the personality of the investigator,

[1] *Born Illegitimate: Social and Educational Implications*, National Foundation for Educational Research, 1971.

his ability to get people talking, and his skill in knitting their remarks and his own observations into a coherent picture of reality.

The survey was undertaken to investigate a small group and its problems and to make an attempt to contact young people unattached to any kind of youth organization. A grant of £6,000 for three years was made to appoint research workers who would investigate four key areas. These were selected to offer contrasting physical, economic and social backgrounds. The number of those observed was small and the focus was selective. One hundred and seventy young people were studied in close personal relationship. Contact was made in three ways: by working alongside or occupying a sympathetic position such as welfare or personnel work; by taking a teaching role in a school; and by meeting the young people during leisure activities, in coffee bars and dance halls. All these methods were tried and tested to see which was the most successful means of contact, that is, which permitted the development of strong relationships as opposed to those of a purely casual nature.

The evidence presented in the study takes the form of workers' reports and observations. Conclusions are naturally dependent upon human factors, the investigator's ability to record and interpret accurately. But the nature of the subject under consideration was such that more formal survey methods might have aroused hostility so that no reliable statistical results could be obtained.

The results provided a useful basis from which interested workers could attempt solutions to a difficult problem.

Example 2: *Criminal on the Road*, by T. C. Willet

The investigator wished to present a picture of the serious motoring offender. The choice as to which offence to consider was determined by the severity of the law with regard to particular offences. Police files were selected as the only source that would provide sufficient information for the testing of the hypotheses, and steps were taken to gain access to these records. A nationwide survey was not considered feasible, so it was necessary to choose a homogeneous police area. This district should be representative of the country as a whole and so should not be mostly rural or mostly urban. Neither should the occupational distribution of its population be biased towards a particular occupational group. Nor should the users of the road be disproportionately of one type — for example goods vehicles or holiday traffic.

Eventually a police district was found in the Home Counties where the police and justices were prepared to co-operate. The scope of the work could now be considered in more exact terms. The minimum period during which trends would become clear was settled as three years. It was judged that there would not be a sufficient number of cases of causing death by dangerous driving, driving under the influence, or of driving while disqualified if the work covered less than three years. It was decided to take for analysis every case under these heads in which there had been a conviction during the years 1957, 1958 and 1959. It was predicted that the number of cases for study would be between 600 and 700, sufficient to give a representative picture. The investigator wished to analyse the incidence of such motoring offences and their treatment over a period of time and also to show something of the development of the law and of the social attitudes influencing it, to give the picture meaning and perspective. A small scale interview study of offenders was also undertaken.

The overall results is an interesting insight into the characteristics of the serious motoring offender.

Example 3: *Adolescent Boys of East London*, by Peter Willmott

Willmott, having successfully completed his research on Family and Kinship in East London, switched his attention in this survey to a socio-logical study of boys growing up in the same area. He wished to test the various opinions that East End adolescents are necessarily problematic and potentially delinquent. He exposes the fallacy and confounds the East Ender's critics. The study shows the normality of adolescent behaviour (that is, the youngster of Bethnal Green behaves in a relatively similar way to others throughout England). Willmott stresses that Bethnal Green is a well integrated working class area and that the cultural pattern is stable and well established. Even deviant behaviour like pilfering and petty crime have been institutionalized into the community's sub-culture, so that the petty thief of 16 quickly develops into the responsible married worker of 19. The sample shows that the adolescent conforms to the exist-ing social order of the area and that it is unusual to find him constantly clashing with the norms and laws as he leaves his teens. The study shows that the family, peer, and street groups exert powerful pressures and sanctions on behaviour.

For the purpose of his study, Willmott wished to select a random sample of boys aged between 14 and 20. He took the addresses of one in every six households from the Electoral Register, obtaining a total of 2,310 addresses. (He later found that of these 14 were unoccupied and 31 demolished.) He interviewed 246 young men (88% of his sample) and he got some of the boys to write detailed diaries concerning their day-to-day lives. He was also interested to test the belief that adolescents in this area would be poor Youth Club attenders (a view expressed by Musgrove in *Youth and the Social Order*) but he finds the opposite is true.

Whilst there may be some criticisms of his survey, he presents a particu-larly optimistic view which further research may substantiate.

Experimentation in sociology

In general it is difficult to carry out controlled experiments in sociology, although it is quite feasible on a limited scale. To test an hypothesis to explain a particular aspect of social behaviour, two groups must be selected, the experimental group and the control group. These are matched for all variables thought to affect their behaviour. That is, the variables of age, sex, class, race, etc. would be held constant in the two groups. But the experimental group would be subjected to the variable believed to cause the change in the behaviour which is the subject of the hypothesis: for example, if the sociologists believes that children will perform better in a task if they are rewarded at regular intervals – then 'regular reward' becomes the factor or variable thought to be the cause of the behaviour under investigation, which is 'improved performance at a task'. If all other variables have been held constant (age, IQ, class etc.) in both groups and if a change does occur in the behaviour patterns of the experimental group (if they do perform better having been rewarded in comparison with those in the control group who have not) then it can be assumed that the new behaviour is attributable to the influence of the variable to which only the experimental group has been submitted – in this example, 'reward at regular intervals'.

Study the following example in the Research Findings.
1 What is the hypothesis being tested?
2 List the variables which were held constant.
3 State the variable to which the experimental group were subjected.
4 What was the outcome of the experiment?

RESEARCH FINDINGS

In a recent study by Heber an experiment was designed to test the hypothesis that IQ level can be improved in children of low social class and who are observed to have low levels of IQ initially, by subjecting them to an intensive and stimulating learning situation. Two groups were selected, an experimental and a control group. These were matched for age, sex, class (all were from social class 5), racial type (all were negro), and IQ level (all had mothers with IQ levels below 80 and their own levels were also below 80).

The experimental group was then exposed to the variable which was believed to affect IQ score. That is to say, 40 children in the experimental group were placed in a stimulating learning situation, whilst all other variables were held constant. The remaining 40 children in the control group were not. When the experiment was completed at the end of 36 months, the result on retesting the IQ levels of all the children in both groups showed that those in the experimental group had increased their scores by an average of 27 points.

Whilst it was believed formerly that there was a correlation between IQ ~el and learning situation this experiment showed that a relationship ~.

' sciences

include those disciplines which study human beings in ~stitutions, and organizations, and include sociology, economics, psychology, and anthropology. They attempt explanation by adopting the scientific method. They seek to replace opinions and un-proven belief with certain knowledge. Each of the social sciences has a particular aspect of man in society which has become its specialized subject matter. Some of the major areas of sociological interest include: (*a*) the family, which is seen as an important social institution, being the means whereby the cultural beliefs of a society are transmitted and the young are socialized; (*b*) social class, which has been shown to have a profound effect on the attitudes and values of individuals; (*c*) the educa-tional system and the way in which its benefits are distributed; (*d*) chang-ing aspects of the population, because the individual is the basic unit in society and the size and density of population are the most important bases for the number and variety of social organization.

Whilst interested in the wealth of a society and the way that it is dis-tributed, the economist is primarily interested in specific economic institu-tions, like factories, banks, trade and industry. Economists certainly reveal some of the concrete facts relating to these features, and often sociologists build upon them. The economist may be concerned with how man's physical wants and needs are supplied, and the sociologist with the effect of the class structure on the way goods are distributed. The economist can tell us about the factors involved in the production and distribution of new cars, whereas the sociologist is interested in the sector of the popul-ation which is car owning, and that which is not. He may wish to know, for example, what is the effect of car ownership on holiday patterns.

There is a close link between some areas of psychology and sociology. Psychology is the scientific study of the behaviour of man, and in particular the behaviour of the individual. The psychologist may perhaps be interested in the reasons why a man becomes a drug taker, with reference to certain defects in his personality, and in the effects of the drug on his behaviour. The sociologist is more interested in the effects of drug taking as a trend in society and which sections of society are more prone to the activity than others. The sociologist may also wish to study the ways in which a society deals with 'deviant' behaviour.

Anthropology is another of the social sciences to which sociology is closely related, in subject matter and in approach. Anthropologists study man as an animal and as a member of a society, but have generally restricted themselves to a study of primitive and preliterate peoples. They have been particularly interested in tracing the origins of human cultures and the stages of their development.

History too, has some areas of similarity with sociology, but differs from it in that it is more concerned to describe events within certain time periods or unique movements such as the Industrial Revolution or the reign of a particular monarch. Sociology does not place such significance on the occurrence of unique happenings, and only a limited portion of sociological interest is devoted to description. It is constantly asking questions about social behaviour and social organization: 'What are some of the different kinds of family organization that are found?' or 'What effects have changes in the divorce laws had on family life in Britain?'

In seeking answers to such questions the sociologist may very well make use of historical data.

Problems facing the sociologist in his quest for data and in adopting the scientific method in sociology

1   It is very difficult to construct large-scale experiments which can be tested and retested, since the social scientist is dealing with large numbers of people. Hypotheses are often put forward which can be tested by accumulating much statistical evidence from surveys, questionnaires, and interviews, and these may themselves be costly and difficult to organize.

2   The collection of data by means of survey and questionnaire must be subject to stringent care. It is possible to get accurate estimates of the views held by a total group (for example – voting behaviour) by questioning a relatively small sample of that group, providing that it is a representative sample of the total population. It must be certain that men and women, northerners and southerners, working class and middle class, urban and rural dwellers, etc. will appear in the same proportion as they do in the whole population. If urban dwellers differed greatly from rural dwellers in their views, then by including mainly urban dwellers in the sample questioned, the interviewer would get a completely wrong idea of the general attitude held by the whole group in whom he is interested. In order to subject results obtained to strict statistical test so that valid conclusions can be drawn, it is necessary to ask several hundred people as a minimum, to complete the questionnaire. A theory of sampling has been worked out by mathematicians in great detail, so that it is possible to estimate the likely error in prediction by means of statistical formulas. The sociologist must ensure that his sampling method obeys the statistical rules precisely. Otherwise, his results will be open to dispute and major error. A classic mistake was made by a researcher in America in the 1930s. He wished to predict the outcome of a Presidential Election. He obtained his sample from a state telephone directory, taking names at random. His prediction was quite wrong although many thousands of people were contacted. He had forgotten that at that time only a particular social class owned telephones. He did not have a representative sample.

3   It is important that bias does not enter into the sociologist's analysis of results. His own attitudes and feelings must not enter into his conclusions. This may occur where the data that have been collected are not conclusive or adequate, in which case accuracy and reliability are lessened. Sociology deals with subjects towards which we may have already our own fixed ideas and attitudes. It deals with questions about crime and delinquency, poverty, the family, politics, and education, and so it is important that we, too, should be prepared to look at data and evidence

which may conflict with our own views without prejudging the issue. Prejudice and bias can be avoided by commenting on facts and statistics as objectively as possible, so that our own feelings do not contaminate our conclusions. If the facts happen to support our existing view we must be just as careful not to go beyond the facts that we have obtained and draw conclusions which are not verifiable. If we do either of these we can be accused of not being sociological in our thinking. The effect of bias is to distort reality.

4   The sociologist is often interested in finding the cause of a particular social phenomenon or the relationship between two social facts. For example, what is the relationship between business conditions and marriage rate, between delinquency and family background, between social class and educational opportunity, between age of marriage and divorce rate? He may try to find the cause of a phenomenon by seeing whether there is a direct connection between two variables. (The two social features that are examined are called variables simply because they vary — age, sex, class, etc.) But unfortunately this is not always as easy or straightforward as it may sound. The sociologist must be careful not to assume that because two variables seem to occur together they necessarily explain the cause of a phenomenon. It has been found that the increase in birth rate in a certain area correlates with an increase in the number of storks visiting the region! Obviously this is a matter of coincidence. The two variables are independent of each other.

Fortunately there are well-tried statistical processes to test the significance of correlations for reliability.

Sociologists, then, must be aware that because two features seem to be mutually interrelated it is not safe to assume that they are so. The interpretation of data to see whether a cause and effect relationship exists requires much care in the analysis of research results by the investigator.

Experiments must be carefully prepared and controlled and if necessary subjected to retest.

Much duplicated research shows a correlation between the variables of father's occupation and child delinquency. That is to say, it has been found that most delinquent children tend to come from social class 5 where the father has an unskilled manual occupation. The correlation in itself does not prove cause and effect. That, ultimately, can be shown most effectively by undertaking a controlled experiment.

Study the following research findings from *The Family Life of Old People*. Read the book itself if possible.
1   List some of the questions that the sociologist wished to answer.
2   Outline the methods that he chose to find the answers.
3   State some of the problems that he encountered.
4   Outline some of his conclusions.
5   What is the significance of his findings for (*a*) Government agencies concerned for the welfare of the elderly, (*b*) the average citizen.

RESEARCH FINDINGS
The Family Life of Old People, by Peter Townsend

A   *Objective*

Primarily to answer the following questions about the life of old people:
How much contact do they have with their immediate kin? Have the
bonds of kinship any material value? What is the difference in family role
of an old woman and an old man? Can more precise definitions be given to
the terms 'loneliness' and 'social isolation'? What are the implications of
widowhood and being single or childless? Is the status of old people
changing? Subsidiary surveys were conducted to explore the respective
functions of relatives and of the social services in helping to meet the
needs of old people, and also to pinpoint those groups making the heaviest
damands on statutory and voluntary provisions.

B   *Method of investigation*

(*a*)   Pilot survey: Trial interviews were carried out in Westminster and
Hampstead but no details are given.

(*b*)   Main survey: Bethnal Green was chosen partly because Willmott and
Young were already conducting a companion survey in the area. Also
because it was an area of considerable change and variety of population,
housing, and industry.

1   *Selection of the sample*   Seven doctors were selected by taking a random sample of one in three of all the G.P.s in the borough. Then the
medical cards of their patients were worked through, every tenth card
being picked out. Cards relating to men of 65 or over, women of 60 or over,
and persons whose age was unspecified were used as the source of the
names and addresses of the sample. After further research, those who were
found to be below pensionable age or dead were rejected, which left a total
of 261 potential interviewees. Of this number 9 died before being interviewed, 24 had left the borough, and 25 others were unable or did not
wish to take part. Of the remainder who were interviewed two thirds were
women. Half of these were widowed and just under one fifth had no sur-
viving children.

2   *Interview technique*   The interviews, which lasted on average two
house, were in the form of 'guided conversations'. They were based on
topics such as household (particulars of persons living with the informant),
type of dwelling, occupation, source of income, expenditure, friends and
neighbours, holidays and pastimes, family life and changes that had
occurred, health, welfare, etc. The great majority of interviews were
conducted between October 1954 and December 1955.

3   *Subsidiary surveys*   Information was collected from a local geriatric
hospital on 300 people from the records of the L.C.C., also from residential
homes on 200 people, and on 400 people being visited by the local home
help service.

4   *Difficulties*   Some interviewees were infirm, forgetful, deaf, or unwilling; however, this only applied to a small proportion of the total
number interviewed.

5   *Accuracy*   Owing to the inaccessibility of the Ministry of Pensions complete list the sample was taken from doctors' records, although such records cover only 98% of the population of London. The representative value of the sample was checked against the 1951 Census and information from the Old People's Welfare Committee, with favourable results.

6   *Statistical validity*   The researchers considered that the nature of the material collected was such that statistical tests could be used only with caution and discrimination.

7   *Finance and assistance*   No figures are given for the cost and financing of the survey. During this period Peter Townsend was employed as Research Officer of the Institute of Community Studies in Bethnal Green. He received the assistance of twelve colleagues, who helped with both the interviewing and the planning of the report.

C   *Some of his conclusions*

He found that people in Bethnal Green in the category he took as elderly were generally supported and cared for by their children. He shows that one of the main functions of the East End extended family was to care for its older members. Its importance far overshadowed the formal social services. His investigation to find the extent to which old people live in isolation (which he defined as having three or less contacts a day) showed that 10% of the 203 old people in his sample were in this situation.

EXERCISES

1   Explain the differences and similarities between a sociologist and (*a*) a chemist, (*b*) a novelist, (*c*) a psychologist, (*d*) a journalist.

2   Write short notes on (*a*) sociology, (*b*) economics, (*c*) social culture, (*d*) social institutions, (*e*) social norms.

3   Why does the sociologist adopt the scientific method in his studies? Suggest hypotheses and methods of finding out:
(*a*)   Why a high proportion of children leave school at the earliest possible age.
(*b*)   Whether social class membership affects voting behaviour.
(*c*)   Whether there is a problem of poverty in your town.
(*d*)   Whether cinema attendance habits have changed over the past 25 years.
(*e*)   The extent to which we live in a 'permissive' or a 'puritan' society.

What are some of the problems that might be encountered in carrying out such studies? Which studies likely to be the most successful in obtaining clear data, and which the least successful?

ESSAY QUESTIONS

1   Explain how your life from the time you were born until the present has been affected and influenced by social factors and by the activities and demands of the state. (Consider behaviour, attitudes, beliefs, etc.)

2   Outline what the subject matter of sociology is. Explain why socio-logists are interested in making their investigations. Try to refer to detailed sociological information that you have read about, in books, newspapers or journals, or which you have seen on television or heard on radio.

3   Describe: (a)   What sociology is.
     (b)   The kind of research that sociologists do.
     (c)   How data are collected.
Refer to specific studies.

4   Outline the basic steps involved in obeying the scientific method. Refer to a piece of research that you have read about, and show how far it does or does not fit in with the stages you have outlined.

Study Notes:
1   Keep a file of relevant and useful newspaper cuttings with an index system which enables you to make easy reference to them.
2   Keep a notebook of useful statistics that you may read about.
3   Study *Whitaker's Almanack*, which is a useful source of statistics (with reference to marriage, divorce, crime, etc.).
4   Try to become familiar with the books that are available in the sociology or social science section of your library.
5   Watch for radio and television programmes that may be useful in illuminating areas to be studied.
6   It is important to read as widely as possible around the topic areas to be discussed and studied.

2 The Family and Marriage

The family in society

The family is both a universal and a very flexible social institution which exists in different forms in all known human societies. Attempts to trace the origin of the family by examining its structure and function in simple or primitive societies have been failures. The assumption that there had been a single evolutionary line of development from a very simple type of family system to a very complex one was shown to be false. Even in very primitive types of society the family system is both very complex in structure and full of variation. Some practice monogamy and others polygamy; some are dominated by the eldest male and others by a female. The type of family arrangement found in a society is a product of its cultural traditions or its dominant beliefs and values. The family system found in the Israeli Kibbutz, for example, in which children grow up not with their parents but in groups of other young people, rather like the boarding school system in Britain, is an attempt to engender community attitudes rather than individualistic behaviour. In rural Japan the grandmother is the most important family member, exerting a strong influence on the upbringing of the children. The mother plays a rather servile role, acting more as a nursemaid than a mother. In some African societies the uncle is given care and control of his sister's children and the father is forced to play a secondary role with little authority. But whatever form the family system takes it remains 'a family' in the sense that it serves the basic needs of the individuals in the society — of care, love, protection, security, training — and it serves to sustain the basic structure of the society, in that it helps to perpetuate its culture, its values, and its traditions.

The interest of the sociologist in the family

The family is closely linked to a whole network of other social institutions. The sociologist is interested to discover the kind of links that exist and the significance for the society of the particular type of family structure that exists in it. He is studying human behaviour with regard to the influence of the family. He may wish to find out whether there is a link between social problems — delinquency, violence, psychological disorder, etc. — and child

19

rearing practices or family environment. The family has been traditionally defended by religious authority in Britain. What has been the effect of
the decline in religious influence and the growth of scientific attitudes
on the family? What has been the effect of rapid social change brought
about by industrialization and urbanization? Statistics show that there
has been a rapid increase in the divorce rate in recent years – is this
evidence that people are becoming more divorce-minded? And what is
the effect of marriage broken by divorce on young children? Do they tend
to suffer emotionally and psychologically as a result? Has the State begun
to undermine the basis of the family system in Britain by taking over many
of its traditional functions? Are there viable alternatives to the traditional
family system of Britain?

These may be some of the questions which the sociologist who examines
the structure and functions of the family may wish to answer. In looking at
the family he is inquiring into its form, how it adapts to historical events
and changes over time, and the relationship between the family and other
social features. To answer the questions he obtains facts and data from
which he can make valid deductions and theories about the family as a
major social institution.

What is meant by 'the family'?

The family may be defined as the relatively small and fairly permanent
group of people who are intimately related and who support and maintain
each other socially, economically, and emotionally. Generally, in Britain,
it consists of husband and wife and a small number of children.

Writing of the family in his book *The Family and Marriage in Britain*,
Ronald Fletcher says:

Family members share the same name, the same collective reputation,
the same home, the same peculiar traditions of their own making and
the same neighbourhood. They share the same sources of pleasure, the
same joys and the same sources of profound conflict. The same vagaries
of fortune are encountered and overcome. Degrees of agreement
and disagreement are worked out amongst them. The same losses and
griefs are shared. Hence the family is that group within which the
most fundamental appreciation of human qualities and values takes
place 'for better or for worse' ... the family is an educative group of
the most fundamental kind.

For the purpose of analysis sociologists identify two basic types of
family organization:

1 *The extended family* All related members live closely together as an
economic unit. It is usually a patriarchal group – dominated by the senior
male member. This type of family system is found most often in pre-
industrial agricultural communities, where it represents the traditional
values and beliefs of the society (such as male dominance, female sub-
servience, family unity) and maintains the traditional functions of the

family unit. It is responsible for the education, training, and welfare of the family members. However, there is some evidence that the extended family still exists in industrial society in modified form. Willmott and Young found that it was a strong feature of social life in Bethnal Green. Married couples in that area often belong to what they describe as 'a combination of families who to some large degree form one domestic unit'.

Commenting on this they say: 'These localized extended family groups spreading over two or more nearby houses are the distinctive features of kinship in the East End.' The extended family is less common in industrial society because people become more mobile socially and geographically. In their search for work and independent accommodation related family members begin to disperse. The family itself becomes a less dominant institution. Its traditional functions are diffused among other specialized agencies: education services, welfare facilities, training schemes, advice centres, and so on are provided by the central government; the family begins to interact with them so that responsibilities are shared.

In the industrial setting the family becomes reduced in size to its basic nucleus — that of the parents and children, generally quite independent of wider kinship relations.

The patriarchal extended family: a Beduin Arab encampment

2   The second type of family system identified by the sociologist is that of the *nuclear family*, parents and children alone. In their comparison of differences in family structure between the village-like quality of Bethnal Green and the more suburban nature of Woodford, Willmott and Young found that 'far less people in Woodford live very close to their parents and other relatives, and there is less day-to-day interaction. Meetings between relatives are less casual, much more dependent upon definite appointments'. It would seem that whereas in Bethnal Green people had

A modern nuclear family: father, mother and (in this case) one child

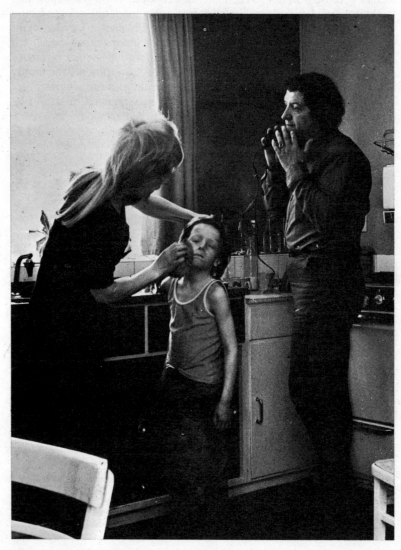

established long-standing roots in the area so that the tendency was to remain there, in Woodford the population was much more mobile, so that there was less sense of identification with the area.

Such independent attitudes are typical of the modern nuclear family, although they may maintain close contact with other family members by means of the telephone and regular visits.

Proximity of parents — Woodford and Bethnal Green
(General samples — married people with at least one parent alive)

Parent's residence	Woodford	Bethnal Green
Same dwelling	9%	12%
Within five minutes' walk	7%	29%
Elsewhere in the same borough	15%	13%
Outside the same borough	69%	46%
Total %	100%	100%
Number in the sample	394	369

Contacts with mothers — Woodford and Bethnal Green
(General samples — married people with mothers alive)

	Woodford	Bethnal Green
Seen within previous 24 hours	30%	43%
Seen earlier in previous week	33%	31%
Not seen within previous week	37%	26%
Total % with mothers alive	100%	100%
Numbers in the sample	346	290

One of the conclusions reached by Willmott and Young as a result of their research was an expectation that 'the stressing of the mother—daughter tie would be a widespread, perhaps universal phenomenon in the urban areas of all industrial countries . . . at any rate in the families of manual workers'. The reason they suggest is that 'manual workers seemed to have more need for the extended family as the "woman's trade union". Working class mothers suffered from more insecurity. They received uncertain and ungenerous house-keeping allowances even when their husbands were not out of a job . . . . If husbands were not killed in war or peace they were always liable to desert. Woman's only protection . . . was herself. The wife clung to the family into which she was born, and particularly to her mother.'

The family in simple society

Simple or primitive societies are those which are non-literate (they may use very simple literary skills in some cases), maintain a static and very basic economy based on barter or exchange, make use of magic and superstitious rituals, and often practise ancestor worship and tribal custom. Economic survival often depends on co-operation rather than competition (although property may be individually owned).

In such societies the family is the most important unit within the social organization. It is an economic and social unit which provides for all the needs of the individual and the groups in the society. There are few social changes and consequently few changes in the structure and function of the family — unlike the rapid changes which occur in an industrialized society and to which the family system must adapt.

Because there are no written rules and regulations to which the members of the society must conform, they are subject to social pressures and group sanctions to ensure their adherence to the accepted norms of the society. The family and other groups, such as friends, neighbours, and relatives, serve as the agencies which educate and socialize the individual. This ensures that the social customs and beliefs of the society are perpetuated and transmitted from one generation to the next.

An example of life in a simple society is provided on page 46.

A 'long house' in Papua. The entire village lives in this building, which consists of a main hall with three tiers of 'apartments' along each side, each occupied by a family group

Functions and characteristics of the family

There are two broad categories to be considered: those concerned with the biological needs of the individual, and those concerned with the social, cultural, and economic needs of the society.

1 THE BIOLOGICAL FUNCTIONS

(*a*)   It is a mating relationship.

(*b*)   It enables the species to be procreated and perpetuated in a regulated and socially acceptable way.

(*c*)   The relationship satisfies human emotional needs and drives, including those of love, protection, self esteem, and security.

2 THE SOCIAL, CULTURAL AND ECONOMIC FUNCTIONS

(*a*)   It is a useful agency of social control which plays an important part in training and socializing the young into the acceptable patterns of behaviour in the society.

(*b*)   It is a means of transmitting the social culture of the society from one generation to the next.

(*c*)   The family unit makes for a stable social system. Individuals are ascribed a name, roles, values, and status, so that each individual has identity and a knowledge of his rights and duties.

(*d*) The family unit meets the economic needs of its members. It provides for the care and protection of the young, of females especially in times of pregnancy, of the elderly, and of the sick or disabled.

(*e*) The family provides a bridge between the individual and the wider society that he will encounter when he enters the world of work as an independent adult. It is an informal agency of education.

Five types of family arrangement

1 In some societies marriage partners are selected by parents or by village elders. In others the individual has free choice of partner.

2 The union of the partners may be monogamous, in which one wife is married to one husband, or polygamous, in which it is socially accept-able for a specified partner to take more than one spouse. Polygamy can take two forms: (*a*) Polygyny, which is marriage between one husband and many wives and may occur either where there is an excess of women in the society due, perhaps, to the fact that young males are likely to meet an early death, or where the ability to marry many wives carries with it added status. Examples are found in Arab societies, and in many primitive cultures where it serves to make provision for the care of widows and orphans, and (*b*) Polyandry, which is marriage between one wife and several husbands. This is a comparatively rare arrangement but is found among the Todas of Southern India and it is practised by the Marquesan Islanders in the Pacific.

3 In some societies descent or inheritance is through the male line only, so that the eldest son inherits title, position as family head etc. This is known as 'patrilineal descent'. Tikopian society is of this type. Where inheritance is through the female line only, where seniority and power is passed to the female members of the family, it is known as 'matrilineal descent'. An example of this type of society was that of the Iroquois Indians. Where descent may be through either or both partners the descent is said to be 'bilineal'.

4 Where marriage partners live by tradition with the husband's family it is known as 'patrilocal residence'. Where they reside with the family of the wife it is termed 'matrilocal residence'. Where the partners are ex-pected to live together and apart from either kin residence is termed 'neo-local'.

5 In some societies the family is traditionally dominated by the father, husband, or eldest male. This was the case in Victorian England, for example. This is known as a 'patriarchal' family system.

Where power and authority is vested in the most senior woman it is termed 'matriarchal'; examples are found in rural Japan and the Trobriand Islands, and it was a feature of the social organization of the Iroquois Indians. Where husband and wife share decision making, so that neither is considered to be socially superior or inferior, the system is described as 'democratic' or 'egalitarian'.

(above) *A typical village in the Trobriand Islands*

(below) *A Victorian family group*

It is interesting to consider that the British system of monogamous marriage, bilineal descent through either partner, and free choice of residence and of marriage partner which is based on democratic principles, is not the most common combination of possible arrangements. Hobhouse, Wheeler and Ginsberg surveyed 434 primitive tribes and found that 66 practised monogamy, 31 polyandry, and the remaining 337 polygyny.

Changes in the structure and function of the family in Britain since 1870

There have been major changes since the introduction of the first Education Act. After 1870 there was a gradual move away from the patriarchal, extended family system towards that of the small, democratically managed nuclear family. Women and children, formerly little more than chattels with few rights, began to attain degrees of emancipation and recognition of their status and needs, which was to have a profound effect on the future structure of the family. The State began to undertake many of the former functions of the family, with the introduction of a formal education system, social welfare facilities for the poor, sick and elderly, and the provision of housing and training for occupation.

Since the family responds to changes in other parts of the social structure, many agents of change can be identified as operating on the family system. Especially significant have been the impact of industrialization, urbanization and the growth of secularization, that is, the decline in influence of religion and the development of scientific attitudes.

1   INDUSTRIALIZATION

The growth of the factory system and the specialization of labour, which began in earnest in the middle of the 18th century, took production out of the home, so that the household economy crumbled. The search for work in industrial centres necessitated the break-up of the extended family unit. Industrial society required legislation to protect the workers employed in dangerous work places and those who would otherwise be exploited. The Factory Acts had begun to limit the advantage of a large family from an economic point of view; compulsory education finally made children an economic liability rather than an asset. Technological society made available improved means of contraception, which enabled people to plan families more efficiently. The advances in medicine meant that it was no longer necessary to have a large family in the expectation that only a few would survive. After 1870 family size and birth rate begin to fall rapidly.

Mass production, one of the results of industrialization, made a wider variety of goods available at low prices. High living standards and the possession of more material goods became important goals. As they obtained more rights and a better education, more women went out to work, which necessitated a more democratic relationship in the home. The Victorian 'patriarchal', father-dominated, family began to disappear in the twentieth century.

URBANIZATION

The growth of large towns and cities occurred in Britain with the development of industry. New centres emerged for work in specialized industries — coal mining, iron and steel, spinning and weaving. They provided great incentives for poor, rural-based families to leave the land and seek

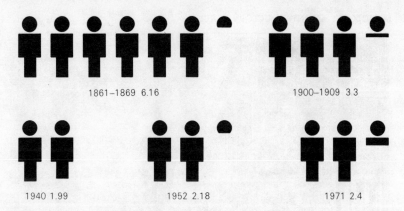

1861–1869 6.16   1900–1909 3.3

1940 1.99   1952 2.18   1971 2.4

(above) *Average family size* **(below)** *Birth and death rates*

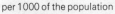

per 1000 of the population

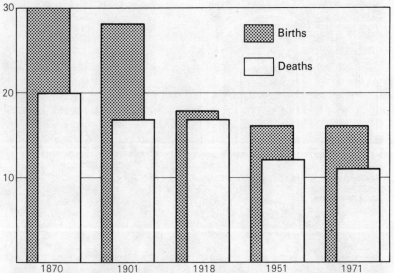

improved standards of living in the urban areas. The population became more geographically mobile after 1825 with the development of the railways. It is estimated that in 1851 50% of the population were living in rural areas; in 1971 there were less than 15%.

One of the effects was to weaken the bonds of the traditional extended family so that the family unit became more precisely focused around the married pair and the children. The industrial city provided the means of care and education, entertainment, and subsequently of welfare that were previously the sole prerogative of the individual family group. An example of the effects of urbanization on family life is given on page 44.

SECULARIZATION

The decline in religious influence in industrial society and the subsequent growth of a scientific and rational approach to questions of day-to-day

Child labour in the 19th century: the market for hiring children in Spitalfields, London

living was hastened by the publication of such works as Darwin's *Origin of Species* in 1857. There followed increasing debate and questioning about traditional values and codes of behaviour.

The growth of rational free thinking and the decline in Church attendance and the power and authority of the Church, together with the decline in the unquestioning acceptance of customary traditions and beliefs, had a profound effect on family life in Britain. Divorce came to be more acceptable; illegitimacy carries less stigma; there has developed an increasing growth of democratic attitudes between partners, so that marriage has become more of a companionship than a necessarily child-centred arrangement.

There is a fundamental dispute between observers of the contemporary family. There are those who argue that it is in a clear process of decay and decline as a social institution and that this can only be for the good — since it is a source of social frustration and psychological disorder in its members and in society at large.

Others see the family as being in some imminent danger of destruction and with it the whole fabric of society. The Reverend E. C. Urwin sees a return to basic Christian principles and life style as the only solution.

There are others again who dispute the view that the family is in any danger at all, and believe that, on the contrary, it is as healthy, dynamic, and functional as at any previous time in history.

THE END OF THE FAMILY?

Dr Edmund Leach in the 1967 Reith Lectures put forward the view that 'British society is a loose assemblage of isolated groups of parents and children. In the past', he said, 'kinsfolk and neighbours gave the individual continuous moral support throughout his life. But today the domestic household is isolated. The family looks inward on itself; there is an intensification of emotional stress between husband and wife and parents and children. . . . The strain is greater than most of us can bear. Far from being the basis of the good society, the family with its narrow privacy and tawdry secrets is the source of all our discontents.'

He argued in these lectures that our present society is emotionally very uncomfortable. 'Parents and children huddled together in their loneliness take too much out of each other. The parents fight, the children rebel.' He believes that 'children need to grow up in larger, more relaxed domestic groups, centred on the community rather than on the mother's kitchen: something like an Israeli Kibbutz perhaps, or a Chinese Commune.'

His theme was directed to the conclusion that 'isolation and the close knit nature of contemporary family life incubates hate which finds expression in conflict in the wider community'. He suggests that most of our social problems could be alleviated by restructuring our family system.

THE FAMILY IN DANGER

Urwin wrote in 1944: 'The family in the modern world, by many signs and tokens, is in a perilous state. Critical observers declare that it is disintegrating and tending to disappear. Some even desire it to do so. The family stands in the spotlight of conflicting tendencies.' The signs and tokens to which he refers include 'the social forces at work in the modern age'; the war had disrupted family life, the divorce rate was rising to unparalleled heights, there were emotional stresses and strains working havoc on the emotions of individuals; and he noted that the sex impulse was being abnormally stirred by films and modern novels, so that the consequence was hasty marriages, and trails of broken homes. He saw the solution as being to ensure that marriage was rooted in a secure religious faith.

Bertrand Russell believed that: 'The modern family has been weakened by the State.... Although the law means to uphold the family, it has increasingly intervened between parents and children and is gradually becoming ... one of the chief engines for the break up of the family systems.'

Current critics point to the increase in the number of men in prison, the number of crimes of violence, and the rise in the rates of illegitimacy and divorce as evidence of the failure of the modern family to socialize its members adequately and to provide a secure moral and social upbringing.

THE VIEW THAT THE FAMILY REMAINS SECURE

Ronald Fletcher in *The Family and Marriages in Britain* sets out a strong defence of the modern British family.

He believes that the family has not declined: 'It is not less stable than hitherto. The standards of parenthood and parental responsibility have not deteriorated.' He produces evidence to show that the changes over the last two hundred years have been for the better, both material and moral. He supports the view of the Church of England Moral Welfare Council Report concerning the family in contemporary society that 'the modern family is in some ways in a stronger position than at any period in our history of which we have knowledge.'

He provides a defence of modern parents and families. He argues that:
1   It cannot be shown that the modern family is less concerned to control its own affairs.
2   The families of the past were not morally superior to those of the present.
3   The family remains an economic unit in the sense that it is a supportive group for all members, and basic necessities such as sewing, washing, and cooking are as important as ever. Much time is spent balancing the household budget.
4   The family remains an important educative force.
Families are responsible to the State to support and help maintain the education system — this is a new responsibility. The family remains an important source of initial moral and social education (socialization and social control).

5   The family is still concerned to maintain the health and welfare of family members – and State provisions are the outcome of policies supported by individual family members.

6   The 'essential functions' of the family, centred on sexual relationships, parenthood, and homemaking, are fulfilled far more satisfactorily in the modern family than they were in the family of the past.

He concludes that the idea that the family in Britain has been 'stripped of its functions' during the process of industrialization is false. 'Both in the sense of being more intricately bound up with the wider institutions of society and with more detailed and refined satisfaction of the needs of its members . . . the functions of the family have increased in detail and in importance. . . .'

The view of Fletcher is supported by Margaret Stacey in her study of the family in Banbury. She also concludes that the family continues to fulfill what have been called 'non-essential functions'. Professor Titmuss believes that contemporary society is in the process of making parenthood a highly self-conscious, self-regarding affair. In doing so it is adding heavily to the sense of personal responsibility among parents, so that standards of parenthood are improving.

However, Fletcher accepts that 'we are greatly in need of more research on the family to clarify further the historical changes to which it has been subjected and to achieve a more reliable knowledge of its variable nature and conditions at the present time in different parts of the country and among different social groups and classes'.

Marriage in modern society

The institution of the family is closely linked to that of marriage, which serves to regularize the union in a socially acceptable way. In Britain marriage may be defined as a voluntary and monogamous union entered into for the mutual lives of the partners. Apart from the social approval endowed by marriage in its cultural sense, it also serves to stabilize the social system in some ways. The move in the U.S.S.R. to eradicate marriage in 1917 was reversed in 1936, when it seemed that the lack of a stable family system had begun to undermine the fabric of Russian life. Marriage provides the partners with particular roles which help to perpetuate stable family life. Rituals and ceremonies help to establish the seriousness of the institution for the society and the nature of the duties and expectations which marriage partners owe to each other on a lifetime basis.

Some observers suggest that attitudes towards marriage are changing so that it will eventually become unnecessary in modern society.

The Report on the Royal Commission on Marriage and Divorce 1956 concluded that: 'Matrimony is not so secure now as it was 100 or even fifty years ago. . . . There is a tendency to take the duties and responsibilities of marriage less seriously than formerly . . . this is insidious and endangers the whole stability of marriage.'

34

IS MARRIAGE A SOCIAL INSTITUTION OF DECLINING SOCIAL VALUE?

Evidence for the view	*Evidence against the view*
1 There has been an increase in the number of divorce decrees made absolute — from an average of 2 p.a. before 1857 to more than 77,000 in 1972.	1 The population has doubled since 1857. Marriage remains as popular as ever. There is a lower percentage of unmarried people than at any other time. More than 70% of divorcees remarry.
2 People are becoming more divorce-minded, which under-mines the stability of marriage.	2 About 60% of divorces occur after ten years of marriage. Other marriages at risk are where the bride is pregnant or the partners are under 21. More than 90 in 100 do not end in divorce.
3 There has been a rise in the number of illegitimate births and in the number of abortions. Women are more economically independent than ever before, so that marriage is no longer an economic necessity. Illegitimacy carries less stigma.	3 Marriage may not be neces-sary for the reproduction of the population, but it provides for it in a regulated and socially accepted way. Research evidence suggests that the illegitimate child suffers severe educational handi-caps.[1]
4 More couples may be seeking companionship rather than a family from their relationship. Attitudes may be changing, in that marriage may no longer be seen as an ultimate goal by which a girl can attain security and status.	4 It is difficult to imagine that marriage will ever disappear. It is an integral part of our social system. It has a normative quality. People conform to it be-cause it is seen as an expected pattern of behaviour. It gives security and status.
5 Marriage has been tradition-ally defended by the Christian Church. But there is a belief that the power and authority of reli-gion is declining in Britain. The result may be that the spiritual and sacramental quality will dis-appear from marriage as the attitudes of people change still further.	5 Although it is true that fewer people are attending church services at present than in the past, there is evidence to show that there remains a deep sense of religiosity in people, in that large numbers continue to seek the Rites of Passage at times of birth, confirmation, marriage, and death.

[1] See 'Handicap of a poor start', Research findings, pages 8–9.

6   There are increasing strains making stable married life more difficult in modern industrial society: boring work; housing problems; poverty; rush hour travel; easier and cheaper divorces. Traditional values are questioned and the mass media help to propagate new ones; 'deviant models' of behaviour – e.g. the unorthodox life styles of film stars and the like – may be seen as representing new norms; and there are increasing facilities for marital infidelity.

6   It is dangerous to look back to the days when there were only a handful of divorces per annum and assume it was a golden age when the moral climate was superior and family life happier. There have always been strains making marriage difficult. We do not know how many unhappy unions were maintained in the past because the partners did not have access to divorce legislation. It may be that the marriage ceremony gives people more resolve to work through difficulties, which may not be so true of those who have not made solemn and legally binding vows.

---

7   Marriage partners may be entering marriage with the view that it is not necessarily a contract for life. If this attitude became widely prevalent it might undermine the basis of marriage and family life.

7   Marriage continues to represent very deep and intimate bonds between partners. There is perhaps a deep psychological need for permanence and fidelity, which would make the idea that marriage was a short term affair unthinkable for the majority entering marriage on a voluntary basis.

Dominian in his book *Marital Breakdown* comments that since the stability of the community is intimately connected with the welfare of the individual family unit, society has a triple responsibility regarding marriage:

1   It has to provide a legal structure that safeguards lifelong stability while making it possible for men and women to start afresh when their previous attempt has not succeeded.

2   It needs to ensure that its citizens are protected as far as possible from contracting marriages whose survival is extremely hazardous.

3   It must provide all possible help to assist marriages in difficulty. (Marriage guidance, psychiatric services, child welfare.)

Prevention, reconciliation, and an effective system for dissolution are society's three responsibilities.

Sociologists have accumulated data which highlight areas of risk. In the U.S.A. sociological studies have associated marriage breakdown with non-church weddings and low socio-economic position; but these have not been confirmed in British studies. However, more research is required in this area.

Marriages at greatest risk of breakdown in Britain
1   Where the bride is pregnant at the date of marriage.
2   Where the partners are under the age of 20 at marriage.
3   Where the couple are childless.
4   Where the couple have been married for ten years or more.

A short history of divorce

Before 1857 there were on average two divorces per annum. It was a complicated and expensive undertaking. The case was taken first to a Civil Court to claim damages, then to an Ecclesiastical Court to prove the offence, and finally to Parliament, where a Private Act of Parliament was required to terminate the marriage. Such a procedure was clearly only available to the most wealthy section of society.

In 1857 the Matrimonial Causes Act was passed, which simplified procedure and allowed the petitioner to sue for divorce in one court at a much reduced cost. Nevertheless it remained prohibitive for the majority until the introduction of legal aid schemes in 1914 and 1949.

The Act of 1857 provided for divorce proceedings on the grounds of the wife's adultery alone, or the husband's adultery but only if aggravated by cruelty or desertion. It was not until the Matrimonial Causes Act of 1923 that a wife could petition on the same grounds as the husband – adultery alone. Further provision was made in 1937 when dissolution was possible on the grounds of adultery, desertion, cruelty, and insanity.

In 1950 existing legislation was consolidated, when it was held that the law must endeavour to buttress marriage, fear was expressed that further reform would weaken marriage as a social institution, and it was recommended that costs should be maintained at a high level.

After 1958 no divorce could be granted unless the court was satisfied that suitable arrangements had been made for the children. In 1963 collusion (agreement between the parties) was converted from being an absolute to a discretionary bar to divorce.

In 1966 *Putting Asunder*, the Report of a group appointed by the Archbishop of Canterbury, put forward the recommendations of the Church of England. It advocated that the irretrievable breakdown of marriage should be substituted for the existing grounds of divorce. Irretrievable breakdown was defined by Lord Walker as: 'where the facts and circumstances affecting the lives of the parties adversely to one another are such as to make it improbable that an ordinary husband and wife would ever resume co-habitation'.

In 1969 the Divorce Reform Act was passed. Its main provisions were:
1   There will be only one ground for divorce in Britain – proof that the marriage has irretrievably broken down. This will be deemed to have happened:
(*a*)   If the parties have ceased to cohabit for two years – in practice have

37

parted or have simply stopped sleeping together – and neither objects to a divorce. (This amounts to divorce by consent.)

(*b*) If the couple have ceased to cohabit for five years even though one does not want a divorce. (This permits divorce by compulsion.)

(*c*) Conduct which a husband or wife cannot be reasonably expected to endure, or adultery which either cannot after reflection forgive, are both evidence that the marriage has broken down.

2 No divorce can take place until the court is satisfied that the best possible arrangements have been made for the children, and the best possible financial arrangements have been made between the parties concerned. The Law Commission believes in principle that suits for damages against co-respondents and actions for enticement against 'the other woman' should be abolished. Insanity disappears as a ground for divorce and is replaced by 1(*b*).

There is much debate as to whether a divorce adversely affects the children of a marriage and causes them emotional problems. Most evidence suggests that it is not the divorce as such which causes difficulties for some children, but rather what happens to them in the home before and after it. In many cases a divorce which separates unhappy and disturbed parents may be beneficial to a child.[1]

The changing role of women in society

WORK

Studies shows that there is an increasing number of women entering the labour force in industrial societies, especially from the married sector. The reasons include the fact that families are smaller and completed at an earlier age, there are wider opportunities for women, and there are demands for higher living standards which two incomes can provide.

One third of the work force in Britain are women (about 9 million). Of this figure approximately 1.75 million women are in Trade Unions, 5 million are married, 3 million are in manufacturing industries, 2 million are in distributive trades, and 2 million are in professional and clerical jobs.

PROPERTY RIGHTS

Before 1857 married women had no legal property rights. In that year an Act was passed which protected the property of deserted wives. In 1870 the Married Women's Property Act gave women further rights to certain kinds of property. The Act of 1882 extended these rights so that a woman had a legal right to (*a*) all property belonging or coming to her, (*b*) all earnings and savings of her work; but it also made her liable to support a pauper husband. Subsequent changes in the divorce law and

[1]See research findings, p. 44.

in thousands

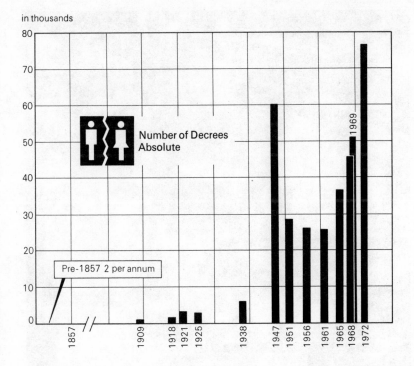

Number of Decrees Absolute

Pre-1857 2 per annum

1969

in thousands

Number of Marriages in Britain

Average age of marriage (1970) :
for men 24   women 22

Women at work: packing bars of chocolate

Property Acts made provision to secure improved rights for women. The most recent, established in the Matrimonial Proceedings Act 1970, asserted the principle that the contribution of the wife who does not go out to work but remains 'a housewife' during the period of the marriage, must be recognized in financial terms if there is a divorce or separation. Parliament implied that a division of assets should be on the basis of a half share to each partner.

POLITICAL RIGHTS

In 1869 women were given the vote in municipal elections. In 1888 they obtained the vote for the new county councils. It was not until 1918 that all women over 30 were given the vote in general elections, and complete equality with men was not obtained until 1928, when all women over 21 were entitled to vote.

EDUCATION

The Education Act of 1870 provided the first national system open to all children. However, even 45 years later, in 1915, educationalists were still concerned about the problem of what should be taught in schools to girls. Welton wrote:

The problem is one which the present rapid changes of opinion as to woman's sphere in the world render especially difficult of solution; particularly with respect to girls of the middle classes. There is an increasing tendency for girls to be prepared to enter various forms of professional and commercial life. This involves a strenuous intellectual application during the years of adolescence, which the generally considerable industry of girls renders particularly trying . . . . There is danger that the old and beautiful ideal of womanliness may suffer in the rough and tumble of competition with boys, with their coarser fibre and greater inertia in all that relates to mental work.

Even for girls who received a formal education before 1870 there were few opportunities to obtain a higher education. In 1840 Queen's College and Bedford College (part of London University) were established. It was not until the 1870s and 1880s that women's colleges were established at Oxford and Cambridge (although full membership was not granted until the 1920s). Teacher's Training Colleges (now known as Colleges of Education) became established after the 1902 Education Act. Before that date there had been a few 'voluntary colleges' founded in the nineteenth century; their national development enabled more women to obtain professional qualifications.

The first students of Girton College, Cambridge, 1871

TIME SPENT IN CHILD REARING

Professor Titmuss comments that 'the typical working class mother of the 1890s married in her teens or early twenties and experiencing perhaps as many as ten pregnancies, spent about 15 years in a state of pregnancy and in nursing a child for the first year of its life. She was tied for this period of time, to the wheel of child bearing. Today for the typical mother the time so spent would be about 4 years.' He goes on to consider the significance of these changes, and notes that 'at the beginning of this century the expectation of life for a woman aged 20 was forty-six years. Approximately one-third of this life expectancy was to be devoted to the physiological and emotional experiences of childbearing and maternal care in infancy. Today, the expectation of life of a woman aged 20 is 55 years, maternal care taking only 7% of this.'

What these changes mean is that by the time the typical mother of today has virtually completed the cycle of motherhood she still has practically half her total life expectancy to live.

WOMEN'S LIBERATION

Some observers believe that women remain 'second class citizens' in society today. They argue that there are many areas of discrimination and prejudice which limit the expectations and ambitions of many girls from an early age. They suggest that the structure of British society is biased in favour of male supremacy and dominance, and that opportunities for women remain limited.

In an article in the *Observer* in 1971 Anna Coote explains how the traditional male and female roles are established at an early age and the consequences of this.

A handful of disadvantages suffered by women are based on the law. The rest are rooted in the traditional assumption that man is superior to women and destined to perform a totally different role in life. Girls are encouraged to accept their expected female role. They are given dolls, dolls' houses, little housewife cleaner sets, toy kitchens containing utensils for the modern miss to cook just like mother. Their sights are set firmly on the home while their brothers play with mechanical toys that turn their attention towards their masculine role in society. School reading books reinforce the distinction between the roles expected of little boys and little girls. Few girls' schools ever have adequate facilities for teaching science – boys seldom learn to cook, make beds, wash or iron.

At most mixed schools (as well as a number of girls' schools including Roedean) the head teacher is a man; the doctor is a man, the TV news is read by a man – and God is a man – so it is not surprising that children develop the idea that authority is naturally invested in the male of the species.

Girls are encouraged to be passive, responsive, eager to care for children. They are taught that their goal in life is a man: as a result

'Women's Liberation': a march down Whitehall calls for equal education, pay and opportunities

most regard employment as a stop-gap between school and marriage, and few bother with further education. While almost as many girls as boys take and pass O levels — the proportion of girls taking A levels is just over a third.

Out of 62,000 undergraduates in 1970—20,000 were girls (17,000 of whom are studying arts, social science and commerce). Out of 10,000 students admitted to engineering courses 240 were girls. Nearly all craft apprenticeships are closed to women. 35% of boys aged 15—18 receive day release training. Only 9% of girls do. Of 130 new Directors of Social Services (a profession largely built up over the years by women) only thirteen are women. There are only twenty-six women M.Ps. That is one to every twenty-four men in Parliament.

When a woman marries she changes her title from Miss to Mrs and assumes her husband's name (although she is not obliged to by law). She assumes her husband's domicile, and her income is regarded as part of his for income tax purposes. If she qualifies for sickness benefit she gets £3.50 instead of £5 for men and single women. It is often difficult for women to make H. P. arrangements, and a single woman often has to provide a male guarantor. Only 12% of all councillors are women. In an article in the *Guardian*, Mary Stott notes that in 1971 there were upwards of 50 Women's Liberation Groups meeting regularly all over Britain. The major part of their campaign was concerned with more nursery education, birth control clinics, provision for unmarried mothers with children, equal pay and job opportunities, and the removal of the legal, tax, and financial disabilities of women.

Does divorce or a broken home lead to delinquency?

Research studies indicate that there is no direct connection between the two factors. Homes may be 'broken' in many ways — not only as a result of divorce. A broken home can be caused by the death of a parent, imprisonment, desertion, incompatibility between parents who may continue to live together. There are many possible consequences: not only social and psychological, but also economic problems may emerge. Living standards may change, a mother may be beset by financial worries which transmit themselves to the children; but that does not necessarily mean that she will care less well for them.

Some studies suggest that one of the major effects on the personality of the child, which may help shape its future conduct, is the degree of disharmony that exists between parents before divorce or separation. In some cases a divorce may usefully remove the children from an environment of conflict and distress. The period of time following the divorce or separation is also significant. A child may be badly influenced by the conflict that can result from contact with a step-parent — or may gain much from a new, harmonious home life. The children found to be at greatest risk are those under the age of four at the time of family breakdown.

Other variables have also been identified, including the sex of the child (boys may be more vulnerable than girls), the personality of the parent or step-parent is important, as is the atmosphere in the home before and after the divorce. It has been found that the young male delinquent is more likely to have a defective relationship with the father than with the mother. In general the concept of the 'broken home' must be treated with care: a child will be distressed where relations between parents are disturbed.

RESEARCH FINDINGS 1

A study by Norman Humphrey entitled *The Changing Structure of the Detroit Mexican Family* is an interesting example of what life in a city can do to a migrant peasant family in North America. When the Mexican family moves into a large urban area the structure of the family is radically changed. Whereas in Mexico a rural based peasant family is patriarchal, with all members having clearly defined customary roles and statuses, the new environment quickly begins to effect changes on the family group. The urban culture imposes new patterns of behaviour, new values and duties which do not match the previous expectations. The result is that the traditional basis of secure family life is undermined.

The father faces the greatest difficulty in coming to terms with the new environment and its pressures. On arrival he may face problems in obtaining satisfactory work or long periods of unemployment. There are housing problems and social isolation, all of which may quickly undermine his role as head of the household and cause a loss of respect and status in both his own eyes and those of his family. If he fails to adjust he may abandon his family or suffer personality changes or other emotional crises.

Traditionally, the woman takes a subservient place in the family hierarchy. Her place is in the home looking after the social and religious welfare of the children. Initially they would be expected to behave in the city environment in the same way as they did in the peasant setting that they have left. But through force of circumstance, the study showed that many came to take advantage of the greater freedom that city life offered. They refused to accept subordinate roles and often became the most dominant members of the family, directing policy and taking decisions. The rate of transformation of roles in the new environment was found to depend on the degree to which its members retained their traditional Mexican cultural values or assimilated those of the urban American.

In general three major changes were identified with regard to the changing structure of the urbanized migrant Mexican family:

1 Both the father's self conception and his actual role and status decline in relation to that of his wife and children.

2 The wife comes to occupy a more dominant position in the family.

3 The status and attitudes of the children come to resemble that of the typical urban American child, of precocious self-confidence.

The problems of loss of identity and the difficulties that immigrants face in coming to terms with a new urban culture are described by Rosemary Collins in an article in the *Guardian* in February 1973. She explains how young social workers in New Cross and Deptford, described as a 'racially tense' area, have established an advice centre for families and individuals who live in the area. A West Indian housewife asked for advice about her son aged 13, who had stayed away from home for three nights although he had gone to school as usual. She had left the boy in Jamaica with his grandmother until a home was ready for him in England and now wondered why he spoke more kindly of his grandmother than of her. She demanded traditional West Indian obedience from him at home, which was at odds with the discipline in his English school and still more unlike the behaviour he saw in the homes of his white friends. Last week he stole something from a shop in order to be caught, because he wanted to be sent away from home. Mervyn Henry, a social worker, explained to her what must be the boy's point of view — that he was alienated both from traditional West Indian values and those of the white community. 'It's easy to explain why boys get into trouble,' he says, 'but it's not so easy to find a solution.'

RESEARCH FINDINGS 2

1   *The family in Tikopia* (Studied by Raymond Firth. 1928/29)
This is a patrilineal society. (Descent is traced only through the male line.)
The average population of a Tikopian village is 50. Each house has a canoe
shed and land and a cook-house, which is owned by a family. In the village
kinsmen are apt to be close neighbours of one another. They accept the
leadership of an elder belonging to the clan. Village land and houses belong
to several clans, one on which tends to be dominant.

One of the centres of attraction linking villagers together is the spring,
the waters of which are piped in hollow tree trunks down to a pool used by
all. The village as a whole works together. Members are also linked
through ties of descent via male ancestors. (Descent also determines
ownership of houses and land, and duty of obedience to a particular chief.)

The economy: Fishing gear may be individually owned. Canoes are held
in the names of the heads of the kinship groups. The catch is shared equally
by the crew. Crops are also shared by those working the land plots.

The household: The household usually consists of several family groups.
For example, two brothers with their wives and children, each taking a
section of the floor. A man may have his unmarried brothers and sisters,
or his father and mother with him. Very few dwellings are occupied by
single persons. Usually the need for co-operation makes it convenient for
a single persons to join another household. There are strong incest taboos,
much like our own, and marriage with a kinswoman closer than second
cousin is frowned on. A Tikopian man has no restrictions on his choice
of wife. There may be much promiscuity before marriage, but little or none
after. No marriage ceremony as such is performed; the couple settle down
together when the woman becomes pregnant in a permanent and socially
recognized union. Terms of endearment (comparable with our 'dear' or
'darling') are not used. They address one another as other people address
them, by the house name of the husband. Neither is there any personal
joking between husband and wife. The father has limited authority. Sons
are expected to look after their parents in old age. Social standing in
Tikopian society is associated with a man's duties in religious ritual.

2   *Born to Fail* by Peter Wedge and Hilary Prosser
This study showed that one in four of 10,504 children surveyed who were
born in a single week in March 1958 were growing up in a family of five
or more children or with only one parent. The same proportion lived in
bad housing, and one in seven was in a low income family. One in sixteen
suffered all these handicaps. The disadvantaged group represent two
children in every British classroom, amounting to 900,000 children in all.
They face adversities which condemn them to a life of adversity and potential failure. One tenth of the group had fathers who were out of work for
more than a year. The chances of this happening to a child outside this
group are one in three thousand. As far as the disadvantaged group is concerned their health was poorer, their school attainment lower, and their

physical environment worse in almost every respect. The research suggests that these children require more social work support and better educational facilities; but above all there needs to be better redistribution of material resources for such families.

EXERCISES
1 Explain the difference between the extended and the nuclear family. What are some of the advantages and disadvantages of the two types of family system?
Into which category does your own family fit more closely?

2 'In rural based societies the extended family is more usual than the nuclear family.' Suggest ways of testing this hypothesis.
What kind of structures are most common in the area in which you live?

3 Outline the differences that have occurred in the structure of the family in Britain since 1870.

4 Suggest ways by which it would be possible to find out:
(a) What are the dominant social attitudes towards marriage and divorce in Britain.
(b) The extent to which these have changed over the past 50 years.
(c) The dominant attitudes of the partners towards marriage in modern Britain and the ways in which these have changed since the turn of the century.

ESSAY QUESTIONS
1 Describe and account for the changes in family life in Great Britain since 1870.

2 To what extent have changes in the attitudes towards marriage, the changing role of women, and the changes in the divorce laws from 1857 made the family a less stable institution?

3 What functions did the family serve in society before the onset of industrialization? To what extent has the State taken over most of these today?

4 Compare the functions of the family in an industrial and in a non-industrial society.

5 Is the family system in Britain today in a state of decay or is it more stable than at any other time?

Typical office workers in the 1930s

Cloth-capped factory hands leaving work in the 1930s

3 Social Class

What is social class?

A layman when first considering the question of social class often believes that a person's income or wealth is the main determinant; and he will usually identify three main groups — variously described as 'upper' or 'aristocratic', 'middle' and 'lower' or 'working' class. Sometimes subgroups like 'unemployed' or 'poverty group' are included. But problems soon arise when he tries to classify people around him into the various class groups on this basis. Does one place the highly paid unskilled worker in a higher class group than the white collar worker, who is usually considered to have more status in the community? And does an unskilled pools winner change his class overnight as the result of the sudden increase in wealth?

Sociologists would suggest that the answer to both questions is 'no', because income alone is not a satisfactory determinant of class membership. The discussion has already introduced the factors of income or wealth, occupation and status; and so class must be a concept which is made up of many related factors.

Some people argue that class is a myth: that it only exists in the minds of the observer — and that if you do not believe that class divisions exist then they do not. Others believe that this is a mistaken view since there is too much objective evidence that class differences are a reality (although they would agree that precise distinctions are blurred except when comparisons are made between extreme ends of the social scale). In discussing class membership there is a certain amount of inevitable generalization and stereotyping involved when describing the 'typical member' of a class group. These factors emphasize the problems involved in trying to decide what class really is. It is no longer possible to identify a member of the 'working class' by his cloth cap and bicycle, nor a member of the 'middle class' by his accent and bowler hat.

Research suggests that members of social class groups have many features in common and these tend to contrast with features of those in other class groups. Apart from income, wealth, occupation, and status they also maintain a set of attitudes and values which are common to their class group.

The sociologist's view of social class

When sociologists use the term 'social class' they are referring to broad social groups which can be ranked in socially superior and inferior positions, both objectively and subjectively, according to particular criteria. It has been found that each class group tends to share certain features in common and that there are distinctions between each of the class groups.

In analysing the class differences that exist in British society sociologists are not suggesting that those in higher class groups are in any sense better than – or superior to – those in lower class groups, but only that their patterns of behaviour are in some respects different from each other. Ultimately, the point of using the concept of social class is simply to try to explain social phenomena and to direct attention to areas of need and areas of concern for the administrators in society. For example, if most delinquents can be shown to come from one social class, or if research shows that children from one class group perform less well in school than those in another, then perhaps aid should be directed to that group. Class is a useful concept when making an analysis of a problem in society because research regularly shows correlations that exist between social class and the feature being investigated.

Every society has a system of ranking: some groups rank higher and some lower in order. The three significant rewards of high social class position are power, privilege, and prestige.

What is the basis of class membership?

Although most people seem to be conscious that they live in a society which is divided into different social segments which can be called 'class groups', it is a difficult term to define with any precision. (It is also a touchy subject in that people do not like to be categorized, and they may not like to categorize others.)

Certainly a person's class cannot easily be assessed on the strength of only one factor such as income or wealth, and so it is helpful to consider several class factors:

1 Occupation
2 Income and wealth
3 Status
4 Attitudes and normative values
5 Life style and life chances
6 Family background
7 Power

That is to say that class is a combination of all of these factors.

Sometimes it is easy to identify a member of a high or low class group: for example, a man earns £10,000 per annum. He is a company director (as was his father). He owns an expensive car; he sends his children to a public school and votes Conservative; he lives in a detached house in the country and his friends are doctors and lawyers. But it is when people display some of the characteristics and not others than identification and categorization are difficult. Often a person's status (the fact that he owns an expensive car or house, etc.) is mistaken for his class. It may be that he does not have any of the traditional 'middle class' attitudes and values, and that he does not mix socially with established middle class people. And so it is likely that whilst he may have high status with regard to some factors, he has low status in others. Because of these problems sociologists tend to use a simplified system which is based on 'occupation' to establish class membership. This is because research shows that there is a good correlation between occupation and the other features of class membership. For example, the status, attitudes, life style, life chances, family background, and degree of social power of an unskilled labourer are almost always very different from those of a professional man, such as a doctor. Although the labourer may be earning a high income his spending patterns will tend to be different from those of a member of a higher social class group. That is not to say that the doctor spends his money in better ways, but only in different ways. And so the method which is most widely used in sociology is that of the Registrar General's classification. This is based on occupation. Other, more precise measures, also based on occupation have been suggested and a scale known as the 'Hall Jones Scale' is sometimes used. In the U.S.A. other methods have been adopted.

THE REGISTRAR GENERAL'S CLASSIFICATION

An example of its use can be seen in *Patterns of Infant Care* by John and Elizabeth Newsom.

Classification by father's occupation

Class	Description
1 & 2	Professional and managerial (sometimes termed intermediate). Includes doctors, teachers, nurses, company directors, shop keepers who own their own businesses, police officers.
3	White collar: clerical workers, shop assistants, tradesmen in one-man businesses, foremen and supervisors in industry. These three groups constitute the 'middle class' of society (about 35% of the population).
3	Skilled manual: skilled tradesmen in industry, drivers.
4	Semi-skilled: machine operators, bus conductors, window cleaners, driver's mates, porters, etc.
5	Unskilled: labourers, refuse collectors, cleaners in industry, messengers, those persistently unemployed. These last three groups constitute the 'working class' element of society, about 65% of the population.

The authors of the study point out that a certain amount of discretion must be allowed in allocating families to particular class groups on a scheme of this kind. Occasionally they used some information about the mother's occupation or former occupation in order to amend the father's classification upwards. Thus the family in which the father was a shop assistant and the mother a teacher was classified as Class 2.

They note, too, that some occupations are so loosely defined that it is difficult to allocate them in any simple way to a class group. In such cases they took additional factors into account. Information about the kind of house lived in, the extent to which the wife seemed to be an educated or cultured person, the number and type of books in the house. But it is almost impossible to be completely certain that the classification is accurate, and anomalies are bound to occur; and to this extent the Registrar General's classification is a useful but crude method. It is operationally most successful at extreme ends of the social scale, in revealing differences in behaviour between those in Classes 1 and 2 and those in Class 5.

THE HALL JONES SCALE

Class	Description
1	Professional and high administrative, including all occupations calling for a highly specialized experience and frequently for the possession of a degree or comparable qualification needing long periods of training and education.
2	Managerial and executive, including those responsible for initiating and implementing policy.
3	Inspectional, supervisory and other non-manual higher grade. Not so much responsibility as in Class 2, but may have some degree of authority over others.
4	Inspectional, supervisory and other non-manual lower grade. Restricted authority over others, but nature of job requires some responsibility.
5	Skilled manual and routine grades of non-manual. Skilled work implies special training or apprenticeship and responsibility for the process on which the individual is engaged.
6	Semi-skilled manual. No special skill or responsibility involved, but the individual is doing a particular job habitually and usually in association with a certain industry or trade.
7	Unskilled manual. Requires no special training and is general in nature, rather than associated with a particular industry.

In a study carried out in the U.S.A. Warner divided each of the traditional classes into two sub-classes:

Class 1 Upper Upper (1.4% of the population)
Class 2 Lower Upper (1.5% of the population)
Class 3 Upper Middle (10.2% of the population)
Class 4 Lower Middle (28.1% of the population)
Class 5 Upper Lower (32.6% of the population)
Class 6 Lower Lower (25.2% of the population)

He found characteristics associated with each of the six classes.

Class 1   The 'aristocratic families' distinguished by wealth.
Class 2   The newly rich.
Class 3   The 'pillars of society' who got things done in the community.
Class 4   Tradesmen and well paid white collar workers.
Class 5   Skilled workers, low paid.
Class 6   Unskilled, the destitute etc.

THE OBJECTIVE VIEW OF CLASS

The problem arises — do I belong to the class with which I identify or with that to which I can objectively be shown to belong? Sociologists suggest that there are objective criteria, of which occupation, status, and life style are good indications, of a person's class membership (i.e. if he is an unskilled manual worker he is listed as being a member of class 5; if he is a successful doctor or lawyer he is classified as being a member of class 1 on the Registrar General's scale.)

THE SUBJECTIVE VIEW OF CLASS

Why is a person not necessarily a member of the class with which he identifies? The main reason is that true class membership implies a total way of life, and an acceptance by others within the class group. A semiskilled worker may believe he is in the middle class, but he will probably not be accepted by other middle class people, and so he will not display the traditional characteristics of the middle class individual. It is likely that most of his attitudes, his life style, and life chances will remain those of the semi-skilled category. (Yet his subjective class membership may, for example, affect his voting behaviour. If he sees himself as middle class he may vote Conservative.)

Wilmott and Young questioned people about the class they thought they belonged to in their study *Family and Class in a London Suburb*. They found that nearly half (48%) of the 355 manual workers in the general sample considered themselves middle class, 3% said 'upper middle', 35% 'middle', and 10% 'lower middle'. They found that 'middle class' identification was just as frequent among the unskilled, the semi-skilled, and the skilled. Of 257 skilled manual workers in the general sample, 49% said they were 'upper middle' or 'lower middle'; of the 98 semi-skilled or unskilled the figure was 43%.

Willmott and Young question who these manual workers are who describe themselves as 'middle class', and suggest that they are generally people who have some of the possessions that go with a middle class style of life: living in their own homes (as opposed to any form of rented accommodation), owning cars, having telephones — and no doubt nowadays owning colour television sets. They found that manual workers are in many ways divided amongst themselves, as are the non-manual workers. But whilst being so divided they found evidence (which was later supported by the findings of Lockwood and Goldthorpe in their study of the affluent worker in Luton) that they might still be united against each other: 'The nearer the classes are drawn by the objective facts of income, style of life, and housing, the more are middle class people liable to pull them apart by exaggerating the differences subjectively regarded. In Woodford this has been done with such success that to a very large extent social relationships are confined to one side or another of the dividing line in the mind. In many ways Woodford is a friendly place; its inhabitants have an active social life. But this friendliness is bounded by class lines. If middle class people have friends they are usually middle class too; if working class people have friends they are usually working class too. There were still two Woodfords in 1959, and few meeting points between them.'

The origin of class

Sociologists suggest that the origin of class divisions can be traced to a variety of factors: to the acquisition of power as a result of military conquest, to the division of labour and the ability to control the factors of production, or to the structure of modern society which requires only a few to administer, who thereby gain highest status. In simple folk societies differences are mainly those of age, kinship, and sex. Differences based on class factors begin to appear as society becomes more complex. Education and training are initially a scarce resource and only available to a select few. The need for a massive work force begins to demarcate one group from another. The more privileged sector may seek to perpetuate its power and limit entry to its ranks. In this respect there develops a close connection between social class, status, and power. The prestige attaching to those high in the social scale becomes hereditary in that it is ascribed to each new member at birth. One of the consequences may be that their path through life may often be economically and socially easier than that of the individual who seeks to obtain status and prestige by means of his achievements.

The Marxian theory of class

Marx (1818–83) described the existence of two main class groups based on economic distinctions. He spoke of the Bourgeoisie – those who owned the means of production, the 'capitalists, landlords, and factory owners' and the Proletariat – those who had nothing to offer in the market place but their labour, the mass of the working people. He argued that to own the means of production is to be in possession of political and economic power. He said that the political organization of a society is the expression of the interests of the ruling élite and gives power to that class. In his interpretation of history (which he claimed was a scientific interpretation) he placed a great deal of emphasis on the struggle between the owners of the means of production exploiting the class of wage earners. He predicted that after a succession of crises capitalism would collapse, a revolution would occur and power would be transferred to the proletariat, and a more egalitarian society would emerge. His concept of class was based on the single economic dimension — that of economic power. But sociologists do not consider that this alone is a satisfactory way of defining class membership. Furthermore, many of the predictions made by Marx in relation to his theory of class and social evolution have not been borne out. One can also question the extent to which it is possible to develop a 'scientific view' of the unfolding of history and a blueprint for the ideal society. If you were to draw up a plan of the perfect society — how many or your friends would find it acceptable? Marx looked towards a society in which there would be complete equality between all citizens, no distinctions of status or class, total co-operation between all members, and the gradual elimination of any form of organized government — the State eventually 'withering away'. Some of his ideas have been put into a novel by William Morris entitled *News from Nowhere*.

Karl Marx

The significance of class

Some sociologists emphasize that class is most significant in relation to the life chances and life expectations that an individual may have in society, so that a person's class position may determine the standards of medical care enjoyed, the type of education received, standards of housing, leisure activities, occupational choice, and life expectation – life chances in a literal sense.

Studies show that the behaviour and attitudes common to different class groups are maintained by traditional class norms. It has even been suggested that the business executive who has 'the wrong address – and the wrong wife' may be subjected to considerable social pressures to change both. And the child with a taste for classical music encountering an environment dominated by preferences for pop will also encounter pressures to conform to the norms of his peers.

Each class environment helps to form the personality and values of its members by means of subtle influences throughout life. Their horizons of expectation, their beliefs about their own capabilities, and the attitudes with which they will face life are fixed in an often permanent way.

The characteristics of class divisions tend to be found in all industrial societies. There are, however, other forms of stratification which are much more rigid and influential on an individual's life style. The caste system is an example of a society in which no social mobility is possible. This is said by sociologists to constitute a 'closed society'.

THE CASTE SYSTEM

The classic caste system is that of Hindu India. Caste membership is by birth and is not alterable during the lifetime of the individual (unless the status of the entire caste is changed). There are five main caste groups:

1 The *Brahmins*, the highest caste, priests and religious men.
2 *Kshatriya*, rulers, administrators.
3 *Vaisya*, merchants and farmers.
4 *Sudras*, manual workers
5 The 'Untouchables', social outcasts.

Any physical contact with those of a lower caste is considered to be a pollution and special religious processes are needed to obtain cleansing. Caste membership determines occupation, marriage partner, income, residence, appearance, and dress.

Class differences in British society are much less marked; white collar workers tend to be more socially mobile and have better work prospects than manual workers, but there are few of the obvious differences that exist in caste society.

Social status

Although the concept of status is closely linked to that of class there is a distinction, which can be expressed in terms of the existence of status groups and class groups.

An Indian potter at work

Status groups consist of individuals each of whom shares in the eyes of others similar standing, prestige, or regard. This may be in terms of their occupation, particular skill, or other behaviour which is highly rated by the group. An individual may have many statuses according to the groups to which he belongs, as captain of a football team, owner of an expensive car, and so on. Status refers to the prestige and respect paid to a person by the group's members. But he has only one class.

Social class is a more collective term to describe the broad groupings into which individuals and groups are categorized in so far as they share similar life chances, attitudes, and values.

While there may be a close relationship between a man's social status and his class it is not a necessary connection. It is possible to obtain many status symbols (a large house and expensive car) but they do not provide sufficient information to pinpoint class membership.

Social mobility

Sociologists study the causes and effects of the movement by an individual up or down the social hierarchy. It is generally measured in terms of the extent to which a person differs in social class or status from his father or grandfather. Many argue that in modern industrial societies movement is comparatively easy. Research by Cyril Burt has suggested that there is a fairly high degree of mobility in Britain — as much as 30%. But a comparative study by Miller in 1960 concluded that no country among the fourteen

57

for which data was available has any considerable movement from the manual strata into the upper levels of society. There is a good deal of occupational shifting within the same occupational class groups, but mobility is reported to be mainly within manual and non-manual occupations rather than between them.

The main avenues of mobility that have been studied include:

1   Educational achievement. This is significant since entry into the higher occupational groups usually requires formal qualifications which only advanced study can provide. Many studies have shown that middle class children are able to make best use of educational facilities, whereas children from class 5 suffer many major disadvantages, thereby limiting their future mobility.

2   Marriage. A study by Berent of mobility and marriage found a high degree of class endogamy (marriage between members of the same class) but suggested that it has declined to some extent since the turn of the century. He also found the educational status of the partners was closely related. He found a tendency for women to marry men in a social class above their own.

3   Occupation. Most studies of mobility use occupation as an index, since there is widespread agreement about the ranking of occupation in order of social merit, and it is generally one of the most convenient methods. The individual who obtains professional status and whose father was in a semi-skilled category can be said to be socially mobile. In general, white collar workers have greater changes of promotion, greater security, and higher status than manual workers, whose opportunities in these respects are limited.

Other influences affecting degree of mobility include:

1   The degree to which the individual is motivated and detached from the normative values of his class. Upward mobility implies an ability to absorb and adopt a new environment. Research suggests that the middle class individual, from classes 1 and 2, has higher achievement motivation than a person from classes 3, 4 or 5.

2   The extent to which a special skill confers high status and gives access to regular contact with those in the highest social strata. (In this respect, professional sport may be providing a new route to social mobility.)

Ralph Turner has suggested that two polar types of mobility are possible. He describes these as:

1   Contest mobility — in which contestants strive by whatever means they can to obtain the main prizes available in a competitive society. They compete on reasonably level terms, accepting the basic rules of fair play — the most competent person attaining the goals of high status and prestige.

2   Sponsorship mobility — in which the individual is sponsored, like one who joins a club on the invitation of the membership. He is selected because he has in the eyes of the other members the qualities desirable in an acceptable club member. On this view recruits are chosen for positions of power and authority by the established *élite* on the basis of some

Professional football as a road to social mobility: Mike England of Tottenham Hotspur at home with his family

supposed criteria of merit, which may be the school attended or the family background and connections.

In fact, upward mobility takes place to a considerable degree by both methods in societies which are socially divided. But Turner argues that in Britian the sponsorship norm is dominant, whereas in U.S.A. it is the contest norm that is prevalent. He says that in Britain children are selected at an early age for the type of schooling that will offer greatest prestige and status (especially public school education). Secondary modern schools may in the past have even served to inhibit mobility, although this is now less true in that they offer a wide variety of academic qualification. He is suggesting that in many cases those who reach high positions of power and authority do so for reasons other than their proven ability, and that in Britain there remains a strong 'old school tie' network.

RESEARCH FINDINGS

The Significance of Class

1   Little and Westergaard describe the British educational system as 'a kind of obstacle race', with fewer and fewer children getting through to the next stage. The lower the child is down the class ladder, the smaller his chances of survival in the educational race. At age 11–13 a class 1 and 2 child has nine times more chance of being at grammar school or public school. At 17 he has thirty times more chance. One in four class 1 and 2 children who reach grammar school go on to university. One in twenty come from the class 3, 4, and 5 groups. The proportion of students at university from the working class groups is the same as it was in 1938 – about 25%. Bernstein's research shows that working class children may

fare badly at school because they do not communicate well in the middle class language used by the teacher. Also working class mothers may hinder their child's development since they do not spend as much time as middle class mothers in talking to their children, nor do they give such constructive answers to their questions. Lack of success within the educational system may cause many working class children to grow to see themselves as 'failures' and so limit their potential horizons. Davie, Butler, and Goldstein show that the chances of an unskilled manual worker's child being a poor reader at 7 are six times greater than those of a professional worker's child.

2   Douglas says that 'the persisting social class differences in educational opportunity are comparable with persisting class differences in infant mortality. During the last fifty years the maternal and child welfare services have been greatly expanded and improved and the chances of survival of infants have been improved dramatically in each social class. However, the relative levels of infant mortality rates have been maintained. Indeed, the unskilled manual workers are relatively worse off today than they were in the past. Where services have been expanded or improved it seems that those who least need them have benefited most. For example, the considerable number of additional maternity beds provided during the last twenty years has been taken up largely by women with relatively small numbers of previous pregnancies whereas those who are having their fourth or later baby – who are in a more risk laden group – are still as likely as they were twenty years ago to be delivered at home. The fact that services are improved or expanded does not mean that they will be available to those who need them most. Put in an educational context, one could imagine circumstances in which large sums of money might be spent on education without improving the opportunities of those sections of the community that are least well provided for today.'

3   David Butler (*Political Change in Britain*) says that 'the most important single consideration determining the way that people vote is class. People tend to vote on class identification.'

4   Class membership may affect the 'social rewards' (or the costs) of people in society. For example, a baby born in class 5 was statistically more than twice as likely to die in the first year of life as one born in class 1 at the dates given in the table.

Class Differences in infant mortality rates per 1000

Class	1921	1939	1950
1 Professional	38	26	17
2 Intermediate	55	34	22
3 Skilled	76	44	28
4 Semi-skilled	89	51	33
5 Unskilled	97	60	40

5   MacDonald showed that there is a correlation between the social class of the juvenile delinquent and the frequencies of the offences they commit. The variable 'father's occupation' was the one most closely associated with delinquency. Most come from households in the unskilled manual group (class 5).

RESEARCH FINDINGS: ATTITUDES AND VALUES

Lockwood and Goldthorpe studied class attitudes and concluded:

In the findings of these studies we have in fact probably the clearest indications that are available of the basic differences in the social perspectives of working and middle class persons and, thus, an important guide to the core distinctions which would be relevant to any discussion of their respective life-styles. For this reason it may be useful to set out here — if only in a very simplified way — certain of the major conclusions which were arrived at in all three investigations.

(a)   The majority of people have a more or less clearly defined image of their society as being stratified in some way or other; that is to say, they are aware of inequalities in the distribution of wealth, prestige and power.

(b)   One 'polar' type of image is that of society as being sharply divided into two contending sections, or classes, differentiated primarily in terms of the possession or non-possession of power (the working class view of wage earning manual workers). Contrasting with this is an image of society as comprising of an extended hierarchy of relatively 'open' strata differentiated primarily in terms of prestige (the middle class view of salaried non-manual workers).

On the basis of the research in question, and of earlier studies of class values and attitude it may be illustrated in the following schematical and, we would stress, ideal-typical manner.

	Working class perspective	Middle class perspective
General beliefs	The social order is divided into 'us' and 'them': those who do not have authority and those who do. The division between 'us' and 'them' is virtually fixed, at least from the point of view of one man's life chances. What happens to you depends a lot on luck; otherwise you have to learn to put up with things.	The social order is a hierarchy of differentially rewarded positions; a ladder containing many rungs. It is possible for individuals to move from one level of the hierarchy to another. Those who have ability and initiative can overcome obstacles and create their own opportunities. Where a man ends up depends on what he makes of himself.
General values	'We' ought to stick together and get what we can as a group. You may as well enjoy yourself while you can instead of trying to make yourself 'a cut above the rest'.	Every man ought to make the most of his own capabilities and be responsible for his own welfare. You cannot expect to get anywhere in the world if you squander your time and money.

	(on the best job for a son) 'A trade in his hands.' 'A good job.'	'Getting on' means making sacrifices. 'As good a start as you can give him.' 'A job that leads somewhere.'
Attitudes on more specific issues	(towards people needing social assistance) 'They have been unlucky.' 'They never had a chance.' 'It could happen to any of us.'	'Many of them had the same opportunities as others who have managed well enough.' 'They are a burden on those who are trying to help themselves.'
	(on Trade Unions) 'Trade Unions are the only means workers have of protecting themselves and of improving their standard of living.'	'Trade Unions have too much power in the country.' 'The Unions put the interests of a section before the interests of the nation as a whole.'

One has here, thus, two sharply contrasting social perspectives, each of which comprises a set of internally consistent beliefs, values and attitudes.

(Affluence and the British Class Structure, 1962)

EXERCISES

1   To what extent would you say that you have been influenced by the class membership of your family?

2   Social class membership can be shown to affect the individual's life in society. Explain how it may influence the following:

(*a*)   Educational performance   (*b*)   Voting behaviour

(*c*)   Job choice   (*d*)   Life chances and life style

3   Suggest ways by which it might be possible to identify a person's class membership in an accurate way.

4   Suggest hypotheses that relate class and leisure activity, class and delinquency, class and higher education. Outline the ways in which these could be tested.

ESSAY QUESTIONS

1   A young unskilled manual worker may be earning £40 per week. A young highly qualified white collar worker may be earning £20 per week. How far does this show that Britain is now a classless society?

2   Is Britain a class or status society?

3   An unskilled manual worker wins a small fortune on the football pools. He buys an expensive car and house and finds that his neighbours are lawyers and business executives. He claims that he is now a member of the middle class. Do you agree?

4   What are the main determinants of social class? To what extent do members of different social classes exhibit different patterns of behaviour?

4 Wealth, Income, Social Policy

The distribution of wealth and income

Facts published in *Social Trends No. 3* in 1973 indicate that a wide gulf exists between the manual and the non-manual workers in Britain in terms of relative wealth.

Percentage of population	Amount of national wealth owned	
	1961	1971
Richest 1%	38%	30%
Richest 5%	50%	56%
Richest 10%	78%	72%
Poorest 50%	7.5%	9.8%

The *Department of Employment Gazette*, November 1971, showed that differentials between high and low wage earners were reduced slightly during the preceding twelve months. The average wage for male manual workers was £29 p.w. and for non-manual workers £39 p.w. The average for female manual workers was £15 p.w. and for non-manual female workers it was £19 p.w. In 1969 nearly half the country's adult male workers earned less than £24 p.w. The figure for women was £13 p.w. In 1970/71 there were 1.2 million men whose weekly earnings were below £20 per week.

In January 1973 a National Opinion Poll showed that two people out of three thought that the present pattern of wage distribution in Britain was unfair. One in four thought it was very unfair indeed. The public broadly agreed with a panel of lay citizens and groups of industrial relations specialists that a coal miner, an ambulance driver and a farm labourer performed a more useful function than a docker or a car production worker, although these latter two groups of workers had higher incomes: the average weekly earnings of car assembly workers were £33, dockers £39, coal miners £29.70, ambulance drivers £26.80, and farm labourers received a wage increase in 1973 which gave them an average of £18.50.

Commenting on the results of the survey Peter Wilsher in the *Sunday Times*, February 1973, points out the problems of making a valid comparison between different occupational groups in order to determine satisfactory rates of pay. It is difficult to measure the value of one occupation against another; what qualities can be suggested as criteria of job importance, and in what order should they be listed? They may include skill, responsibility, productivity, age, long service, danger – but are there others which are more important? Yet there is no doubt that the majority of people feel deeply that a scale ought to exist: 'The notion that useful vocations like nursing and garbage collecting should take a back place in the pay queue – while pop singing and property development reap the prizes ... does set a lot of teeth on edge.'

In 1971 the Trades Union Congress lifted the Unions' target to £20 for a 40 hour week. This is a basic wage exclusive of overtime and special bonus payments. The aim is to eventually reduce the working week to 35 hours.

It is in the face of facts such as these that the question of a more equitable distribution of income and wealth arises. Great wealth is a source of power and privilege. It is hard for the average individual to accumulate great wealth – which is passed on from one generation to the next in very wealthy families by inheritance. If a man of 25 invested £100 per year at an interest rate of 6% he would receive £100,000 at the age of 95!

Those who are opposed to any kind of redistribution of income claim:
1   It is human nature to accumulate wealth – there are always some cleverer than others who would obtain the income of the less clever.
2   If people are taxed too heavily it removes the incentive to work hard.
3   The present distribution of income and wealth is reasonable.

Those who argue in favour of a major redistribution claim:
1   The rich gain their wealth from inheritance and as proprietors of business enterprises. They do not work any harder for their high incomes than the poorest paid. Two thirds of those with more than £100,000 inherited more than £25,000 of it.
2   Sixty years ago Lloyd George said 'A fully equipped Duke costs as much as two dreadnoughts – and Dukes are just as great a threat and they last longer.' We have not moved far in producing greater social equality since then.
3   It has been said that 'our tax system breathes through its loopholes'. Rich people can escape their taxes, death duties, etc. by employing skilled accountants to find the loopholes. 'Only the stupid, the absent minded, and the unlucky pay estate duty.'
4   Since wealth provides power, then such power ought to be held in a publicly accountable way, which privately held wealth prevents.

The source of wealth in a society

The economic system of a society is responsible for the creation and distribution of wealth. The wealth so distributed is known as income. In advanced western societies income is derived from:
1   Labour, known as 'earned income', and obtained in wages and salaries.

2   Property and investments, which may be in stocks and shares, Building Societies, land and business premises. This is known as 'unearned income'. In non-capitalist or socialist societies income cannot be derived from this source.
3   State benefits, sometimes known as 'social income', including pensions, allowances, and other benefits.

Who are the rich?
The very rich can be classified into four main groups:
1   Old landowning families. For example, the Duke of Westminster (whose son the Earl of Grosvenor inherited £11 million on his 21st birthday and threw a party on his 90,000 acre estate for his tenants to celebrate the fact) and the Duke of Wellington, who sold a part of his Hampshire estate for £1,150,000 in 1970.
2   Inheritors of industrial empires. For example, successive generations of the Pilkington family, whose glass manufacturing industry is believed to be worth more than £150,000,000. Bobbie Butlin took over control of his father's Holiday Camp empire in 1968, when the annual profits were nearly £20 million.
3   Builders of first generation empires. For example, business men like Harry Hyams who started from scratch in 1945, Sir Charles Clore who started with little and is now in control of the Selfridges Group, many High Street shoe shops, Garrards, the Crown Jewellers, car distributors and ship builders, Sir Isaac Woolfson, and Sir John Cohen who established the Tesco supermarket chain, have all become multi-millionaires in their own lifetimes.
4   Major shareholders and participants in family trusts. For example, variations in settlements involving more than £3 million for the family of Lord Cowdray were approved in 1970.

There is no significant evidence to show that the very rich are losing their wealth as a result of changes in the structure of taxation since the war. It has been noted, however, that among the wealthiest 1% of the population very few hold individual fortunes. Personal holdings are spread around family members to reduce the amout paid in taxes. In the industrial giants — firms like I.C.I. and Shell — control has passed into the hands of paid directors who may have only small shareholdings.

In 1966 the Central Statistical Office published the figures in this table.

Assets	Value	Numbers owning
Landed property	£23,000 million	6 million
Stocks and shares	£13,000 million	2 million
Cash in the bank	£10,000 million	18 million
Private property and income	Less than £1000	7 million
	Between £3,000–£5,000	2.5 million
	Between £100,000–£200,000	30,000
	More than £200,000	14,000

Statistics for 1961 from the Inland Revenue showed that the millionaire group had increased from 63 to 81. There are some extreme cases of highly paid executives – in Britain the highest is thought to be £260,000 p.a. In the U.S.A. the Chairman of General Motors earned $889,963 in 1972. In Britain salaries of between £8,000 and £40,000 are equivalent to an after-tax figure of between £4,000 and £12,000. The richest 80,000 people pay 75% tax on the last slice of their income, and the rate on unearned income is even higher. However, those in the highest income brackets do enjoy valuable fringe benefits – expense accounts, the use of the firm's cars, and high social prestige and honour. They tend to get a better yield on their investments because they are better advised than the average person and they can afford to take greater risks.

Supplements to income

SUPPLEMENTARY BENEFITS

Between 1948 and 1966 the National Assistance Board was responsible for assisting people whose resources fell below a standard approved by Parliament. In 1966 the Board was replaced by a scheme of Supplementary Benefits administered by the Ministry of Social Security. Supplementary pensions and allowances are cash benefits for people who are not in full time work and whose income from pensions, wages, and other sources is not enough to meet their needs. It is paid of right and does not depend on having paid contributions into the scheme. Claim is made by completing a form obtained from a post office.

Here are some examples of the benefits available (1973):

	Weekly rate	Claimant over 80
Married couple	£13.65	£16.60
Single householder	£8.00	£10.65
Person 16–17	£5.15	
Dependent child 13–15	£4.35	
Under 5	£2.40	
Blind married couple	£15.70	£18.65

Those who receive supplementary benefit are automatically entitled to free prescriptions, free dental treatment, dentures, and glasses, free milk and vitamins, and free school milk.

FAMILY INCOME SUPPLEMENT

This is a benefit of up to £5 a week for families with one or two children and up to £6 a week for larger families. It is only available to those in full time work (30 or more hours a week).

Here are some examples of the amounts available (1973):

Number of children in family	Levels of income below which the family qualifies	Maximum payable
1	£25.00	£5.50
2	£28.00	£5.50
5	£37.00	£7.00
6	£40.00	£7.00

Who are the poor?

The surveys made at the end of the nineteenth century first revealed the extent of poverty in the major cities of Britain. It was found that more than 30% of the populations of the cities of London and York were living in poverty 'so abject that they were unable to maintain a standard of living sufficient to supply the bare necessities of life'.

A further survey in 1936 showed that there had been little change. It has been shown that the most rapid decrease in inequality of income distribution occurred between 1938 and 1948. But since then there has been a less rapid closing of the gap between rich and poor. Recent research suggests that the gap between the extreme ends of the social scale is increasing. The poorest section is not benefiting by changes in the structure of taxation or social welfare as much as the more affluent sector, which also makes better use of available services and facilities.

A survey made in 1966 and published by the Ministry of Social Security as *Circumstances of Families* in 1967 calculated that there were nearly 500,000 families containing nearly 1,500,000 children that were either living on supplementary benefit or had incomes below supplementary level. Of these, 140,000 families did not qualify for supplementary benefit because the father was in full time work and 20,000 could not claim benefit at the full rate because of the wage stop.[1] These 160,000 families whose incomes could not be raised to the minimum level included about 500,000 children.

A survey in 1968/69 by the Department of Health and Social Security showed that more than 75,000 men in full time work were living below the poverty line. The poverty line depends on the circumstances of each family. The Supplementary Benefits Commission makes fixed allowances for married and single people, for each child, and for rent. The total is the poverty line for the family concerned and represents the level below which the State believes it should not be allowed to fall. For example, a married couple with 2 children aged between 6 and 11 with a rent of £5 p.w. would qualify for a supplementary benefit payment of £17.50 a week, which would become their poverty line. (1973)

The Child Poverty Action Group Report 1971 stated that: 'The poor

[1] The wage-stop: a rule which lays down that the Supplementary Benefit must not bring the total income above what the person receiving it would earn in full-time employment.

Below the poverty line in Salford

can expect to get poorer and families in most need will suffer increasing hardship.' The report suggests that the increased charges in school meals, prescriptions, and dental treatment will lead to greater hardships for those on low incomes, because they will either pay more or else make less use of services. Evidence of malnutrition among school children is already alarming. It estimates that there are about 25,000 children in Manchester and Salford who come from families living on or below the poverty line. Schemes for exemption and remission are dismissed by the report as ineffective because they involve an extension of means testing.[1]

It has been shown that up to 1961 'the poorest families paid out 28% of their wages in tax. By 1966 the burden increased for everyone below £1,700 p.a. While the poor and moderately well off (often with incomes boosted by the earnings of working wives) have failed to capture any significantly larger share of life's good things for themselves, the wealthiest section has maintained its hold of the major part of the wealth of Britain.'

The poor may be categorized as:
1   The unemployed. There were more than 1 million in 1971/72, the highest figure since before the last war. The number dropped to approximately 700,000 in 1973.
2   The low paid. There were more than 2 million adult men earning below £25 per week in 1973.
3   The elderly. There are more than 8 million people over the age of 60.
4   One-parent families.
5   The sick and disabled.

Research by Nicholas Bosanquet published in 1973 shows that as many as 10.6 million people in Britain were living at about the level of income which can be described as the poverty line: 76p per day for each married adult and 40p for each child — to cover all outgoings except rent. This represents the Supplementary Benefit allowance. On this basis a fifth of the population live in the world of the hard pressed. He shows that the gains to poorer families at work were rather small between 1960 and 1973, and suggests that without a policy to help the low paid there is likely to be an increasingly bitter struggle for income between manual and salaried employees.

How can income and wealth be redistributed?

From time to time suggestions are put forward for ways of alleviating the problems of poverty and low standards of living.
1   It may be possible to improve the system of social welfare and to increase benefits, especially family allowances and pensions.
2   The tax system could be changed to increase the burden on the rich and reduce it on the poor. Some recent attempts in this direction have not completely succeeded. The Budget of 1972 removed three million

[1]Means testing: adjusting payments according to the means of the applicant.

people from paying any tax, but the paradoxical result was that they did not benefit as much as the average wage earner who paid 2% less in tax than he did previously. The very rich benefited most of all. Those earning more than £15,000 p.a. in unearned income received an extra £1,430 p.a. and those whose unearned income amounted to between £20,000 and £50,000 received an extra £1,700.

3   A negative income tax system has been suggested, which would cover 90% of the population. For them, the main personal allowances for taxation would be abolished (child and family allowances). People would receive a 'tax credit'. For most tax payers there would be little change in their take home pay since they would get back what they had lost in allowances. But for those paying little or no income tax, the tax credit would give them more than they would lose. This system would increase their take home pay.

4   Trade Unions advocate the introduction of a national minimum wage to eliminate the group of low wage earners from potential poverty.

5   The sociologist Peter Townsend argues that Britain needs a central department of social planning to weigh up the allocation of resources to education, health, housing, and social security (advised preferably by social scientists), and to explain itself publicly in a series of forward plans. More than anything else, he says, Britain needs a comprehensive policy for families.

Why does poverty continue in Britain?

1   Many people still believe that if you are poor 'it is through your own fault'. It is widely believed that poverty ceased when the Beveridge Report was implemented in 1948. In fact there are many reasons for poverty which are beyond the control of the individual and which were not eradicated by Beveridge – parts of his report were never implemented. He demanded family allowances, for example, at 'subsistence' level. But year after year family allowances are left unchanged despite continuous inflation. If Beveridge were fully implemented now they would have to be around £2.50 per week, instead of 90 p current in 1973.

2   There is much evidence to suggest that a great number of those in need often do not apply for the help that the State provides. In some cases they are not familiar with the procedures, in others they do not wish to submit to detailed investigations of their background or means, and would rather do without than accept 'charity'.

3   There are weaknesses in the benefits regulations. There is the wage-stop regulation which requires assistance to be below normal earnings. Benefits are not granted to a family where the head is in full time work. Most children in poverty have a parent working long hours at a low paid job.

4   Poverty is often inherited. The child of a poor family attends irregularly a school with poor amenities and probably a high turnover of staff. He

The Citizens' Advice Bureau is one agency that helps people who are not familiar with the procedures to claim the benefits to which they are entitled

leaves as soon as possible to enter an unskilled job. He marries early a wife from a similar background and produces a family in a crowded flat or house, has frequent job changes, and is often out of work. His children follow the same path.

5   Governments regard the problem as one which is gradually being defeated. In 1937 it was reported that 4½ million people in Britain were suffering from malnutrition. In 1973 Sir Keith Joseph, Secretary for Health and Social Services, introduced a new scheme to help those in poverty by providing £10 million to raise Supplementary Benefit levels. He said, 'There is no definitive overwhelming evidence about the state of the very poor that they are poorer than they were. There is mildly encouraging evidence that there are fewer of them and they are relatively less poor.' The poor would benefit very much from the increase of £3.50 in the needs allowance and from the increase in rate limits of £1.50 for rent rebates. They had benefited from the postponement of the 2p increase in school meals. He announced aggregate improvements of the order of £55 million. This would go to abate family poverty.

Professor Abel-Smith suggests that any sensible policy to deal with poverty should be preventive. He says that we need more decent housing for low wage families at rents they can afford. Educational opportunities must be made equal in practice as well as theory. It must be made to be seen to be a continuing process. The child with little parental support needs the best school and the best teachers. Retraining and rehabilitation centres and services need to be extended and developed. More flexible retirement policies are needed. Families of excessive size need to be deterred. Making family planning an integral part of the Health Service would be one step in the right direction. While fatherless families cannot by wholly prevented, their number can be reduced. Expenditure on divorce is over 40 times greater than that on marriage guidance. High costs, legal delays, and the log jam of pending cases often represent major obstacles to the formation of new marriages. The most obvious remedy is to concentrate help where it is most needed. But any policy which expects the poor to volunteer for a means test will fail to reach thousands needing help — benefits being seen by many as charity rather than as of right. In the meantime, until some workable system is found whereby only the needy are helped, the only practical way of helping the poor is by giving benefits to all, including those who do not need them. This is the traditional answer: higher family allowances, pensions, benefits for the sick, the unemployed, the disabled, etc. We are forced to accept solutions which seem both wasteful and costly. It is because of this dilemma that no government has solved the problem.

Social policy: the coming of the Welfare State

Social policy may be defined as 'the policy of the government with regard to actions having a direct impact on the welfare of citizens by providing them with services or income'. The most significant of these include public assistance, health and welfare services, facilities for education, and the protection of citizens. Social policies are designed to deal with social problems that are seen to exist as a result of statistical information, carefully researched reports, and other evidence. But what is seen to be a problem in one society may not be seen to be a problem in another: in this sense all 'problems' are relative to the time and place and economic development of the society.

There was very little attempt to introduce social policies which might benefit disadvantaged citizens until the nineteenth century. Development in this period led the way for the major transformations which occurred in the twentieth century. Poverty had always been regarded as a social fact rather than as a social problem. Traditionally the extended family was the main source of social welfare for the young and the aged. The dominant attitude had been that people should look after themselves, and there was little sympathy for the underdog.

With the growth of industrialization and urbanization new liberal social attitudes began to emerge which supported the view that there were some members of society who did need help and that it was the duty of the State to provide it. The Napoleonic wars in the first twenty

A 'refuge for the destitute', c. 1840

years of the nineteenth century imposed more hardships and showed
the necessity of State aid. A high proportion of the population were found
to be susceptible to changes in price levels; the war caused inflation and
poor harvests led to the Speenhamland system, by which the amount of
relief offered to the poor was tied to the cost of bread. But it proved to
be a demoralizing system, since wages were kept to a very low level.
Economists and humanitarians like Adam Smith and Jeremy Bentham
spoke and wrote about the way the poor should be treated.

Governments which saw a need to improve the methods used to assist
the poor, had no expert knowledge and no facts and figures. In 1830
there was a serious revolt by labourers which has been described as the
last violent protest in English history against rural conditions. A Commission was appointed to look into the workings of the Poor Law, which
dated from 1590. It was influenced by the concept of 'the greatest good
of the greatest number'. Whilst favouring Government intervention in
matters of poor relief, public health, and education, it laid down certain
principles to be followed:
1 There should be no relief for the able bodied.
2 A person accepting relief should be kept on standards below those
of the poorest independent worker, so as to encourage a return to work as
soon as possible.
3 The workhouse test should be applied: those who were offered a
'house' and accepted were those in genuine need.

It was not realized until the turn of the twentieth century that the cause of poverty had not been solved by the pronouncements of the commission and that the problem of poverty remained.

Boards of Guardians were established which administered relief in 15,000 parishes in England and Wales. These endured until the 1929. Poor Law Boards were replaced in 1919 by a Ministry of Health. The Report of 1834 embodied the underlying social attitudes of the day: any one who is poor, is poor because he is idle. It was not believed that there were any other reasons. 'The most important duty of the legislature,' it said, 'is to take measures to promote the religious and moral education of the labouring classes.' The aim of education was seen to be to teach the poor their duty and place and to inculcate in them true social and moral principles. Reading was encouraged, but not writing, for as one educationalists of the period said, 'to teach a pauper to write is like putting the torch of knowledge into the hands of rick burners'.

Dates of significant events in the field of social policy

1870   Forster's Education Act. Education was recognized as necessary in order to provide a skilled work force in an industrial society. The view that 'a free society could not be orderly unless it was literate' became more widely accepted.

1880   The *Spectator* described Britain as 'a place never more happy and tranquil'.

1885   Paupers were no longer disenfranchised.

1886   Serious riots occurred in Trafalgar Square.

1888–92 First major strikes by dockers and girls in match factories.

1889   Surveys were carried out which revealed the extent of poverty in London and York by Rowntree and Booth (whose book was entitled *Darkest England*). These revealed that 10% of the population was in primary poverty (having insufficient income to meet the basic requirements of physical efficiency) and 18% were in secondary poverty (unable to meet the bare necessities of life). Three quarters of those in poverty were poor because they were low paid or unemployed. The majority of the remainder had large families or were in poor health.

1901   The spirit of the age is reflected in the comment of *The Times*: 'Subsidized school meals will tempt parents to starve their children at home.'

1902   Balfour's Education Act reorganized the framework of education in Britain.

1904   Report on Physical Deterioration: recruits to the Boer War had been found to be of poor standard.

1905   The Unemployed Workmen's Act. Recognized the right of men to expect work. Attempts were made to tackle unemployment as a national problem.

1905–9 The Royal Commission on the Poor Law: 'A grand inquest on the state of the nation in matters of poverty.' Social policy was given new impetus and direction – whereas 'the object of the Nineteenth Century was to accumulate wealth the duty of the Twentieth is the more noble task of securing its better distribution.'

1906   The Liberals took office. Lloyd George said, 'In so far as poverty is due to circumstances over which the man has no control, then the State should step in to the very utmost of its resources.'

1908   Pensions were paid to those over 70 whose income did not exceed £31 a year. It was seen as a means of 'strapping a life belt to the toiler'. Those who had been in prison were not entitled to a pension until ten years after their release.

1908   The Children's Act: protected the health and rights of children. The State accepted obligations to provide for deprived children.

1909   The Royal Commission Report on Poverty was published.
1   The majority wished to keep the old Poor Law.
2   The minority (Sidney and Beatrice Webb) advocated prevention and said special agencies should be set up to deal with poverty. They believed that State intervention would not limit freedom but expand it for those who could not protect themselves.

1909   Lloyd George's Social Welfare Budget. But the distinction between the deserving and the undeserving poor remained. Pensions were not available to anyone 'who habitually failed to work or failed to provide for the future' (although Booth had already shown that one third of those in poverty had been thrifty in work).

1909   Churchill said, 'The social conditions of the British people in the early years of the Twentieth Century cannot be contemplated without deep anxiety.'

1909   The Labour Exchange Act. Set up the first Government Department to provide information and assistance as a public service.

1909   Beveridge wrote his book *Unemployment a Problem of Industry*. He saw defects in the view that all citizens could provide for themselves unaided against the problems of life.

1911   The National Health Insurance Act. Provided unemployment assistance. 'The greatest scheme for reconstruction yet attempted.'

1913   First payments were made to the unemployed. Small amounts were paid in (3d. from the employer, 4d. from the employee and 2d. from the Government) in return for ten shillings a week.

1918   Fisher's Education Act.

1918–39 The interwar years saw the consolidation of existing schemes. There was little development owing to severe economic crises and high inflation.

1919   The Housing and Town Planning Act. 'Homes for Heroes.'

Housing estates were built, together with new council houses.

1924   Wheatley's Housing Act. This made local authorities responsible for working class housing with Government subsidies. 500,000 council houses were built. (By 1934 there was still a shortage of 100,000 houses.)

1929   The Local Government Act abolished Boards of Guardians (established in 1834). The need for State assistance became more obvious.

1932   Unemployment reached 22% in England, 36% in Wales, and 13% in London (compared with 4% in 1973).

1942   Beveridge announced his plan 'for turning the idea of social security from words into deeds and for ensuring that the needs of all citizens will be met.' These included:

(*a*)   All in insurance for cash benefits.

(*b*)   Children's and Family Allowances.

(*c*)   Free medical treatment.

Insurance was to be obtained by single weekly contributions paid through an insurance stamp.

Lord Beveridge, architect of the 'Welfare State'

1944   Butler's Education Act. Introduced the tripartite system.
1946   The National Health Service provided 'free medical service'.
1947   The Town and Country Planning Act.
           The introduction of the Welfare State by Beveridge was seen
as a means of redistributing income to ensure the abolition of
social evils (unemployment, poverty, etc.). It was described
as 'the bravest and boldest attempt to set down on paper the
nation's peace aims in terms of a new social order'. It marked
the complete antithesis of the Victorian principles — help was
to be made available to all as a right of citizenship.

There has been a subsequent move away from 'benefit as of right' to
'benefit on a selective and discretionary basis'. Selectivity is said to ensure
that only those in real need get help; it provides greater finance for the
scheme and wider choices for patients. Those who do not favour selectivity
argue that means tests are degrading and the result is that many people
fail to apply for benefits to which they are entitled. But twenty-five years
after Beveridge there is still evidence of poverty existing in Britain. In
the Golbourne district of London more than 230 people were living to an
ancre in 1970, which was eleven times the average for greater London.
Evidence from such areas indicates that many people are trapped in a
cycle of poverty. The message of one grafitti writer is
          I don't believe in nothing
          I feel they ought to burn the world down
          Just let it burn down baby.

The interest of the sociologist

The sociologist is interested in the way in which problem areas are
identified and located in a society and the ways they are dealt with.
He is also interested in the impact that they have on the organization
and structure of the society. A sociologist may have a specific aim to
produce relevant facts and data with regard to areas of concern, or he
may wish to interpret the effects of particular policies.

Research studies have shown that social policy is affected by several
factors:
1   The answer given to the question 'to what extent should a man be
responsible for his own welfare?' had changed considerably between
1834 and 1948.
2   The current beliefs about the function and role of Government. Is
official intervention as far as social welfare is concerned acceptable or
desirable? Does it limit or increase social freedom?
3   The state of scientific and social knowledge. Problems can be recognized only when there are sufficient data and information about them.
4   The economic state of the country. Successful welfare policies can be
financed only by a strong and growing economy.

These factors interact and are subject to constant change. Social policy is never static, since both needs and resources alter. In Britain there has long been a difference of opinion about the desired ends of social policy: whether social action should be concerned primarily with those in greatest need or whether it should be undertaken to establish social rights for all citizens. Most social policy is the result of a compromise between these conflicting interests. In general, social policy is concerned with an attempt to protect those who are thought or seen to be weaker members of society (the young, the elderly, those in difficulty) and to promote the welfare of all citizens by providing services to meet all of their possible needs.

RESEARCH FINDINGS
The Aged in the Welfare State, by Townsend and Wedderburn
This survey formed part of an international study of old people aged 65 and over which was carried out in the U.S.A., Denmark, and Britain with the main object of measuring the extent of disability and incapacity among the aged in relation to their family and social relationships, occupation, housing, and levels of income.

The research workers in the three countries accepted precisely comparable methods of procedure and research, agreeing on a common questionnaire covering health, family and social activities, income, occupation, and retirement.

In Britain the main field of interest dealt with experiences of health and welfare services. This study contains information selected because of its particular relevance for immediate policy decisions concerning welfare services.

The methods of research
Information was collected from persons aged 65 or over on relationships between their individual disability or incapacity and (*a*) family and social activities, (*b*) occupations, (*c*) housing, (*d*) levels of income.

Two separate samples of people in Britain were selected at random, over 4,000 being interviewed in private households during two periods of 1962. Information was collected during 1963 about another 2,200 living in all types of institutions except general hospitals. A questionnaire lasting about one hour was drawn up. Two thousand local authority administrative areas were used as sampling units. At the second stage addresses were selected with equal probability from electoral registers in the areas to be sampled. At each address where elderly people lived (approximately one third) all were interviewed. Of those eligible, 4,067 (84%) gave full interviews, 11% refused to be interviewed, and 2.4% proxies were used because the person was unable to answer, being too ill. Approximately 4% refused to answer financial questions. In these cases the interviewers tried to obtain information about those who refused, but it was rather inadequate.

The result
As a result of the study much valuable information was obtained from

which it was possible to suggest and implement new policies to assist those in particular difficulty, and to recommend ways of preventing problems arising in the future.

RESEARCH FINDINGS

The Poor and the Poorest, by B. Abel-Smith and P. Townsend

The Poor and the Poorest, published in 1965, was the result of the authors' belief that 'existing income and expenditure data could be re-analysed to produce valuable information about poverty and the social aspects of income distribution'. They maintain that two assumptions commonly held may not be as true as is widely believed. These are (*a*) that we have abolished poverty and (*b*) that income is more equally distributed than at any other time. The purpose of their study was to 'find out from surveys done by the Ministry of Labour the number and characteristics of persons with low levels of living'.

In order to obtain their information they analysed and re-analysed data collected by the Ministry of Labour in two sample surveys — one conducted in 1953—4 and the other in 1960. The 1953—4 survey involved a sample of 20,000 households out of which 12,911 responded. The 1960 survey consisted of a sample of 5,000 out of which there were 3,540 respondents. For the purpose of their research they divided the population into three groups: (*a*) those whose basic resources fell below basic National Assistance scales; (*b*) those whose resources were less than 20% above National Assistance scales; (*c*) those whose resources amounted to less than 40% above National Assistance scales.

Owing to the size of the 1953 sample the authors decided to take a random sub-sample from the original sample, which entailed a 25% sample of households in the lowest income groups. On the basis of the results of the sub-sample estimates were made for the whole sample. They readily admit that estimations based on a small sub-sample are not statistically sound; but in spite of problems of comparison and under-representation the authors concluded that in 1953 10% of the population were earning little above the basic National Assistance rate, and that by 1960 this figure had increased to 18%.

EXERCISES AND ESSAY QUESTIONS

1   Discuss this statement: 'Although Britain is a wealthy and industrial society the gap between the rich and the poor remains. There is still much inequality in the distribution of wealth.'

2   By what means could wealth and income be redistributed or shared more equally? Is it socially desirable that they should be subject to stricter Government regulation?

3   'It is only human nature to accumulate wealth. If you are poor it is your own fault. The rich are rich because they work harder.' Discuss.

4   Select two of the following periods. Outline the main developments that occurred in social policy and explain their significance:
(a) 1834–1900, (b) 1900–1920, (c) 1920–1948, (d) 1948–1973.

5   In what ways did the attitudes towards disadvantaged citizens change after 1834? What caused the change?

6   'The underdog does not need the sympathy of successful people.' How far does this summarize the attitudes prevalent in the nineteenth century? In what ways did these views become modified in the twentieth century?

7   What is the interest of the sociologist in social policy? Outline details of two studies that you have read about with regard to poverty, ill-health, housing, or unemployment.

5 Education

What is education?

There is no general agreement about what is meant by education, and there is no absolute agreement about its aims. In general, it can be said to include: processes of learning, acquisition of knowledge, training in skills, morality, development of individuality and cultivation of character, the ability to organize experience so that priorities are made clear to the individual, making him more critically aware of his environment so that he can act effectively. All this is concerned to train the individual for his future work role.

There are many agencies of education in a society; it is not confined to 'the school'. It is a part of a complex process of socialization that transforms the child into a social being.

1 The school is the formal institution which is designed to provide detailed knowledge and to train the child into the accepted patterns of behaviour, which will enable him to participate effectively in the life of the society.

2 There are more informal agencies which include:

(a) The family, which provides initial socializing influences and reinforces the cultural values and formal learning processes. It helps to establish the 'horizon of expectation' of each child.

(b) The friendship group, neighbours and relatives, which helps to pattern the behaviour of the child, ensuring conformity to acceptable norms and attitudes.

(c) Youth clubs and other organizations attended on a voluntary basis, which provide introduction to useful leisure activities and training in participation and organization.

(d) The mass media, radio, TV, papers, books, journals, etc., which provide information and ideas absorbed by the individual in an informal way. They may help to develop critical faculties so that the individual comes to be more selective in his choices, and better informed.

(e) Current attitudes in the community, the norms of behaviour which the individual will adopt as a result of growing up in that community: these are the 'folkways' of the community and vary from area to area (traditions, customs, values, etc.).

In complex technological society there is a process of change and adaptation. The educational system is designed to introduce the individual to the complexities of the society and to enable him to deal more effectively with the problems and innovations he will meet in the wider society of adulthood.

Industrial society requires a well educated work force. Developed industry is the source of wealth and high living standards. It is argued by many educationalists that if vocational training were ignored the economy would suffer. (Some critics believe that this view may serve only to organize human beings to become 'cogs' in a social machine so that they come to behave with the precision and regularity of cogs.) Ivan Illich put forward the view that schools are not essential even in a modern state. He advocates 'de-schooling society' on the grounds that you cannot teach unwilling pupils and that those who can make best use of the school become the most privileged members of society.

The philosophy behind the introduction of compulsory education in the nineteenth century was that life in an industrialized, urban based setting required at least the basic skills of reading, writing, and arithmetic; the knowledge on which increased specialization rested demanded training that few parents could provide by themselves.

Educational expansion was generated by economic needs and by the social interests of a growing society based on technology. Education was seen to be a useful tool for social stability. 'A set of good schools civilizes a whole neighbourhood', said a Commission Report in 1858.

Effective political participation required an educated populace. The vote was of little consequence to the illiterate man. Education has been said to be 'the key that unlocks the door to modernization.' Today, questions about social justice and equality of opportunity – and the part that the formal educational system can play in attaining them – are more to the fore.

Brief outline history of education in Britain

597 St Augustine is believed to have established Church schools at Canterbury – to teach converts and train priests.
With the spreading of Christianity similar schools were set up in cathedrals and monasteries for vocational training.

1000 Some Grammar schools established (to teach Latin grammar and literature). Schools such as St Peter's, York, and Beverley Grammar School are thought to date from pre-Norman times.

1150 Oxford University founded.

1200 Cambridge University founded.

1382 Winchester College founded.

1440 Eton College founded.

12th – 14th century Growth of powerful merchant and craft guilds. Some of these established schools to teach crafts and skills. Many schools and colleges were endowed by individuals and by the guilds.

15th – 16th century	Between 300 and 400 endowed Grammar schools had been established. Not until the twentieth century was the country again so well supplied, in proportion to its population, with the means of education.
1545 – 7	Reformation. Dissolution of the monasteries put an end to much religious education.
16th – 17th centuries	The damage was repaired to some extent, town councils and merchant guilds established more schools and colleges.
1650	60 free schools established and maintained out of public funds.
17th – 18th	Grammar school and university education fell to a low ebb. Need for cheap labour paramount and little reforming zeal in Government.
1750	The Industrial Revolution produced a new middle class which began to patronize private schools.
1754	2,000 Church schools established, known as 'Circulating Schools'. Teachers circulated from one to another.
1800	Lancaster and Bell proposed the monitorial system to teach the 3 Rs. Founded the 'National Society for promoting the education of the poor in the principles of the Established Church throughout England and Wales'. 'The British and Foreign Schools Society' was founded.
1807	Samuel Whitbread proposed a Bill for a national system of elementary schools (rejected by the Lords).
1833	House of Commons granted £20,000 for education (and increased the grant to £30,000 in 1839).
1832–70	Pressure for Reform and for expansion of education for all.
1868	Taunton Report: discussed the question whether education should be the responsibility of the parent or the State.
1870	Forster's Elementary Education Act. School Boards were elected to provide schools out of public funds. Education established for the first time on a national scale and directed by the central government.
1880	Mundella's Education Act. Education made compulsory. Leaving age 10.
1889	Technical Institutions Act. Councils empowered to spend a limited amount of money on vocational education. Leaving age 12.
1902	Balfour's Education Act. School Boards replaced by Local Education Authorities, which were empowered to provide secondary education. Until 1902 less than 1% of those educated at elementary schools proceeded to Grammar schools. Leaving age 13–14.
1907	Provided for medical inspection in schools and provision of meals.

1918	Fisher's Education Act. Older and more able pupils to be given training in advanced practical work. Leaving age 14.
1926	Hadow Report. Introduced concept of 11 + and two stages of education: Primary and Secondary.
1938	Spens Report. Advocated tripartite system: Grammar, Secondary Modern, Technical.
1944	Butler's Education Act. Implemented Hadow and Spens. 146 Local Education Authorities were to produce a system of education suited to age, aptitude and ability of child. Three stages of free education: Primary, Secondary, Further. Religious Education lessons were made compulsory. School leaving age 15. The Act advocated 'parity of esteem' between children regardless of the school they attended.
1946	16 June: Circular 147 advocated the introduction of Comprehensive education defined as 'the secondary education of all children in a given area without organization on three sides'. First Comprehensive schools in London and Essex and parts of Wales.
1959	Crowther Report. Recommended that scientific education should be broadened; numbers in full-time education should be doubled; looked at the failure rate of day release students; part-time education for those of 16–18 who had left school at 15.
1963	Robbins Report. Looked at the aims of higher education. Advocated expanding university places.
1964	Newsome Report, entitled *Half Our Future*. Concerned with children of average and less than average ability. Attacked concept of 11 +. Introduced C.S.E.
1967	Plowden Report. Concerned with primary education and the transition to secondary education. Two hundred recommendations including abolition of 11 +. More financial aid for schools in poor areas and teacher incentives.
1972	School leaving age raised to 16 (advocated in 1944 Education Act).

The historical background in which education has developed in Britain has resulted in a complex structure in which religious and elitist attitudes and independent and State agencies have played significant parts.

The long history of religious influence was brought to bear in the Education Act of 1944 which established the desire 'to revive the spiritual and personal values in our society', since religion was seen to be 'the sanctifier of human activities, the protector of group continuity, and the builder of morals and solidarity'.

Religious knowledge and the basic elements of religion, ritual, feeling, belief, and organization, were to be taught. The Act required that 'every school day shall begin with a corporate act of Christian worship'.

The belief in the need to educate a small *élite* as future leaders or administrators is likewise rooted in history. Initially education was the prerogative and privilege of the wealthiest sector in society – those who could afford to pay the necessary fees or engage private tutors. Subsequently, after the introduction of a national system of education for all, the view was modified to that of providing a specialized education for the intellectual *élite* who could be selected on the basis of an intelligence test. It is a view which is widely debated still; it is seen by many to be socially unsatisfactory and by others to be socially necessary.

The private sector of education, fee paying preparatory schools and Public schools, is rooted in the guilds, the merchant philanthropists, and the religious orders of the Middle Ages. They endowed schools in order to prepare their pupils for entry into their ranks. It remains a significant feature of the British educational system, despite periodic attempts to limit its influence and authority. There are nearly 300 independent public schools in Britain, and although only 5% of the school population attend them they continue to provide a high proportion of students for universities and other areas of higher education.

The State intervened to provide an adequate system of education for all its citizens in 1870 when the first Education Act was passed, although education did not become compulsory until 1880. Subsequent Acts of major importance were passed in 1902, 1918, and 1944 – all of which came at the end of wars in which Britain was directly engaged. The educational and physical condition of recruits to the forces was found to be of such poor standard that major amendments to the educational system were seen to be necessary.

The structure of education
in England and Wales today

The Education Act of 1944 established 146 Local Education Authorities.[1] These hold almost complete power over the system of education adopted in their area. This explains the great variety of secondary schooling which is found throughout the country. In some areas there are Comprehensive schools, in others Grammar and Secondary Modern schools, and in others Middle schools and High schools.

The way in which they carry out their duties is supervised by the Secretary of State for Education (previously the Minister of Education) in the Department of Education and Science.

The Act of 1944 specified that 'the duty of the Minister is to secure the effective education by Local Education Authorities under her control [the first Minister was a woman, Ellen Wilkinson] and direction of the National policy for providing a varied and comprehensive educational service in every area'. The school leaving age was fixed at 15, with the recommendation that it should shortly be raised to 16.

[1] The number was reduced to 104 in the reorganization of local government that took effect in April 1974.

Under the Act the statutory system of education was reorganized in three progressive stages: Primary (age 2—11), Secondary (12—15), and Further education. The Primary stage was divided into Nursery (2—5), Infant (5—7), and Junior (7—11).

The Plowden Report, entitled *Children and their Primary Schools*, suggested that these schools should be given higher priority in the total educational budget. Educational Priority Areas should be designated where both the environments of the children and the school are poor, and teachers in these areas should receive additional payment. Class sizes should be reduced and corporal punishment abolished, and the worst deficiencies of Primary schools should be overcome. The recommendations have not yet been fully implemented.

Ellen Wilkinson with the 'Jarrow Marchers', 1936

SECONDARY EDUCATION

The major concept introduced in 1944 was that of tripartite education: 'At the age of 11 all children should pass into Secondary schools of which there should be three types: Grammar, Secondary Modern and Technical. All children should enjoy parity of esteem. There should be a common curriculum for the first two years to facilitate transfer for late developers.' (In practice only a small percentage were so transferred. The statement also implied a possible element of unreliability in the intelligence test.)

The Hadow Report of 1926 established that a selection process based on the level of intelligence of the child at 11 could be used to sift the highly intelligent child from the average and below. Children should receive an education suited to their 'age, aptitude and ability'. Those who did not show high levels of intelligence in the tests were to receive training in craft skills which would enable them to take their place in society as the necessary manual workers and technically skilled workers. There were in fact no academic examinations in Secondary Modern schools until the mid-1960s. The consequence was that more than 75% of the school population was leaving such schools without any academic qualifications.

Until 1966 about 25% of the school population attended Grammar schools, although this figure varied from area to area, depending on the number of Grammar schools and places available. In some parts of Wales the figure reached more than 40%, but in other areas of the country it fell as low as 10%.

The principle of selection was that of the 11 + intelligence test which was designed to measure the child's IQ (intelligence quotient) in the belief that it was fixed by the age of 11 and could be reliably measured.

The method has subsequently come under attack both on social and scientific grounds. The system was said to be both socially divisive and an unsound way on which to determine an individual's future.

INTELLIGENCE TESTS

In 1905 the French psychologist Binet devised the concept of 'mental age'. The dull child was said to be slow in his development – and to have a response of a child younger than his chronological age. The bright child was said to exhibit the behaviour of a child older than his own chronological age.

Terman later introduced the concept of an index of mental development:

$$\text{Intelligence Quotient (IQ)} = \frac{\text{mental age}}{\text{chronological age}} \text{ multiplied by } 100$$

If a child's mental age (as shown by an IQ test) was 15 and his chronological age was 10 his IQ would be 150 ($\frac{15}{10} \times 100 = 150$).

The average score is 100.

Those who oppose the use of IQ tests object to them on several grounds.

1   All they measure is the capacity to conform to the tester's rigid restrictions, and they do not measure the true range of a person's wide potential because they ignore his creative and imaginative ability and his social and physical aptitude.

An IQ question which asked, 'Select the odd word from this list: house; igloo; office; hut' gave 'office' as the correct answer because it is the only one that you do not live in. But some respondents wrote 'igloo' because it is the only one made of ice, others 'house' because it is the only one in which you would have an open fire; and others 'hut' because it is the only one in which you would keep your garden tools.

2   IQ may not be a fixed factor and may be open to improvement by means of coaching, incentive, and other motivation. This explains why children from classes 1 and 2 tend to do better on the tests than those from other class groups; their background, their parents, and their expectations place more value on doing well at such tests.

3   It is argued that a child's future should not be based on the result of tests of this nature which do not take account of the child's health or frame of mind on the day of the test.

Apart from the doubts raised about the methods of selection, the division between the Grammar school and Secondary Modern school came to be criticized on other grounds.

1   It was argued that the system perpetuated social class divisions, the school population being divided into the *élite* who were being prepared for positions of administrative responsibility and the remainder who were largely to become the manual workers in the community (with less opportunity for mobility, power, or social prestige).

The following table indicates the educational advantage held in 1955/56 by children from the highest social class groups compared with those from the lower categories.

Performances at Grammar School Selection, during grammar school and admissions to University, by occupation of father (boys, England and Wales 1955—56).

Occupation of father	Top group at entry to Grammar school %	Grammar school record of two passes at A level %	Students admitted to University from all Grammar schools %	Students admitted to University from all (incl. Public schools) %
Professional, Managerial & Clerical	33.5	52.5	63.5	74.0
Skilled Manual	45.3	38.8	30.3	21.7
Semi-skilled Manual	16.3	47.1	4.9	3.4
Unskilled Manual	4.9	1.6	1.3	0.9
Total %	100.0	100.0	100.0	100.0

School Leaving Age

Father's occupation	Number in sample	15 or below %	16 %	17 %	18 or over %
Professional	929	25	24	17	34
Clerical	882	59	22	9	10
Skilled	3666	78	15	3	4
Semi-skilled	946	85	11	2	2
Unskilled	852	92	6	1	1

From 15–18 1959 Crowther Report, Volume 1. Percentage distribution of National Service recruits to the Army and R.A.F. by age on leaving school and father's occupational background.

2   The Crowther and Robbins Reports expressed the fear that the aim to expand higher education was handicapped by limitations imposed by the Tripartite system, since opportunities for those attending Secondary Modern schools to obtain qualifications were few. The Comprehensive school was designed to help overcome this problem and to provide access to higher education for more pupils.

Percentage of pupils remaining after minimum leaving age in Comprehensive schools and Tripartite schools (Coventry and Leicester), 1964.

	Comprehensive	Tripartite
Coventry	57.6	39.3
Leicester	49.2	33.4

3   From the point of view of the child in school it may be that the prospect of the test puts a strain both on the child and the teacher, making the day-to-day education less spontaneous and interesting.
4   Much research suggests that assignment to a low status school or stream as a result of the test affects an individual's view of himself, so that failure is associated with a negative image of the self, which serves to limit horizons and expectations. This may be reinforced by the teacher who comes to see the child as a failure; and the child comes to perform in accordance with this expectation. (See research findings, page 104).
5   Although there was provision for the transfer of 'late developers' few ever were transferred. The result was that many able children either left school without adequate qualification or else did not receive the type of education which would have suited them best.
6   Secondary Modern schools were only occasionally endowed with facilities or buildings to match those of the Grammar school.

THE COMPREHENSIVE SYSTEM
This has become a political shuttlecock because it is promoted or denigrated according to the political party in power. The Labour Party favours the system because it is in accord with the principle of social equality, whereas the Conservative Party does not believe that the traditional Grammar school should be abolished when it has been a part of the system for so long and has been well tried and tested.

The Comprehensive system operates on the basis that all children leave the Junior school together and enter a Comprehensive school without any kind of entrance test. The scheme has some variations in different parts of the country, but the principle remains the same; all children should be educated in the same school and receive the same opportunity to obtain qualifications and training in skills to which they are best suited. In Leicestershire there is a scheme which enables parents to choose whether or not to send their children to the Grammar school. Pupils enter a High school at 11 and choose at 14 whether to transfer.

The aims of Comprehensive education are:

1   To abolish the 11 + and the stigma of 'failing the exam'.

2   To develop greater social intermixing.

3   To provide greater opportunity for pupils to find their levels of ability and obtain suitable qualifications.

4   To overcome the dangers of traditional streaming methods employed in Secondary Modern schools, which research has shown to be faulty.

Comprehensive schools either stream according to subject ability: if a child is able at English he moves to the A stream for that subject, if he is average at History he moves to the B stream for that subject, and if he is poor at Maths he moves to the C stream for that subject: or they do not stream at all, so that children are in classes of mixed ability and the teacher cannot influence performance by his prior expectation.

5   To provide a wider range of facilities and a staff who can offer an equally wide range of subjects to meet the needs of all pupils.

Some of the disadvantages of the system:

1   Comprehensive schools are generally very large, with more than 1000 pupils. It is argued that this makes it impossible for the staff to know the children personally.

2   It does not allow for parental choice. (Although, technically, parents are permitted choice under the Tripartite system it is generally difficult to exercise it.)

3   It is believed that able pupils may suffer if educated in the classroom with less able pupils.

4   It is seen as a largely experimental system which has yet to prove itself. Grammar schools have been in existence for hundreds of years, whilst Comprehensive schools have only been in operation since 1946.

Some results from studies suggest that whilst there may be fewer outstanding pupils being produced compared with the numbers who passed through Grammar schools in the past, average levels of ability are higher: fewer pupils leave school without any qualification, and more obtain higher standards than previously. A study in 1973 by Guy Neave, of the Sociology of Education Unit in Edinburgh University, showed that the Comprehensive school provides the best means of increasing the number of working class children reaching University. The proportion remained fairly constant between 1928 and 1968 at 28% (although the working class sector forms approximately 70% of the population). It is now approaching

38%, and the newer Comprehensive schools are doing better in this respect than the older ones.

INDEPENDENT SCHOOLS

These schools are organized independently of the State system, and most of them do not receive any money from the State. Their finances come from endowments and from the fees that they charge parents to educate their children.

1   Preparatory schools: Mainly for boys ages between 8 and 13. They prepare their pupils for entry into the Public schools.

2   Public schools: Those independent schools which are represented at the Headmasters' Conference. There are about 190 of them.

3   Direct Grant schools obtain some finance from State funds on condition that they offer 25% of their available places to children from the State system.

All Independent schools (including those maintained by a religious denomination) must register with the Department of Education and Science and conform to the regulations laid down as far as standards and facilities are concerned.

Advantages of the Independent school:

1   They have smaller classes, generally, than schools within the State system.

Tuition in a preparatory school

The public school: old and new buildings at Marlborough College

2   They generally have good facilities – especially for sport.
3   They can attract highly qualified staff.
4   They confer high status on their pupils.
5   They offer great social advantage, since the business and social connections of the parents are very extensive – hence the 'old school tie network'.
6   They are successful in obtaining a high percentage of university places for their pupils.

Criticisms:
1   They make for social distinctions between children.
2   Only 5% of the school population attends Independent schools, but they obtain nearly 25% of University places. (Some schools have long-standing connections with particular universities or colleges, facilitating entry for their pupils.)
3   Their existence may make for less social equality in the educational system, and the existence of the 'old school tie network' for inequality in the world of business. This is confirmed by a study published in October 1973, *Élites and their Education*, by David Boyd. He shows that

since the war there has been little change in the proportion of public school people reaching the upper ranks in the occupational hierarchy.

OTHER FORMAL AGENCIES OF EDUCATION AVAILABLE AFTER THE AGE OF 16

1   Colleges of Further Education

			Number of students, 1965
(a)	National Colleges	to provide advanced technical studies for	1,500
(b)	Regional Colleges	particular industries	89,000
(c)	Colleges of Art		120,000
(d)	Agricultural Colleges		1,500
(e)	Farming Institutes		9,000
(f)	Others: Commerce/Technology		1,440,000
(g)	Evening Institutes		1,250,000
(h)	Independent Colleges		17,000
Total			2,928,000

2   Polytechnics

A White Paper in 1966 entitled *A Plan for Polytechnics and other Colleges* advocated the designation of 30 major centres in which a wide range of courses catering for students of all levels of higher education aged 18 and over. Many have been established in which C.N.A.A. degrees (Council for National Academic Awards) can be obtained. This degree awarding body was established following a recommendation in the Robbins Report.

3   Colleges of Education

Numbers of students training to become teachers have increased rapidly in recent years:

1962:   48,000
1964:   70,000
1966:   84,000

In many colleges it is possible to obtain a B.Ed. degree after a four-year course.

Since 1948 the number of teachers in full time service has increased from 200,000 to nearly 350,000 in 1973.

4   'Day Release' and the apprenticeship system

Apprenticeship, which is taken up at the age of 16 and which lasts five years, is defined as 'the contractual relationship between an employer and young worker under which the employer is obliged to teach the worker'. The contract between them is known as the Indenture. This is designed to give security to both parties, since once signed it is difficult to break unless agreement is reached between them.

Whilst the apprentice is serving his time he is encouraged to attend a local College of Technology on a system known as 'day release', which

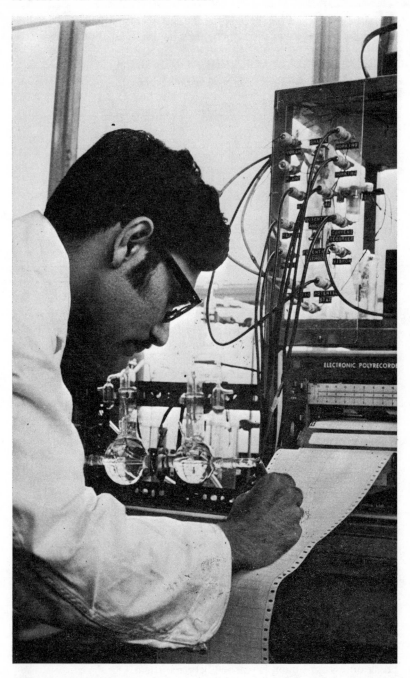

Research at a polytechnic

means that he will attend either one day a week throughout the year, or for several weeks at a time, in order to obtain qualifications by examination in his particular craft. Of boys aged between 15—18, 35% receive day release education, and of girls in the same age group, 9%.

5   Adult Education

Classes for adults of both educational and recreational interest are provided by Local Education Authorities, the Workers' Educational Association, University Extra-Mural Departments, and other voluntary bodies. It is difficult to estimate the total number of students enrolled by such organizations, although in 1966 there were nearly one and a half million attending evening institutes and half a million attending other courses, provided by University Extra-mural Departments.

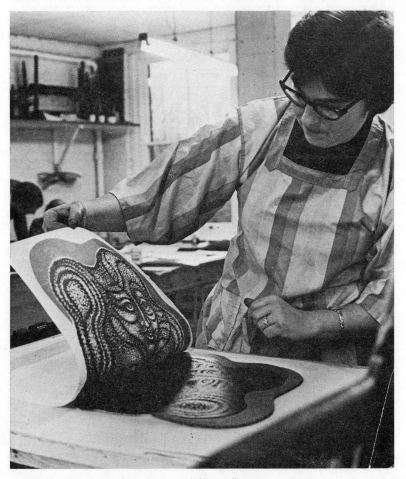

Adult education: a pupil inspects a pull from a lino cut

6 Universities

There are 44 universities in Britain with a gradually increasing student population. Courses normally last 3 years, and formal qualifications are required for entry.

Full-Time University students in Britain

	Men	Women	Total
1938—9	38,368	11,634	50,002
1947—8	59,065	19,442	78,507
1953—4	60,793	19,809	80,602
1957—8	71,855	23,587	95,442
1963—4	92,636	33,809	126,445
1967—8	145,280	55,007	200,287
1971—2	160,000	60,000	220,000

Social Class by father's occupation of undergraduates in Britain 1961—2.

Non-manual Occupations	Men %	Women %
Higher professional	17	20
Other professional and managerial	40	43
Clerical	12	11
Manual Occupations		
Skilled	19	16
Semi-skilled	6	6
Unskilled	1	1
Not known	1	3

7 The Open University, 'The University of the Air'

The Open University was established in Britain in 1970. No formal qualifications are necessary to gain acceptance on any of the courses offered. Anyone studying for one of the degree courses gains a degree after accumulating six credits (those with prior qualifications, such as Teacher's Certificates or Higher National Diploma are exempted from two credits.) Study is done by correspondence and by TV and radio broadcasts, which bring distinguished lecturers within the reach of all students.

In 1963 the Prime Minister, Mr Wilson, said that he believed the group who would benefit most would be those 'who for one reason or another, have not been able to take advantage of higher education'.

	Numbers applying	Numbers accepted for degree courses
1970	42,000	24,000
1971	34,000	21,000

It is not certain as to whether the main aim of the creators of the Open University is being met — to open higher education to those social groups who have been disadvantaged by a poor formal education in school. There is some evidence to suggest that those who are taking greatest advantage of the system are those who have already reached the point of entry to higher education.

Education and society

The educational system of a society reflects its dominant values.

Thus in ancient Sparta the dominant belief was in citizenship. The State was more important than any individual member. Sparta educated its boys to become warriors to defend the State. Any newborn male child who did not appear to be strong and healthy was left to die of exposure or given to the slaves. From the age of 7 to 18 their training for war began. After that age they were cadet soldiers on probation. They were not granted citizenship until they had proved their ability during the next ten years.

In fifth-century Greece Plato argued that education should teach a man to fight against all that is ugly and false, and seek always after the good and beautiful. All men should receive training to enable them to play their part in the State and to fit them for their allotted class, which Greeks of the time believed to be permanent and natural arrangements.

The social attitude of England in the seventeenth and eighteenth centuries is reflected in Milton's comment: 'I call ... a complete and generous education that which fits a man to perform justly, skilfully, and magnaminously all the offices, both public and private, of peace and war', and in Locke's view: 'That which every gentleman desires for his son, besides the estate he leaves him is contained in these four things, virtue, wisdom, breeding, and learning'.

In U.S.S.R. the aims and ideals of Communism are propagated through the educational system – just as the principles of western democracy are perpetuated in schools in Britain and America. Mr Kruschev said in 1958: 'All school children should without exception take part in socially useful labour on enterprises, collective farms, and other places of work ... all children finishing school should go to work in production. No one must evade this stage.'

Children in Russian schools are expected to follow very precise rules which they must know in detail:

Here is a list of rules for pupils in the U.S.S.R., from *Soviet Education* by Nigel Grant.

It is the duty of every child:
1   To acquire knowledge persistently in order to become an educated and cultured citizen and to be of the greatest possible service to his country.
2   To study diligently, to be punctual in attendance, and not arrive late for classes.
3   To obey the instructions of the school director and the teachers without question.

Bas-relief of a Spartan warrior

The 'motor transport study room' in a Moscow school

4   To arrive at school with all the necessary textbooks and writing materials; to have everything ready for the lesson before the teacher arrives.

5   To come to school clean, well-groomed, and neatly dressed.

6   To keep his place in the classroom neat and tidy.

7   To enter the classroom and take his place immediately after the bell rings; to enter and leave the classroom during the lesson only with the teacher's permission.

8   To sit upright during the lesson, not leaning on the elbows or slouching; to listen attentively to the teacher's explanation and other pupils' answers, and not to talk or let his attention wander to other things.

9   To rise when the teacher or director enters or leaves the room.

10   To stand to attention when answering the teacher; to sit down only with the teacher's permission; to raise his hand if he wishes to answer or ask a question.

11   To take accurate notes in his assignment book of homework scheduled for the next lesson, to show these notes to his parents, and to do all the homework unaided.

12   To be respectful to the school director and teachers; when meeting them to greet them with a polite bow; boys should also raise their caps.

13   To be polite to his elders, to behave modestly and respectfully in school, in the street, and in public places.

14   Not to use coarse expressions, not to smoke, not to gamble for money or other objects.

15   To protect school property; to be careful of his personal things and the belongings of his comrades.

16   To be attentive and considerate to old people, small children, the weak and the sick; to give them a seat on the bus or make way for them in the street, being helpful to them in every way.

17   To obey his parents, to help them take care of his small brothers and sisters.

18   To maintain order and cleanliness in rooms; to keep his clothes, shoes, and bed neat and tidy.

19   To carry his student's record book with him always, to guard it carefully, never handing it over to anyone else, and to present it on request of the teacher or school director.

20   To cherish the honour of his school and class and defend it as his own.

In America the first requirement of education is that it should prepare children to play their part in a democracy and to defend the freedoms established in the Constitution.

The elitist attitudes which have been a historical part of the British educational system have gradually given way to a widespread belief in the need for greater social justice and equality. These ideals which are developments of the second half of the twentieth century in Britain are embodied in recent educational reports. Thus in the Crowther Report 1959: 'Education is a national investment. The nation needs scientists, technicians, administrators and craftsmen in order to be able to compete in industrial productivity with other nations. The country needs good citizens able to play their part in a democratic community.' and in the Robbins Report 1964:

'There are four main aims of higher education:

1   Instruction in skills suitable to play a part in the general division of labour.

2   Promotion of the general powers of the mind.

3   The advancement of learning.

4   Transmission of a common culture and common standards of citizenship.'

The other evidence of a change in values which is reflected in the changes introduced into the educational system is the development of the Comprehensive system of education in Britain since the late 1940s, when there were a handful of comprehensive schools, to the present date when there are more than 2,000 such schools.

Since the 1944 Education Act, education in Britain has developed in both quality and quantity. In 1938/39 educational services cost £114 million. In 1968/69 they cost £1,891 millions. By 1980 it is estimated they will cost £5,248 millions. It is forecast that by that date 850,000 places will be needed in higher education to meet the needs of qualified school leavers. But debate still continues about whether the provision of education should be regarded as an economic investment or whether it should be an instrument designed to promote social justice and equality in society. There are some critics who express their views in what they term 'Black Papers,' that standards are declining as a result of recent changes in the educational system. They point to the decline in reading standards, the increase in violence, and the continued failure of working class children to make use of higher educational facilities, and suggest that the traditional system was more effective and productive. Sociologists are naturally interested to investigate such claims and to try to discover why some children are successful and others relatively unsuccessful after ten years or more of full-time education.

THE OPINIONS OF SOME EDUCATIONALISTS

At a London Conference of the National Council for Education in 1972 two eminent academics attacked the changes that are occurring within our educational system. Professor Brian Cox of Manchester University argued that the values of the 'neo-progressive' should be rejected. Their beliefs include: no competition and so no examinations; rejection of the Grammar school concept of correct English and emphasis instead on the vitality of working class speech and culture; anti-streaming, anti-selection and anti-any form of hierarchical organization.

Professor Pollard of Hull University called for a thorough investigation of Comprehensive education. He said that present evidence was not inspiring. The introduction of the Comprehensive system had been the greatest ever unresearched leap in the dark.

In an article in a booklet entitled *The Challenge of Change*, published in January 1973, Sir Alec Clegg, then Chief Education Officer for the West Riding of Yorkshire, suggested that a group of violent, resentful children who see themselves as the rejects of a qualification conscious society, is becoming more conspicuous in schools. He compares the group to the black minority in the United States, and gives a warning that its violence and resentment will grow as automation replaces the conveyor belt, creating utterly dull jobs for many young adults. He calls for a widening of the principle of Educational Priority Areas residential provision for specially disturbed or grieviously deprived children; a greater use of social workers in infant and junior schools; and a fuller keeping of school records, especially about personal and social problems.

In an article in the *Guardian* in 1972 Bryan Allen, Headmaster of a Comprehensive school in Essex, argued against the compulsory raising of the school leaving age:

It is fashionable among some quarters, he wrote, when thinking of suitable courses for non-examination pupils, to use such superficial phrases as developing 'outward looking curricula' or introducing 16 year-olds to 'the complexities of the world' .... How much better it would be if the leaving age were flexible, say from 14 to 17, so that schools could take account of physical and emotional maturation. Some few children might even profitably leave school at 12, and I am writing as a juvenile magistrate in London . . . . Any curious visitor to a large secondary school who seeks the fourth-year examination classes . . . will be led in due course by the noise to a group of gum chewing, whistling, bored, bulky teenagers, sitting on the back seats of their classroom, taking little notice of the teacher possibly with his connivance — anything for a quiet life. Unable to concentrate for more than a few minutes at a time they can hardly wait till term ends to get away . . . .

In his book *The Pre-School Years*, Willem van der Eyken writes:

For millions of children growing up in Britain in 1972 life is still a matter of relative poverty. Professor Peter Townsend (1967) has reported that between 7 and 8 million persons, or about 14% of the total population, live below a specifically-defined 'national assistance' standard. As these lower income-groups often have the largest families, it could be that something like one fifth of the child population of Britain grows up in an environment that in certain fundamental respects can be classed as 'deprived'.

Moreover, even if the home is not in this category, the area in which the child lives may well be. The Plowden Committee Report drew specific attention to what it called 'educational priority areas'.

Some of these neighbourhoods have for generations been starved of new schools, new houses and new investment for everything.

RESEARCH FINDINGS 1

A survey carried out by the West Riding Educational and Health Departments discovered that the reading ability of infant school pupils in the area of the study corresponded closely to those of pupils in school 50 years ago. The survey covered 864 children in 19 Infant schools. There were 440 boys and 424 girls in the sample. The average age of the children was 7.2 years. Each child was given the 'Burt Test List' of words to read. The average score of correct words was 32. The scores were then converted into average reading age; that of the boys was 7 years and the girls 7.5 years. Commenting on the results, the investigators say that the Burt Test is the oldest still in use and enables comparisons to be made between scores of children today and those of children on whom it was first standardized. They conclude that 'the reading standards of the children tested were found to be wholly satisfactory; their scores matching those of children on whom the test was first standardized with surprising closeness.' The National Foundation for Educational Research has also carried out studies in 1971 which show that reading standards are much the same as they were ten years ago.

RESEARCH FINDINGS 2

The importance of language as a factor in explaining degree of educational attainment has been shown by Bernstein in his research (1961, 1965, 1970). He suggests that the middle class child is more successful in school because there is less conflict in values between teacher and child, since both are likely to be from the same social class background. Furthermore the child is predisposed to respond to the language of the teacher. The middle class child is more able to conform to authority and to the role of the teacher, and more able to manipulate the two languages of school: that of his peers (the language of the playground, of his friends of whatever background) and that of the school, which is a more formal language of the teacher, adults, and literature. This leads to appropriate behaviour in a wide range of social circumstances. The middle class child responds to the social structure of the school, to its rules and regulations. He is able both to respond to it and to exploit it.

He describes the middle class language as an elaborated code. The language of the lower working class is termed a restricted code. Although syntax and grammar may often be incorrectly used meaning is generally understood. Users of the restricted code do not make use of the elaborated code and so have more difficulty in communication in formal learning situations. Children limited to the restricted code do not perform as well in school; they ask fewer questions; they show less curiosity; they show less interest in literature; they are less able to understand and communicate with the teacher; they are particularly handicapped when dealing with those aspects of the curriculum which require an understanding of abstract concepts, theories, and generalizations.

RESEARCH FINDINGS 3
Studies to see whether there is a correlation between aspects of a child's home background and his school performance have been made by many investigators. They include Fraser (1959), Douglas (1964), Wiseman (1964), Vernon (1969), Peaker (1967), Pidgeon (1970).

The results have been to show some of the important variables affecting school performance. They include:
1   Parental attitudes towards child's education. Their lack of interest or failure to encourage is a significant factor in poor performance.
2   Family size. Children in large families were found to spend less time in conversation with adults and were consequently less able in school performance.
3   Educational level of the parents. Homes which contained books and in which parents were able to assist their children in their school work were shown to provide them with educational advantage.
4   Degree of parental and maternal care. Children from homes in which these factors were evident showed high levels of good health and brightness in reading and were less prone to get into serious trouble with the authorities.
5   Neighbourhood background. Children from backgrounds in which delinquency, crime, and high rates of illegitimacy were common, and

from poor homes and socially deprived areas showed poor levels of performance in school. They had little motivation and low levels of achievement.

Peaker found in one of his studies (1967) that a correlation also existed between the attainment of children in Primary schools and the school environment itself. Some of the influencing factors include the size of class, the size of the school, streaming, the reputation of the school, its facilities, teacher characteristics (poor schools tend to have a high turnover of staff), and the leadership or standing of the headmaster in the eyes of staff and pupils. Wallace's research in America (1966) showed the significance of the peer group on the development of attitudes. Group pressures work to ensure that group norms are adhered to, so that initial high standards are lowered to meet the requirements of the group.

RESEARCH FINDINGS 4

Elder's research showed that assignment to a low status school or academic stream affects an individual's view of himself. Those who have a low opinion of themselves as students or pupils generally perform in accordance with their self-assessment. Low self-esteem is associated with anxiety, defensiveness, low achievement, and low future aspirations. The consequences of failure at 11 and of allocation to low streams in the Grammar or Secondary Modern school are likely to be substantial. In addition to the psychological harm produced, this selection procedure contributes little towards developing every child's sense of self-esteem. The acceptance of a negative self-image is associated with the under-utilization of mental abilities. Instead of coping with and exploring the tasks of school, the pupil with low aspirations tends to avoid such demands. Elder found that the mobility aspirations of individuals in different streams reflect closely their respective status levels in school. A stream children are more upwardly mobile in their aims than C stream children.

He also suggests that the lack of meaningful courses for Secondary Modern school pupils is an important factor in the desire to leave school at the earliest possible time. 'Boredom and complaints about lethargic teachers were a common response among 200 pupils from five such schools in Sheffield. The pupils preferred to get out into the world and devote their energies to something new, rather than vegetate in school. It was also thought better not to take any examinations rather than take some and fail. The seeming irrelevance of school for the life situation of many children has left a void in their lives which has been filled in large measure by commercialized youth culture. This culture and the seeming irrelevance of the school are major pressures encouraging pupils to leave as soon as possible.'

EXERCISES

1   Outline the results of some studies that you have read about which show the significance of the educational structure on a child's performance: consider streaming, the 11+, Comprehensive schools, Independent schools, etc.

2   Write short notes on: (*a*) Primary education, (*b*) The Plowden Report, (*c*) Intelligence tests, (*d*) The Open University, (*e*) Further education.

3   Research into the major Education Acts since 1870; give a detailed report on any one.

4   To what extent do you agree or disagree with some of the opinions of educationalists expressed on pages 101—102?

5   Do you approve or disapprove of the 'Rules for Pupils' in the U.S.S.R.? Explain your answer.

ESSAY QUESTIONS

1   Explain what is meant by the Tripartite and the Comprehensive systems of education. What factors have tended to make English secondary education move towards various kinds of Comprehensive schemes?

2   What are the main functions of the educational system in Britain?

3   What are the likely social benefits and what are the possible problems which may result from raising the school leaving age?

4   Contrast the formal and informal agencies of education that exist. Explain how even in simple societies there are very adequate processes of education.

5   How far does the British educational system ensure equality of opportunity?

'The newspaper reading habit is deeply ingrained in the daily routine'

6 The Mass Media

The mass media are the various systems by which communications are transmitted to large numbers of people at the same time, and which have developed since the innovations produced by the industrial and technological revolution. Mechanical and electronic systems have enabled news, ideas, opinions, and other information to become available to the mass of the population (and with the growth of the 'phone in' programmes on the B.B.C., members of the population can make their views widely heard) with great rapidity. The mass media include primarily broadcasting, the press, journals and magazines, films, records, and advertising.

Sociologists are interested to examine the various media of communication that exist, to understand their functions and their possible influence and power. They may wish to assess their significance for the individual and for the society as a whole.

In making an analysis it is useful to consider:

1 The possible functions of the media — to inform, entertain, educate etc.
2 The possible influence of the media — on attitudes and values, fashion and taste, and their significance as a source of power and social cohesion.
3 The factors that affect the media — the economic considerations, the need for advertising, the strength of public opinion as shown by the existence of pressure groups which work for change, the availability of legal sanctions, and the influence of powerful individuals, such as Lord Reith, the first Director of the B.B.C.

The press

One writer makes the point that 'no other people on earth are such avid readers of newspapers as the British' — a fact confirmed by UNESCO statistics, which indicate that Britain leads the international table of number of daily copies of newspapers read per 100 of the population. In 1966 personal expenditure in Britain on papers was £203 millions, in 1971 £310 millions. It is estimated that total readership of papers exceeds fifty million per day and seventy million on Sundays. Many households take more than one paper each day. It is believed that nearly 90% of the adult population reads at least one national paper every day. It has been said that 'no other product of modern civilization has achieved so complete a saturation of its potential market', although one might now add that television has equalled this degree of 'saturation'. The success of the newspaper industry is comparatively recent and is particularly marked in Britain.' In 1920 one adult in two read a daily paper, while every four read five Sunday papers. By 1947 every ten adults read twelve daily papers and twenty-three Sunday papers.' In 1971 the total circulation of national Sunday papers was more than 22 million.

Studies show that per head of population the people of Britain read almost twice as many of their newspapers as the Americans, for example, and nearly three times as many as the French. There has been a slight decrease in circulation figures in recent years which may be due to the influence of other media — especially television, whose instant coverage of news events may make that of the newspapers on the following day seem stale and dated. Magazines and journals may also provide better coverage of the 'entertainment' aspect of newspapers, which is limited by lack of colour and by the format of the paper. Nevertheless, the decrease in overall circulation figures is slight, and readership figures have probably been hardly affected. Occasional strikes may affect circulation figures in so far as they cause people to stop and ask whether their daily paper really is essential, and so may cause a change in readership and buying habits to some small degree. Steady price increases may also have an adverse effect, so that the cost of the paper over a week, together with the rapidly inflating cost of the Sunday paper, may represent the alternative cost of a book which may be seen as providing better and more lasting value. But in general the newspaper reading habit is deeply ingrained in the daily routine of the population.

It is ironical that although readership and circulation have increased very rapidly over the last fifty years only two new newspapers have appeared (the *Daily Worker/Morning Star* and the *Daily Recorder* — 1953). The *Sun* replaced the *Daily Herald* (1964), whilst several have disappeared through economic failure: *Morning Post, News Chronicle, Daily Dispatch, Westminster Gazette, Daily Sketch, Daily Herald, Evening Star, Sunday Dispatch, Sunday Chronicle, Sunday News*. Provincial journals have also disappeared at a much faster rate than they have been replaced. More than 250 such papers and journals have ceased publication in this period. It seems that the population is reading more copies of fewer papers. Five national daily or Sunday papers have closed since 1960 and seven provincial morning papers have closed since 1950. Whilst all papers are striving to maintain their independence (and so reject the suggestions that Governments should finance ailing papers) with the arrival of a mass readership the character of journalism has changed. News is no longer the major prerequisite of a successful newspaper: the meteoric rise in circulation of the *Sun* newspaper from 800,000 in 1969 to 2,800,000 in 1973 is evidence of this.

Facts with regard to the popular press were revealed in a survey conducted at the end of 1971 by I.P.C. (owners of the *Mirror*). The *Daily*

Express emerged with the highest reader satisfaction from news items —
31% voting in favour. The *Mirror* follows with 27%, the *Daily Mail* has 25%,
and the *Sun* is bottom with 22% of readers reading the paper for its news
coverage. In its advertisements the *Sun* claims to have the highest proportion of young readers: 26% are in the 15–24 age group and 45% are
under 35.

In 1972 the *Press Directory* listed 142 daily and Sunday news papers in
Britain, 1,211 weekly papers and 4,796 periodicals.

Average daily circulation of national daily papers, January–June 1972

Daily Mirror	4,289,233
Daily Express	3,348,752
Sun	2,625,532
Daily Mail	1,710,141
Daily Telegraph	1,442,000
Evening News (London)	900,749
Evening Standard (London)	519,154
Guardian	391,075
Times	345,016
Financial Times	187,781

THE START OF POPULAR JOURNALISM

The Education Act of 1870 provided the impetus for the expansion of
newspaper readership. The new readers required 'a respectable cheap
substitute for the daily reading matter of the superior classes, looking, as
all the best substitutes do, as much like the original as possible but easier
on an unsophisticated palate'.

Popular journalism has its beginnings in this period following the
1870 Act. Houlton in Manchester developed an evening paper to meet the
growing interest in sport: the first Football Cup Tie was in 1871, the
first Australian Test Match in 1878, and the beginning of professional
football in 1885. Newnes established a journal called *Tit-bits* in 1881
from all the most interesting books, periodicals, and newspapers of the
world, which contained items of news on everything except politics. By
1896 the circulation was three times greater than that of the *Telegraph*. He
introduced sales promotions campaigns — and for the first time advertisers
realized the potential audience they could reach by advertising in such a
journal. There followed other papers based on this style (including the
London *Evening Star* — which ceased publication in the 1960s), which
were the first to acknowledge and exploit the existence of a new newspaper reading public.

Alfred Harmsworth (later Lord Northcliffe) and his brother Lord
Rothermere extended the market. In the 1890s they established such
popular papers and magazines as *Answers, Comic Cuts, Chips, Forget-me-not,
Home Sweet Home, Funny Wonder, Union Jack, Marvel, Sunday Companion,
Boy's Friend*, etc. They were all very successful financially. Northcliffe also
appreciated the importance of advertising and of publicity stunts to attract

Lord Northcliffe

Lord Rothermere

readers. (He offered a pound a week for life to any reader who guessed most accurately the amount of money in the Bank of England on a particular day. More than 700,000 entered.) In 1896 he purchased the *Evening News*, which gradually achieved the largest circulation of any evening paper in the world. The *Daily Mail* was established in May 1896. All its news stories were short, and it carried serial stories, political gossip, society news, stock exchange prices, sporting news, and features for women. The *Mail* dominated newspaper circulations until the 1930s, as did Northcliffe's successful *Sunday Dispatch*. He established the *Daily Mirror* as the first popular picture paper. He saved the *Observer* from extinction and became principal proprietor of the *Times* in 1908.

His was the greatest newspaper empire in the history of journalism, though it is matched in more recent times by that of Lord Thomson, the present owner of the *Times*.

It is perhaps not without significance that the most powerful of the newspaper owners became immensely wealthy and acquired titles: Lord Northcliffe, Lord Rothermere, Lord Beaverbrook, and Lord Thomson — and the latter two were Canadians. Francis Williams writes: 'Not since Napoleon has any man enriched the nobility with so many of his relations as Northcliffe did. By the time he was done he and his brother were Viscounts, another brother was a Baron and the two youngest were Baronets.'

FACTORS THAT AFFECT THE KIND OF PAPERS WE HAVE

1 *The concentration of ownership: the influence of the proprietor* In Britain, newspapers have been owned traditionally by individually wealthy men or have been held within an influential family. Such people have had a great influence on the policies of the paper, particularly with regard to their political attitudes; and in some cases their influence can still be seen today, although the power of the individual owner may have been much modified by the economic needs and demands of present day publishing.

In his biography of Beaverbrook, A. J. P. Taylor writes: 'Beaverbrook was a financier and politician before he became a newspaper owner. He was elected Conservative M.P. for Ashton-under-Lyne in 1910, when Bonar Law, later Prime Minister, was his business associate and intimate friend. Before long, he included Lloyd George, Churchill and Birkenhead in his political friendships, and he played an important part in the destruction of Asquith's government at the end of 1916. In the following year, by acquiring control of the Daily Express, he passed into a category other than those of financier and politician....'

Raymond Williams notes that 'in 1965, seven out of eight of our national morning papers were controlled by three groups, headed by Beaverbrook, Cecil King, and Rothermere, while seven out of eight of our national Sunday papers were controlled by two of these: Beaver-

(above) *Lord Beaverbrook*

(below) *Cecil King*

brook and King. The two London evening papers were controlled by Beaverbrook and Rothermere.' In 1973 there were nine major press groups. The largest of these is the International Publishing Corporation, which controls two out of five of our national daily and Sunday newspapers. It also has a virtual monopoly of all large circulation women's magazines and is the largest single owner of technical and trade journals. In all it controls more than three hundred publications. Although ownership and control have changed to some degree over the past few years, the majority of the press remains concentrated in comparatively few hands, so that individual proprietors may still hold considerable power. Beaverbrook was editor-in-chief of the *Daily Express*, and almost daily he indicated to his editors or executives of each of his newspapers the outline of leading articles, diary stories, and features, many of which were transmitted to him for approval before publication.

Lord Thomson, proprietor of Times Newspapers, said in 1966: 'I have my views on various questions and I make sure that he [the editor] knows them, but I never see them appear in the paper unless he agrees with them ... he is the editor and nothing goes in the paper unless they are also his views.'

2 *The influence of the editor* The chief responsibility of the editor is the preparation and implementation of policy. The individual power and influence of the editor in shaping attitudes and social trends is less in evidence now than in former days, except perhaps occasionally in the case of the quality papers and political journals, where his comments, if he is renowned and respected, may continue to exert some influence. For example, William Rees-Mogg, then political editor of the *Sunday Times*,

Lord Thomson

is thought to have influenced the decision of Sir Alec Douglas Home to resign as leader of the Conservative Party. The success of the popular press is shaped largely by its reputation as a source of entertainment. It is for the editor to maintain that image. His own views may be revealed in the editorial columns, but it is doubtful whether they carry much weight with his readers, who do not take his paper for its news or editorial content.

Editors are not subject to codes of professional ethics of good conduct (unlike lawyers, teachers, or doctors). The only restrictions on what they print are Government D Notices, which indicate secrecy in the national interests, the laws of libel, and the supervision of the Press Council, which investigates complaints from the public.

It has been said that 'the editor of a modern newspaper, particularly of one with a circulation of several millions, is the impresario of a vast entertainment enterprise ... the dual role of the press to inform and entertain, to appeal to the enlightened forces of public opinion whilst drumming up the largest numbers of paying customers, is not solely a modern dilemma; it has always existed, but it has been vastly increased by the enormous cost of producing a modern newspaper'. A newspaper is an industry in which shareholders have invested many millions of pounds. It must make profits or perish. In this respect it is the function of the editor to make profits at all costs.

3   *The power of the advertiser*   Charles Wintour, himself the editor of an important evening newspaper, states that although the revenue from advertising varies from an average of 76% in the quality Sunday papers to 38% for popular dailies, and no national newspaper would have the slightest hope of economic survival if all advertising revenue were withdrawn from it, nevertheless 'I have never known of any attempt whatsoever to affect the politics of a newspaper ... It is my opinion that in general advertising influence is negligible and even where it is not, that it is harmless'. He suggests that to a considerable degree newspaper managements and advertisers are in partnership. Even after much criticism in the *Evening News* of cigarette smoking the tobacco companies increased their advertising expenditure from £192,000 in 1970 to £305,000 in 1971.

He writes, 'Where the influence of advertising may be most felt is in the basic strategy of a newspaper. The advertiser wants a coherent group of readers, not a wide scatter.' It may therefore help the editor to ensure that his paper is appealing to those sections which are particularly important to the advertiser — especially to women readers — and he may seek remedial action if weaknesses are revealed.

Changes in style and presentation have been caused largely by economic pressures — the need to attract advertisers and particular types of regular readers. As a result of the constant need for advertising, the quality papers have come to blur the distinction between news and advertisements. Colour supplements often produce articles written by experts on behalf of sponsors. The *Daily Mirror* and the *Sun* have a combined readership of more than twenty million. The dilemma facing the rivals to these papers is that advertisers want proof that sales are increasing before they are prepared to back the paper. It has been found that some types of newspaper presentation attract more advertisers. A former managing director of Gallup Polls said after studying 3,500 advertisements he came to the conclusion that whichever criteria one took, on average a single column inch in a tabloid[1] achieved greater communication than in a broadsheet[2].

There are three major types of advertising:
1 Classified (specific notices advertising jobs, articles for sale, etc. in ordinary type).
2 Display advertising (usually general and persuasive in tone using large type and illustrations).
3 Company advertising (designed to promote a particular company by advertising its product which may be of no use to an individual buyer – industrial ventilation products, for example. The aim is to add prestige and build an image.)

1965 Table showing the percentage of advertising in National Dailies

	Times	Guardian	Telegraph	Mail	Express
Classified	77	75	73	44	22
Display	23	25	27	56	78

	Sun	Worker	Mirror	Sketch
Classified	18	100	9	41
Display	82	0	91	59

The type of advertising used depends on the nature of the readership of the newspaper.

THE FUNCTIONS AND INFLUENCE OF THE PRESS
1 It is a major source of information which may not be available in such detail from any other source. It is able to cover a wider range of items than any other available medium and offer detailed comment. (News broadcasts on television and on radio may give more dramatic coverage but may offer less interpretation and comment.)
2 It is a source of entertainment.
3 It may help to form attitudes and opinions, fashions and tastes. It may serve to propagate cult behaviour by providing details on which some readers may model themselves.
4 It has an educational function, providing data which would be otherwise unavailable or difficult to locate.

[1] Tabloid: a paper with small pages, e.g. *Sun, Daily Mail*.
[2] Broadsheet: a paper with large pages, e.g. *Daily Express*.

5   It is a major outlet for advertising.
6   It may be used to promote a campaign by a pressure group.
   The impact and influence of a newspaper or journal depends on how news and information is presented. Important factors in this respect are:
(a)   The amount of space devoted to the item.
(b)   Its position in the paper.
(c)   The circulation and readership of the paper.
(d)   The style of the report.

POSSIBLE DANGERS OF THE PRESS

1   Tendency to bias or inaccuracy according to the political slant of the paper, or the desire to sensationalize an incident
2   Too much trivia and banal items at the expense of real news.
3   The intrusion into private lives when such intrusion is unnecessary for the purpose of the story.
4   The concentration of ownership in few hands, which may give too much power to too few people.
5   The lack of professionalism in journalism: it is only recently that journalists could undergo any training.
6   The power of the individual journalist as epitomized in the career of the American Walter Winchell. Commenting on his influence shortly after his death John Crosby wrote: 'He invented keyhole journalism. He could sell 40,000 copies of some awful book with a single mention in his column. And he did. He could ruin an actor's career by accusing him, probably falsely, of being a Communist. And he did. He was the true father, not only in America, but all over the world, of gutter journalism. . . . So pervasive was his influence that even the most respectable journals invaded private lives far more deeply than before his time. Winchell abolished privacy for ever. He established the "gossip column" which is now carried by all papers. At its height his column was carried by more than 1,000 papers throughout America and his radio programme had an audience of more than thirty million.' (The film *The Sweet Smell of Success* was based on Winchell's career.)

Broadcasting

Radio began in the 1920s, financed by income voted by Parliament based on income from licence fees. A Charter was established in 1927. The British Broadcasting Corporation was set up. Lord Reith was the first Director until 1938. He had great influence on the policy and image of the B.B.C. He was serious-minded and fought to maintain monopoly. (This was perhaps accepted by successive governments as a safeguard against the lowering of standards or expression of any extreme views.) In the 1950s pressure groups began to try to break the monopoly. There was no party involvement until 1952, when the Conservatives took up the 'commercial cause'. In 1954 the I.T.A. (Independent Television Authority) was established, with its Chairman and members appointed by the Postmaster General. Programmes are now transmitted from approximately thirty-seven stations by fourteen programme contractors, whose revenue derives from sale of advertising time. There were immediate inroads into B.B.C. viewing figures. Great profits were made. Because of concern in this area the Pilkington Committee was formed in 1962.

THE PILKINGTON COMMITTEE ON BROADCASTING

The report of this Committee took the view that broadcasting should be a public service. It praised the B.B.C. and criticised the I.T.A. The Com-

Lord Reith   *[BBC Copyright Photograph]*

mittee supported the view that television has an important social role. It argued that there was too much violence, sex, and distortion of ordinary moral standards in television programmes, and that the range of programmes was too limited and too trivial. Blame for low standards was placed on the I.T.A. They also studied relationship between the ownership of the Press and commercial television. They admitted that while there were risks involved in the concentration of control of newspapers and television there was no evidence that this power had as yet been used to exert undue influence on the public. Only Thomson Newspapers had a major interest in a television company.

The Television Act of 1963 laid down levels of profits that could be made. In 1968 new attempts were made to restrict profits in commercial television (profits of between 300 and 1500 per cent were being made), and to raise the level of programme material. But for commercial companies the criteria of success of a programme is the number of viewers attracted to its commercials. From that figure can be calculated the cost per 1,000 viewers to advertisers. When the cost per 1,000 is too high there is pressure to change the nature of the programme and replace it or make it more popular so that the advertiser will be encouraged to renew his patronage.

COMMERCIAL RADIO
In March 1971 it was announced by the Minister for Posts and Telecommunications, Mr Chataway, that the first local commercial radio stations would be established in 1973. Eventually sixty would be in operation. They would operate under the control of the Independent Television Authority — to be renamed the Independent Broadcasting Authority (I.B.A.). Two million pounds were advanced to set up the first London station. 'Few would deny,' he said, 'that competition in news and current affairs had been beneficial in television. It was desirable, therefore, to have an alternative and competing service in radio.' He went on to explain that 'the I.B.A. would have the same responsibility for ensuring balance, impartiality, decency and good taste in radio as I.T.A. had in television.' Critics asked:
1 Will the I.B.A. maintain control over the standards, styles of presentation, and quality of presentation when there are sixty stations to administer? They point to the criticisms raised in the Pilkington Report which suggested that in television the search for profits had the initial effect of lowering standards. This is of concern with regard to radio in so far as demand for commercial radio grew with the popularity of the 'pirate stations' which were based entirely on a constant diet of pop music.
2 Is it socially healthy for an audience to be inundated with advertising material?
3 Could such stations provide a platform for radical dissent by extremist groups who could afford to pay advertising fees? How much independence should the I.B.A. have, and how much control should Parliament be able to exert?

What kinds of answers would you give to such questions?

In October 1973, Paul Ferris, reviewing the first four days of commercial radio said: 'They were painfully disappointing. This was nothing to do with the inevitable minor snags and hitches. As for commercial radio's news and comments service, which was supposed to blanket London with programmes for the people, it simply doesn't stand up to the claims it made, and must justify if it's to carve out an electronic niche for itself. . . .'

TELEVISION

In his book *The Least Worst Television in the World* (1973) Milton Schulman (a longstanding theatre critic and former television executive) argues for 'more participation, more access. Getting the wide range of British life from arts to farming represented on the screen demands not just a fourth channel and not just more hours. None of this can be done while entertainment programmes dominate most of the important time segments, and actors, comics, singers, quiz masters are considered the main inheritors of the medium.' He suggests 'during peak times all channels must provide at least 33% serious programming' — that would be a starting point towards reversing 'the accelerating trend towards irresponsible and trivial television'. He goes on: 'Allowing popular channels to compete against specialist or cultural ones will merely mean the bulk of the viewers will be subjected to all the dubious influences that an entertainment biased system produces and will also further fragment society between those who get their views from a frivolous sector of the box and those who acquire them from a more socially committed and demanding sector.'

Schulman's belief is that the offerings of I.T.V. and B.B.C. are increasingly trivial and violent, and his readings of social research and of actual social history in the TV age lead him to believe that its influence is malign and must be curbed.

THE INFLUENCE OF TELEVISION[1]

Everyone has his own image of the medium. For some it is the unrelenting agent of permissiveness, at work from morning till night at the business of corrupting the established values of the nation, mocking the sacred, dignifying the profane. For others it is the blinkered guardian of the privileges of the establishment, hopelessly entangled with yesterday's society, with outmoded customs and dead traditions. To some broadcasting is staffed exclusively by trendy lefties . . . to others, producers are no more than the carefully programmed mouthpieces of the governing classes, licensed to do no more than is necessary to give the illusion of free debate.

They cannot all be right. I reject these interpretations and so, I

[1] Lovel Hill in the *Listener*, 7.12.72.

119

think, do all reasonable people. If you look at the sum of what the B.B.C. puts out — all the radio services, both TV channels — which many of our critics do all too rarely, you will conclude that it could not be produced by a single kind of person or even by two or three kinds of person, differing in many respects from one another. It is, I think, the diversity of our programmes which represent one of our strongest claims on the time and attention of our audience.

If you search the libraries for books about the influence of television, you will find quite a number, but if you're looking for some single, coherent view of what influence television exercises, you are likely to be disappointed. Not for want of spending money: in this country the I.T.A. spent a quarter of a million pounds in five years and came up with not very much. In the U.S.A. a Commission has just spent a million dollars and has come up with the same amount. So we can't, I'm afraid, look to the academics for very much guidance.

If you take the supposed ill effects of television, they would arise from its success in persuading people to act in ways disapproved of by society. From time to time, we read of some offender who claims as his defence, 'I saw it on the telly'. Let us allow him the benefit of the doubt and assume that what he is saying is not just a later rationalization. Immediately someone can be heard suggesting that measures ought to be taken to curb the power of television to influence in this way. But, of course, they overlook the many millions who saw the same thing and didn't react by imitating what they saw. Indeed there are so many millions who didn't that one is entitled to look for the special circumstances that prompted the one who did.[1]

The cinema

Here is one opinion on the influence of the cinema and television, put forward by Knight:

The culture provided by all the mass media, but particularly by film and television, represents the most significant environmental factor that teachers have to take into account. The important changes that take place at the secondary stage are much influenced by the world offered by the leisure industry which skilfully markets products designed for young people's tastes. The media help to define aspirations and they offer roles and models. They not only supply needs (and create them) but may influence attitudes and values.... We need to train children to look critically and discriminate between what is good and bad in what they see. They must learn to realize that many makers of films and television programmes present false or distorted views of people, relationships and experience in general, besides producing much trivial and worthless stuff made according to stock patterns.'

[1] The point he implies is that whilst television may not cause deviant behaviour, it may reinforce it where it already exists.

THE INFLUENCE OF THE CINEMA

It is certainly a major leisure activity, although attendances have declined significantly since 1946, when more than thirty million people attended on average each week.

Year	No. of cinemas open	Attendances per week (average)	
1946		30 million	
1950	4,584	28 million	
1960	3,034	10 million	
1963		7.4 million	
1969	1,581	3.8 million	Gross takings:
1972		3.4 million	£57.7 million

(Source: Official statistics; *Board of Trade Journal, Annual Abstract of Statistics*)

Studies have shown that the group going most frequently is a largely working class section of the population aged between 16 and 24.

Some critics see the cinema as an almost mindless activity and the source of trivial and corrupting ideals. 'The cinema has several advantages over the novel: the public have not to make any effort on translating words into images — that is done for them. . . . Attending the cinema . . . is a passive and social amusement.'

Others see the cinema in a more favourable light: 'Film as art exploits virtually all the modes which are also exploited by literature: irony and satire, metaphor and symbol, dream and vision . . . allusion and quotation. It exploits these modes through its specific and peculiar formal structures. By examining these modes of operation in film, attention may be focused upon their comparable operation in literature.'

The debate about the possible dangers of the values of the cinema, like that relating to the significance of television, rests on the answer that the critic gives to the question: do the mass media reflect society as it is, acting as a social mirror, or do they create the behaviour they portray and the social climate of the day? If the latter argument is believed to be true, then censorship may be justified on the ground that people must be protected from dangerous influences. Certainly advertisers must see the mass media as a useful way of influencing attitudes, since they spend vast sums in successfully endeavouring to do so.[1] The cinema is a particularly useful medium in this respect, and most of its advertising is aimed at the age group which attends most frequently.

DISTRIBUTION

The types of film that are made for national circulation depend on their predicted success at the box office. Once a successful formula is found it is repeated and developed until a new one replaces it. In recent years the themes of sex and violence have been successfully adopted, replacing Hollywood romance and musical comedy in popularity, although

[1] £160 million in 1973.

'westerns' and cartoons seem to have endless appeal to audiences. But the need for box office success means that experimental film makers, or those making films about non-commercial subjects, are at a disadvantage. They will find difficulty not only in obtaining financial backing to make their films, but also in showing their films to audiences.

The major cinema circuits are controlled by two powerful organizations—Rank and A.B.C. If they do not believe a film will be financially successful they may decide not to show it in any of the cinemas they control.

SEX, VIOLENCE, AND CENSORSHIP

'Film makers in many parts of the world had more freedom from censorship and there was growing evidence that films showing explicit sex and violence were in demand almost everywhere; since attendances at cinemas had seriously declined, world markets had to be satisfied if films were to make profits, and such evidence could not be ignored.'

John Heilpern comments that out of the ten most popular films in Britain in 1971 only two were overtly violent: *Soldier Blue* and *Get Carter*. The most popular film in America was *Love Story*. Top in Britain was Walt Disney's *The Aristocats* followed by a number of remakes of popular

The Odeon, Lewisham, a Rank cinema

122

The ABC cinema, Walsall

television shows. 'How long, asked one critic, before the film version of "News at 10"? What's worrying people, then, isn't as yet the quantity but the intensity of violent films.' In 1971, thirteen critics wrote to *Times* condemning *Straw Dogs*, as did Stephen Murphy, the new film censor.

John Trevelyan, the previous censor, has outlined the history of the British Board of Film Censors:

It was set up in 1912 in order to solve a practical problem. The Cinematograph Act of 1909 had been intended to reduce the risk of fire in cinemas by requiring that all buildings used for this form of entertainment should be licensed by the local authorities, but the courts held that the Act had given them wider powers, including that of censorship of what was shown on the screen. It was obviously impracticable for film companies to submit their films to a large number of local authorities individually, and so the Government of the day accepted a proposal from the film industry that an independent censorship board should be set up to do the work while reserving the right of the local authorities to act individually if they chose to do so. This curious arrangement has survived to this day. . . . From a study of the Board's history and records it is clear that from 1913 when it started until about 1950 it considered itself the guardian of the nation's morals and the protector

123

Violence on the screen: a still from 'Al Capone'

of authority, but in the course of the next twenty years its attitudes and policies changed.

By a process of gradual evolution it became a reflection of the public social conscience, interpreting in its decisions what appeared to be changes in public attitudes and not attempting to impose on adults a conformist morality.

Commenting on the increasing escalation of violence in films (*Cool Hand Luke*, 1967, *Bullitt*, 1968, *Wild Bunch*, 1969, *Clockwork Orange*, 1971, *Straw Dogs*, 1972) and television Professor Himmelweit puts forward the pessimistic view that 'the audience might be affected eventually . . . by its total amount . . . which contributes to the image that problems can only be solved by violent means – since it is often displayed by the law as much as the offender. It may be helping to create the assumption that violence is routine in daily life.'

TRENDS WHICH CAN BE IDENTIFIED

1 The film industry remains important, although it operates on a reduced scale. The Hollywood image has disappeared. It continues to throw up stars, personalities, and great actors and actresses who may influence the attitudes and values of their audiences. Trends may be set in terms

of fashion: white boiler suits came into vogue after *Clockwork Orange* was shown; hair styles: Tony Curtis was a major influence in this respect in the 1950s; and normative behaviour: when the film *Rock Around the Clock* was shown, cinema seats were ripped up and young people were dancing in the aisles wherever it was shown.

2   It is used increasingly as an educational aid in schools and colleges, and small scale film making is a popular school and club activity.

3   There is a debate about the possible benefits and dangers of popular commercial films, which are often criticized for cashing in on an unhealthy interest in sex, sensationalism, and sadism.

4   Film making is more widely accepted as an art form, although experimental films are hindered by the concentration of ownership of the main cinema circuits.

5   The number of people attending the cinema on a regular basis is declining as television and other commercial enterprises develop to cater for the leisure needs of people; nevertheless the cinema remains a significant leisure pursuit for a large proportion of the youthful section of society.

Advertising
THE BIRTH OF A BRAND LEADER

What consumers buy, according to Alan Hedges, are units of satisfaction. It is a quality which he believes is incorporated in the packaging and promotion of a product, as well as what is in the box or bottle. As director of research and marketing with a large advertising agency it is part of his job to probe the components of satisfaction.

A market research operation which he found satisfying was one he conducted for 'Tree Top' fruit squashes. The promotion was based on one of the most thorough pieces of ground research ever undertaken. It serves to demonstrate the essential tools for boring into the heads of housewives and others.

In 1962 a subsidiary of Unilever had a dominating share of the domestic fats market, with products like Stork and Blue Band margarine, and it decided to diversify a little. It was looking for a product with a long life cycle and an expanding market within the food and drink area. It was thought that the soft drinks market would provide an opening.

The first job for the market research team was to assess and appraise the market potential: the kinds of drinks available, the companies involved, level of sales, and how the market might develop over ten years. They concluded that any new soft drink would be sold mainly through grocers and consumed mainly in the home, and this meant either squashes or fizzy drinks; but further research showed that fizzy drink sales would not be large enough to support an entirely new brand. The branded share of the soft drinks showed a fragmented pattern – at that time Suncrush was the brand leader with 18% of a twenty-two million pound a year market, and there was substantial price competition.

Consumer research began with group discussions led by a psychologist. Groups of eight to ten children from selected suburban areas were invited to interviews to talk about fizzy drinks, and groups of housewives to discuss squashes. Participants in these discussions were paid an attendance fee of £1. What emerged was that while women recognized that children like fizzy drinks, they themselves regarded them as an indulgence and wholly unappetizing — unlike fruit squashes. They seemed to be haunted by visions of recurring wind and of teeth riddled with cavities. The company, therefore, ensured that advertising would carry a strong inference that the product was good for children.

Squash advertising had never before implied that squashes are 'good for you'. Questionnaires were drawn up for the major part of the research operation, which took the form of a detailed survey of consumer practice and attitudes to try to validate the hypotheses drawn from the discussions. Teams of interviewers were sent out to a random sample of areas with instructions to find certain numbers of consumers determined by sex, age, and class. This method of quota sampling is less expensive than random sampling.

Analysis of the replies showed that there was low brand loyalty to the existing products and that squash purchasers (identified as primarily lower middle class and upper working class housewives) were prepared to pay a higher price for a higher quality product. They equated higher quality with the notion of 'fruitiness' — 'thicker and more like real fruit'. Most of the squashes available at the time were thin in flavour, texture, and colour.

Hedges said: 'We knew we had to produce a dense, highly coloured squash which would command the price premium we believed consumers would be prepared to pay. We set out to create a degree of brand loyalty coming into a low brand loyalty market. And we had to package our squash in a way which was consistent with these aims.'

While chemists experimented with different formulations which were sent out for taste tests, bottles of every possible shape and size were collected. The aim was to find a distinctive shape which would stand out on the shelves. But when they preference tested the bottles in pairs — all filled with the same volume of liquid — it was found that many of those with the most interesting shapes appeared to contain less liquid than they in fact did. So they prescribed a bottle which was as tall as possible but still looked bulky enough to give the impression of volume. The design finally chosen was off set by placing the label high up. A long measuring cap was used to conceale the air gap which sometimes caused people to think the bottle had not been properly filled. The packaging was complete and later won an award. The name 'Tree Top' was chosen because it was easy to remember and implied that the best of the fruit went into the drink. The entire market research operation cost £40,000. Within a few years 'Tree Top' had become the best selling soft drink and was established as the new brand leader.

The influence of the mass media

1   They are a source of information, opinion, education (news, Open University, etc.).

2   They may be used to disseminate propaganda.

3   They may be used to maintain the status quo. (News can be slanted to make any who seem to be undermining the established order appear as 'wrong doers' – e.g., strikers, politicians with extreme views. Political leaders often engender a sense of unity in a population by suggesting that there is an external threat, and by sometimes identifying it. General Amin expelled Ugandan Asians 1972 and won popularity.)

4   The media can help to shape ideas, attitudes, values, and norms. (The appeal 'Your country needs you' caused any who did not respond to be seen as social deviants.)

5   The media are particularly important in reinforcing ideas already held. (Speakers who uphold the individual's beliefs are listened to with care: those who put forward opposite views are ridiculed.)

6   They are a major influences with regard to fashion (dress, hairstyle, etc.), the success or failure of records, films, theatre productions.

7   They are a major source of entertainment and leisure activity: one medium may give rise to another – e.g., the record industry produces a pop star, many disc jockeys, magazines and journals, etc.

8   They may help to break down traditional prejudices and fears (although it could be used for the opposite purpose – as in Nazi Germany – to intensify hostility against race, religion, political groups, etc.)

9   They may be used to mobilize public opinion and obtain changes in the law or in attitudes: e.g. The Queen's Pardon for Timothy Evans came after much pressure from writers and journalists to reopen the case. The 'Buy British' campaign was encouraged by the press – as was the 'Dig for Victory' campaign during the last war.

10   The media may be accused of deliberately presenting a dream-like world to the public which is so far from reality that reality is obscured. Romantic literature and popular entertainment programmes may serve to hide an unpleasant real world. Advertising, in particular, presents an appeal based on 'this is what things could be like . . . if you use this product': it may also serve to reinforce beliefs about what the real world 'ought' to be like: 'A woman's place is in the kitchen using this washing up liquid.'

11   Ownership of the press and the film circuits is concentrated in a few hands. In other areas production is in the hands of small groups who are not subject to any professional ethic: there is no controlling body as there is in the legal and medical professions. Judgement on what is news or what is acceptable is in the hands of individuals with little specialized training.

12   The media rely on commercial success, especially through the economic support of advertisers. Box office appeal is all important in the cinema. The press and magazines appeal to particular age groups and classes of readership to ensure a regular audience.

13   The media can manipulate the audience to the extent that beliefs and expectations can be built up until a point of hysteria is reached in the audience. In 1938 a radio production by Orson Welles of *The War of the Worlds* in America caused people to believe that an invasion from Mars had begun. The mass media have gone a long way in establishing the idea of a 'youth culture' in western societies. Television programme directors may have a preconceived idea of what is going to happen at a pop festival or a demonstration and will only film events which seem to support the idea, omitting other, possibly innocuous, behaviour. The reporting of events may trigger off events of a similar type: a report of a Buddhist monk burning himself to death in Vietnam in 1963 had the effect of causing similar suicides in the west, where that form of protest was previously unknown.

The presence of reporters and journalists may cause publicity seeking behaviour on the part of groups involved, and may make them to respond in the expected way (photographers may even ask for suitable poses). One television interview in which two Rockers said that reinforcements would be arriving was followed by a sudden influx of Mods and Rockers, large numbers of whom may have been attracted by the excitement the interview promised.

RESEARCH FINDINGS

In April 1973, the Professor of Film and Television at the Royal College of Art argued that far from being 'a power house of anarchy and sub-

The ubiquitous camera at a pop festival

version, television is controlled by boards of men and women selected from the most respected sections of society and staffed by people who accept the conventional views and wisdom of their society. Television, far from leading public opinion, almost always operates discreetly below the level of what people will tolerate.'

Violence on Television

1961   A conference was held, called by the Home Secretary, of representatives of the Churches, educational and social services, the press, broadcasting, and others. They discussed the incidence of delinquency and the extent to which it derived from the general moral climate of society. After the meeting the I.T.A. offered to finance research on the impact of television on society, with particular reference to the incidence of delinquency.

1962   Social scientists met at a conference in Sunningdale to decide on what research projects could be usefully undertaken. They widened the scope to include the part that television plays, or could play, in relation to other influences, in communicating knowledge and fostering attitudes: the development of children's moral concepts as well as forms of adult behaviour which are likely to be influenced by television.

1963   The Television Research Committee was established, to control the spending of the I.T.A.'s £250,000 grant.

1966   The first progress report was published.

1968   The second progress report was published. It noted that half the grant was allocated to the Centre for Mass Communication Research at Leicester University under the direction of Professor Halloran. It provisionally suggested that it might be wrong to concentrate too much on the idea that violence in the media leads to real violence.

1969   In the U.S.A. the National Commission on the Causes and Prevention of Violence suggested that a connection does exist. It pointed out: 'Every year advertisers spend $2,500 million in the belief that television can influence human behaviour. The television industry enthusiastically agrees with them, but none the less contends that its programmes of violence do not have any influence. The preponderance of available research strongly suggests that violence in television programmes can and does have adverse effects on audiences – particularly child viewers.'

1969   The Home Secretary announced that studies on the causation of violence were to be conducted under the sponsorship of the Home Office by Professor Radzinowicz at Cambridge University.

1970   The T.R.C.'s third progress report suggested that there was a certain section – impossible to say how large at present – which found it difficult to distinguish between fantasy and factual reality. There was a vulnerable element in the population. Children from lower class homes were likely to talk less about what they saw on the screen with their parents than those in middle class homes and they were left without any filtering equipment for scenes of violence. Exposure to realistic violence could produce anxiety states. Professor Halloran emphasized that the values of the television men who made the decisions should be examined as much as those who complained about programmes. He was concerned that the violence codes of the B.B.C. and I.T.A. should be 'subject to continuing systematic review in the light of relevant research results'. (The Television Act of 1964 placed a statutory obligation on the I.T.A. to produce a code on violence. The code emphasized that violence should never be used simply to attract the interest of viewers. The B.B.C. has a guide which was introduced in 1960 and is similar to the I.T.A. code, but producers are left with wide powers of discretion.)

The conclusions of the 220 page document on Television and Delinquency were generally guarded. 'The whole weight of research and theory in the juvenile delinquency field would suggest that the mass media are never the sole cause of delinquent behaviour. . . . At the most they play a contributory role . . .'

1971   A series of U.S. Government sponsored studies by Liebert and Baron produced evidence to link violence on television to aggressive behaviour in children. 'Repeated exposure to television aggression can lead children to accept what they have seen as a partial guide for their own actions. There is a direct causal link', was their conclusion.

1971   The B.B.C. commissioned a study of how families react to violence

Violence in the traditional 'Western' tends to be stylized rather than realistic: a still from 'How the West was Won'

130

on television. In a lecture Kenneth Lamb, the B.B.C.'s Public Affairs Director, said the object of the short term research project was to help broadcasters who have to make immediate decisions about programmes.

1972   Publication of the B.B.C. Report *Violence on Television*. The Report of over two hundred pages is divided into two parts: Part 1 represents the results of an examination of 1,558 programmes monitored by 105 experts. There were 1,889 violent incidents giving an average of 1.3 per programme or 2.2 per hour. There was found to be more violence on Saturdays than any other day of the week. 'An hour of news had seven times the incidence of violence found in fictional programes.... A little more than one third of all violent incidents occurred in fictional drama, 86% being of intentional physical violence, and as many as 33% including 'killings'. On average there were about twice as many violent incidents in imported American programmes as there were in British ones. The observers found that 96% of all fictional pro-grammes which contained violence were justified in showing what they did. There were more fatalities on I.T.V. Guns were the most frequent instruments of aggression in American programmes, whereas the British used their fists more often. 'If there were such a thing as "a typical hour" of British television it would contain two major sequences concerned with violence or aggres-sive behaviour. One would be a report of real life violence while the other would be a fictional portrayal consisting of direct, inter-personal physical assault, shown in detail. It would be true which-ever of the three channels was viewed or whether the hour occurred before or after the 9 p.m. watershed.'

Part 2 is concerned with attitudes towards violence on the part of the audience. Information came from discussions with fifty families (consisting of mother, father, and up to three children) questionnaires to 600 – 900 households on twelve evenings when selected programmes had been screened, and further interviews with one hundred viewers. The results showed that although 57% thought there was too much violence only 18% actually perceived violence in particular target programmes. Most viewers claimed that 'realism' was an essential element in their perception of televised violence (meaning that incidents should be graphic, in a contemporary setting, and with characters with whom it is easy to identify). The analysis of programme material indicated that most violent incidents did not meet these requirements: being non-graphic, remote in time or place, and concerned with themes that rendered the characters distant from the ordinary viewer, so that much of the violence on tele-vision is not perceived as 'real' by most viewers. The authors say that possibly the amount of violence had affected the viewers' threshold of tolerance and that they had become 'saturated'. More viewers were upset by bad language and sex than by violence. Concern about violence is more common among women than men and among the elderly than the young. Those with aggressive personalities are least concerned.

The report confirms previous findings by other investigators – that television tends to reinforce those attitudes already established in the viewer, so that in America, for example, where the carrying and use of guns is commonplace, television portrayal of this helps to contribute to the acceptance of violence or gun play. Although much violence had little significance for most viewers the report admits that 'it does not imply that such portrayals are harmless'. It names the top ten violent programmes as: Mannix, The Untouchables, The Baron, The Avengers, I Spy, Dr Who, Hawaii Five-O, The Virginian, Callan, and Star Trek.

EXERCISES

1 Carefully define 'the mass media'. Which are their most important functions?

2 Why are sociologists interested in the mass media?

3 Complete the following table:

Medium	Main functions	Possible influence or significance	Factors which affect medium	Trends
The press				
Broadcasting				
The cinema				
Advertising				

4 Write notes on: (a) Lord Northcliffe and Lord Rothermere, (b) Lord Beaverbrook, (c) Lord Thomson.

132

5 Why has the audience for the mass media increased rapidly during the last 100 years?

6 Explain the significance of the following: (*a*) Concentration of ownership of the press: the influence of the proprietor, (*b*) The influence of the editor, (*c*) The influence of the advertiser.

ESSAY QUESTIONS

1 What do sociologists mean by 'the mass media'? Select any two examples and discuss their influence and significance for society.

2 How important are the mass media in influencing people's attitudes and behaviour?

3 Discuss the sociological arguments for and against introducing commercial radio into Britain. What has been the social significance of commercial television?

4 Does violence on film and on television influence the people that watch it?

7 Youth Culture

The mass media constantly make reference to the existence of a 'youth culture'; is this a myth created by the media – or a reality? If so what is the nature of the youth culture? The term refers to those patterns of behaviour, values, attitudes, and ideas which are generally accepted and pursued by that section of society that we term 'youthful', which are radically different from the accepted culture of the society, and especially that of the older generation.

There is a problem of making a clear definition of what is meant by the term 'youth'. Does it refer specifically to teenagers of 13–19? Or to those from school leaving age to 24? There is no precisely defined group to which the term applies; but it may be useful to make an arbitrary classification and suggest that youth culture refers to those patterns of behaviour found to be most prevalent in young people between the ages of 12 and 25.

There are three aspects to consider:

1 'Youth culture' can refer to the behaviour of the mass of young people (more than 8 million aged between 12–25) a large proportion of whom are virtually economically independent, in terms of their wage packet, and who spend more than £1000 million a year on records, magazines, cosmetics, cinema, travel, etc. For this section of society large commercial enterprises have developed to provide their leisure facilities and their economic wants. The general cultural pattern is described by Abrams: 'A high proportion of non-working time is spent outside the home and in the company of the teenager's own peer groups – at cinemas, cafés, attending mass spectator sports, taking part in team games, walking and cycling'. In this sense the term refers to all that behaviour which is common to the youthful section of society and which is generally alien to that of the remainder of the population by virtue of the nature of the activities pursued. Those features of social life which may be considered to be a significant part of the youth culture include: (*a*) The cinema which draws its audience almost entirely from this age-group, and on which 4 million teenagers spend £3 million a week. (*b*) Radio, which has increased its teenage audience via Radio 1. (*c*) Records: 'A new kind of entrepreneur has been produced who may run a pop group, write songs,

design badges, and have an interest in a boutique at the same time. And climbing on the band wagon are commercial impressarios and disc jockeys who are hippy for this season but might next year be offering to promote the Hallé Orchestra if that proved to be more marketable.' In 1964 more than 85 million records were produced, in 1970 112 million, and in 1971 120 million. (d) Cosmetics, on which teenagers spend £22 million a year, that is, they represent 30% of the total market. (e) Clothes, on which it is estimated that they spend more than £160 million per year.

Observers suggest that teenage culture on a general level is largely commercial. You cannot easily participate without spending money. It can be described as 'immediate, intuitive, and dynamic': it moves according to fashion and whim.

2   In a more specific sense the term may refer to the activities and the behaviour of particular sections of the youth in society: there are some who have developed comparatively coherent and articulate philosophies of rebellion against the traditional cultural values of their society, who advocate particular ways of change, and whose life styles are in accordance with their beliefs. These may include student militants and others with strong political views. There are others, less politically motivated but none the less in rebellion against the accepted social order, whose answer is to opt out. This sector may include the 'bohemian', the 'beats' of the 1950s and more recently the 'hippies'. This is the most literary of the youthful subcultures, producing its own literary cult figures and much literature, music, and art of high quality.

3   A third sector may be termed the 'deviant' youth culture – which includes such groups as 'Teddy Boys', 'Mods and Rockers', 'Skinheads and Greasers', etc. Such groups are generally the product of the subculture of the environment from which they come, and there is little if any rational, considered philosophy in their behaviour patterns.

'Youth culture' is generally used as a blanket term, and it is not always clear which aspect is being considered. For the purpose of analysis it is helpful to consider it in its more specific sense.

The interest of the sociologist

The sociologist wishes to investigate the attitudes and values of the youthful section of society to see in what ways they differ from those of the generally accepted and dominant norms of society. They are interested to see to what extent 'youth culture' is a valid and useful concept, and to find ways of making an analysis of the relevant factors. They may ask – are there many youth cultures, rather than one overall culture? Are young people in rebellion against middle class values and middle class ideals? Is youth on an unknown spiritual quest? Do deviant groups represent a threat to society and how does one explain their existence? Are young people becoming more conformist and unquestioning? To what extent do the mass media and mass entertainment serve to create a youth culture?

The skinhead and his girl

SOCIOLOGY: AN INTRODUCTORY COURSE

The sociologist investigates all the relevant features connected with the subject matter, collects evidence and data, and seeks to produce theories to explain the phenomena that he observes.

There are variations in behaviour between various sections of the youth in society which have been observed by sociologists. The factors affecting the cultural behaviour of young people include:

1   Income, occupation, and class background.
2   Age: the interests of a young person of 15 will be different to those of a person of 25.
3   Local environment (housing estate, rural area, etc.)
4   The growth of the entertainments industry – especially since the war.
5   Affluence compared with austerity before and just after the war.
6   Wider educational opportunities which put more young people in touch with theories and ideas not available to the prewar generation (university, college, etc.).
7   The influence of the mass media and the 'stars' who provide models of behaviour (pop stars, football stars, etc.).
8   Twenty-five years of peace have meant that a generation has grown up without fear of war or influence of conscription. Hence a greater sense of freedom to choose patterns of behaviour rather than have them imposed or ordered.
9   The snowball effect of following fashions and trends: once a part of the cultural scene, the individual becomes a slave to its trends and movements.

The factors which make for the distinction between the culture of the youthful section of society and that of its elders include:

1   The provision of entertainment especially for them.
2   The search for beliefs, identity, values.
3   The ability to undertake activities not open to older people who may have defined responsibilities (travel, sport, etc.).
4   Normative patterns of behaviour are different in that they are based on different values: young people are open to a wider variety of influences (the media, school, 'current ideas' – young people seem to be in nationwide contact with each other).
5   There is a continuous battle with the 'pressures to conform' of parents, teachers, and society. (Hence the 'generation gap' – the dominant values of society are those of the 'middle aged' section of society in that there are more people of this age group than any other.) –
6   Young people are more economically independent than at any previous time.

POSSIBLE EXPLANATIONS OF THE GROWTH OF YOUTH CULTURE IN BRITAIN

People aged 14 in 1945 were underprivileged and disillusioned in the difficult post-war years. They became a 'cautious generation'. Those aged about 7 or 8 in 1945 were not so aware of material hardship, and later

138

The CND Aldermaston March, Easter 1963

became idealistic, wanting to put the world right. From these two groups developed a synthesis in the mid-50s when those aged between 18 and 25 developed a social awareness and a sense of rebellion, while the remainder sank into an acceptance and conformity. It has been said that working class youth provided the clothes — jeans, duffle coats — and the middle class the ideas — the beginnings of an articulate philosophy of rebellion against the moral codes of their affluent ('You've never had it so good') elders, and the growing emphasis on materialism and techno-logical achievements. This element of dissident youth was held together by the unifying elements of political belief (the C.N.D. Movement, for example, the growth of jazz clubs and later pop music, and the literature of rebellion — Kerouac, Ginsberg, 'angry young men' like Osborne, Colin Wilson, etc.); the development of new attitudes in the cinema (the 'Nouvelle Vague') and the theatre (*Look Back in Anger*, etc.). With the growth of magazines and journals aimed at a young audience ideas and attitudes spread more rapidly.

In the 1960s with university expansion, many young people developed more coherent poltical attitudes.

The mass media began to turn their attention more to the activities of youth and may have helped spread ideas concerning cult behaviour (battles on beaches between Mods and Rockers, skinhead dress and behaviour).

Some observers suggest that at the present time there are more factions dividing youth and fewer unifying causes — that youth is becoming less humane and idealistic and more materialistic and inclined to accept the affluent society.

Youth groups within society

Only a small minority seem to have worked out a coherent new phi-losophy by which to live on a permanent basis. Of those who have, Rosak suggests that theirs is an attempt to 'develop a counter-culture to that of the technological age. It can be compared to the Romantic literary movement in literature of the early nineteenth century. They are seeking to oppose the dehumanizing influences that are at work. In the new youth culture, youngsters experiment with drugs and alcohol and new kinds of religion to experience life in a world of their own making.' He writes: 'The counter-culture is based on creativity, opposition to the impersonal forces of technology, and on a spiritual vision — making for a new heaven on earth.'

He is writing of a very small section of youth who are not overtly political in their attitudes, and are not seeking a violent revolution to attain their ends. They are prepared to find their salvation through their own endeavours, without necessarily seeking to obtain converts to their cause. In this respect they may be seen as the 'drop-outs' or hippies who adopt an alternative life style based on specific principles.

But the sociologist Bryan Wilson, writing of the non-political section of youth, describes the hippy movement as 'an expression of rebellion by urbanites who are clearer about what they are against than what they are for. In the U.S.A. their slogans focused on the war in Vietman, restrictions on personal freedom, the brutality and corruption of the police. They are against the prevailing order without knowing how to live when there is no social order. Unconventional conventions are accepted: the discovery of the self with the aid of drugs, perhaps a Buddhist text or even the Gospel of St John is a religious quest among the more sophisticated hippies. The millenium of the socialist society is too remote for their enthusiasm. Drugs represent the rejection of the values of parents, the middle class, the masculinity cult, athleticism, the clean and decent 'all American boy'. The hippy rebellion is directed against the customs and conventions of society. The hippy culture rejects the mass media but ironically is manipulated by it and indeed could only occur in conditions of affluence and with the facilities that a wealthy economy provides.'

However, it has thrown up its own literary spokesmen, and is largely responsible for much of the 'Underground Press', *Oz, Time Out*, and *Rolling Stone*.

The 'alternative society': a protest against traditional values — and traditional dress

The literature of the youth culture

In September 1957 a novel was published which the *New York Times* called 'the most beautifully executed, the clearest and most important utterance yet made by a young writer; a book likely to represent a generation as *The Sun also Rises*, by Hemingway, represents the twenties.' It was called *On the Road*, and described the experiences and attitudes of a restless group of young people 'mad to live, made to talk, mad to be saved'. The author, Jack Kerouac, said they were members of the 'beat generation'. To be beat is 'to be at the bottom of your personality looking up; beat means beatitude — it describes the state of being emptied out — a state of mind in which all unessentials have been stripped, leaving it receptive to everything around it, but impatient with trivial obstructions.' What Kerouac seemed to offer was 'some insight into the attitudes of a generation whose elders were completely flabbergasted by the social changes going on around them'. Implicitly modern jazz, rock'n roll, drug addiction, delinquency, and all the attendant phenomena that have characterized much of contemporary youth in extreme, seemed to be the primary preoccupation of Kerouac's characters.

What differentiated the characters in *On the Road* from the non-conformists of other books was Kerouac's insistence that they were actually on a quest, and the specific object of that quest was unknowingly spiritual. He believed that beyond the violence, the drugs, the jazz, and all the other experiences in which it frantically seeks its identity, this generation will find a faith. Everywhere young people are reacting to the growing collectivity of modern life, and the constant threat of collective death, with the same disturbing extremity of individualism.

A similar argument is put forward in a book entitled *Youthquake* by a priest, Kenneth Leech, published in 1973. He has tried to chronicle an era in the growth of a youth counter-culture specifically from the angle of the spiritual quest. He points to the prevalence of pop songs and musicals with religious themes, and the growth of new religious groups among the young as evidence of the underlying search for spiritual answers. Young people seem to be saying more and more that it is how a man lives and not why that is important.

There is another section of youth which is politically motivated and whose behaviour and life styles are determined according to these beliefs. They inevitably form a small group in Britain. There are those who work within the accepted political parties — the Young Conservatives, Young Socialists, and Young Liberals — and there are some who are described by James Jupp as the more militant section of youth. These, he says 'see modern society as a confidence trick offering high standards of material comfort in exchange for slavery to the industrial machine. The only sections of society likely to revolt against this are the unbribed poor, racial minorities, and youth.' Older members have too much to lose to criticize too strongly. 'The idea that youth is both enlightened and capable of liberating itself and others is irresistible to young idealists.'

Jupp writes: 'A whole generation has been created in the past 10 years which is sceptical and hedonistic, critical of the adult world and essentially apart from it. But most will come through unscathed, ready for the embrace of the affluent society.'

He suggests that such extreme attitudes are passing ideals which are eventually replaced by more orthodox views and behaviour. Nevertheless, they do form a significant part of the youth culture particularly of students in colleges and universities. In the 1950s and 1960s the supporters of the C.N.D. movement might have fallen into the politically motivated category.

Stanley Cohen has tried to explain the presence of youthful deviant groups in society — the reason for the presence of Teddy Boys, Mods and Rockers, Skinheads and Greasers. In his book *Folk Devils and Moral Panics* he writes:

Societies appear to be subject, every now and then, to periods of moral panic. A condition, episode, person or group of persons emerges to become defined as a threat to society. The moral barricades are manned by editors, bishops, politicians and other right thinking people . . . ways of coping are evolved . . . the condition then disappears . . . sometimes the panic passes over and is forgotten . . . at other times it has more serious and longlasting repercussions and might produce such changes as those in legal and social policy. . . . One of the most recurrent types of moral panic in Britain since the war has been associated with the emergence of various forms of youth culture (originally almost exclusively working class, but often recently middle class or student based) whose behaviour is deviant or delinquent. To a greater or lesser extent, these cultures have been associated with violence. . . . In the gallery of types that society erects to show its members which roles should be avoided and which should be emulated, these groups [Teddy Boys, Mods and Rockers, Skinheads and Greasers etc.] have occupied a constant position as 'folk devils': visible reminders of what we should not be.

Cohen's idea is that society requires scapegoats when things are going wrong in order to create a sense of unity and self-righteousness. The burning of witches in the middle ages is an example of his folk devil theory.

What is the function of the youth culture?

Some sociologists have described the youth culture as one that emphasizes disengagement from adult values, daring, immediate pleasure, and comradeship in a way that is true neither of childhood nor adulthood. The youth culture is not always specifically anti-adult, but is belligerently non-adult. The rock 'n roller, the college student, the juvenile delinquent, the beatnik, the hippy, all form part of the general youth culture.

Others say that the period between childhood and adulthood is an uncertain one. The individual's role and status are ambiguous. He is neither child nor adult, no longer totally dependent, yet not allowed to become totally independent. The family can no longer adequately prepare its members for their adult roles, with the increased division of labour and the growth of specialized organisations; young people look more and more to their peers and evolve and draw on their own distinctive cultures.

They see all expressions of youth culture (whatever form they take) as a part of the transition from childhood to adulthood: it is a way of coping with the uncertainties and difficulties of this stage of development. The result is that young people create and draw on their own distinctive culture, often with the aid of the mass media and encouraged by commercial enterprises. The fact that young people are free with their money (which gives them a greater degree of freedom than at any previous time) may be a point of friction between the generations.

'Participation in a youth culture may serve a useful function for the young person. The peer group that carries the culture provides support in certain situations; and may offer compensation for some of the strains to which the young person is exposed. It also allows him to break away from the dependence of the family so that he can express his own identity.'

It has been shown that, for those with less critical awareness, adopting the deviant values of a group may represent a way of gaining acceptance in the group, a means of showing manliness, bravado, etc., and initiation into the presumed world of maturity and adulthood.

In its general sense youth culture may be all youthful behaviour which does not conform to those accepted standards of adult society resulting from the affluence of youth and the changing historical and social context in which current youth is growing up (violence but no war, wealth and success are the watchwords). The behaviour of young people is inevitably different from that of the older generation because it is in a period of transition from childhood into adulthood and young people are acquiring independence. They must come to terms with these changes by experimentation and by adopting the values of their peers with whom they are in close contact.

In its more specific sense youth culture varies from group to group and is an expression of the values and attitudes and norms of each group: some develop political values, others are deviant, others are non-political and non-deviant: whichever group the young person mixes with will affect his values and his view of the world.

RESEARCH FINDINGS 1
An investigation into the behaviour of young people, 1963. (Schonfield: *The Sexual Behaviour of Young People*).

A detailed investigation was made to obtain facts about the moral attitudes and behaviour of young people aged between 15 and 19. The scope of the research was to find out as much as possible about the activities of teenagers within a specified framework.

1   The interview was obtained direct from the teenagers themselves.
2   The interviewers were specially recruited and trained for the work.
3   The research was based on a series of random samples.
4   The questions on moral attitudes were preceded by a large number on family background and leisure activities.
5   A sufficiently large sample was interviewed, so as to be able to describe certain norms of behaviour within the teenage group.
6   Care was taken to exclude all value judgements on the part of the interviewer in the course of the interviews.

After careful consideration it was decided that, providing the interviewers are trained and the schedule of questions is tested the interview situation remains the best method of obtaining information about moral behaviour and attitudes.

In the pilot research visits were made to a jazz club, a youth club, and various schools and universities so that a detailed reaction to the methods of the research team could be obtained. The young people in the random samples were not volunteers. They received visits from the research team and then had to be persuaded to answer questions. The method of obtaining interviews was very expensive but provided a more representative picture of the whole teenage population.

The first area to be sampled was designated as London C. The sample was drawn from all National Health records in the area, which covered 97.5% of the population throughout the full age range. Twenty doctors were selected by random sampling. The cards of all their patients were studied, which produced a list of 2,478 teenagers from which a stratified sample was drawn to produce almost equal numbers in four age and sex groups: girls born in 1943/44 and 1945/46 and boys born in the same periods.

The next two areas to be sampled were South A and South B, where samples were drawn from school attendance lists. The numbers sampled were 2,304 and 3,510. Since two samples were required, one representing the middle class section of the town and the other the working class section, it was decided to use the Index of Jurors as an indication of social class. This is an index which gives the percentage of the electors who are on the electoral register of each ward. It had been shown in 1951 (by Gray, Corlett, and Jones) that if an electoral ward has a high index of jurors then a large proportion of the electors will be in Class 1 and 2 of the Registrar General's scale of social class. Similarly, a low index of jurors indicates a high representation of social classes 4 and 5.

For the other areas a third sampling method was devised. A market research agency was employed to locate all the teenagers living in selected areas, one with a large middle class population (North A) and the other with a mainly working class population (North B). Using the Index of Jurors as a guide, two wards were chosen for the middle class sample and three wards for the working class sample.

Similar results were obtained from the three samples, which were all derived in different ways. The research provided a detailed insight into the moral behaviour of the teenagers questioned which, because of the nature of the scientific sampling method used, provided a picture of the behaviour patterns of the youth of the country as a whole in terms of their values and culture.

RESEARCH FINDINGS 2
George Greening's study of the attitudes of young people was primarily designed to investigate religious attitudes, but it also provides other interesting details.

760 young people aged between 17 and 21 who were members of classes 3, 4, and 5 were questioned:

Activity	%		
Membership of a social club	35	Approve of divorce	80
Play a sport regularly	50	Approve of corporal punishment	55
Approve of gambling	63	Approve of capital punishment	56
Support of political party	24	Favour church weddings	73
Favour trade unions	62	Favour easier licensing laws	
Favour student power	28	in public houses	63
Favour racial integration	60	Approve of drug taking	10
Favour the welfare state	86		

Suggest other hypotheses that could be tested in light of these findings. For example: 'There is likely to be a strong element of hostility towards college students in classes 3, 4 and 5.'

EXERCISES
1   Define the term 'youth culture'.
2   What are the problems in making a definition?
3   Write a short passage describing the average young person who emerges from the study by George Greening. (See also page 211.)
4   What are the factors that distinguish between the culture of youth and that of the older generation?
5   To what extent does it seem that young people are less idealistic in the 1970s than they were in the 1950s?
6   What are the major influences which affect the behaviour of young people? Suggest ways by which a sociologist could investigate these.

ESSAY QUESTIONS
1   Young people are no better and no worse than at any other time. Discuss this statement in light of (a) the generation gap, and (b) the increase in crime and violence.

2   What do sociologists mean by 'youth culture'? How do they account for the growth of 'youth culture' in modern industrial societies?

3   To what extent is it true to say that the mass media have created a youth culture in Britain in recent years?

4   The age of majority is now 18 and the school leaving age is 16. Discuss the possible effects that these changes might have on our society (with reference to voting behaviour, age of marriage, size of family, etc.).

5   What categories exist within the ranks of young people?
What are their distinctive features?
Are there any common factors?
Complete the following table.

Group	Social Class	Age Range	Behaviour Patterns	Comments of Sociologists
Politically Motivated Youth				
Non-conforming Youth (But Non-political)				
Deviants ('Folk Devils')				
Religious/ Spiritual Youth				
Orthodox and Conforming Youth				

The assembly line: hard and repetitive work, but well paid

8 Work

The sociological significance of work

The sociologist is interested in understanding the relevance of work as an economic activity for the individual and its significance for society. It can be assessed in terms of what it does for him and what it does to him. For some it may provide a valuable and enjoyable experience in which the individual's understanding and personality are enlarged and his life enriched. For others it may be an unpleasant and dehumanizing experience which crushes any sense of personal worth and any possible future enjoyment in work — and yet they may continue for a lifetime in such employment.

Why should this be so, and what are some of the explanations giving rise to these experiences and attitudes? This is the field of study of the sociologist.

Attitudes towards work

Sociologists have identified some of the major attitudes that exist with regard to work, which help to explain the behaviour of individuals in relation to their occupation.

1 *The extrinsic attitude* Those who hold this view tend to believe that the only real point of work is to obtain as high a standard of living as possible; hence a person should take the best paid job that he can regardless of the nature of the work, since it is a means of obtaining the material goods he needs. The belief that it is always better to take a boring or unpleasant job that is well paid in preference to an interesting but less well paid occupation may be termed an 'extrinsic attitude', since the reward gained from the work is extrinsic to the work itself.

2 *The intrinsic attitude* Those who hold this view tend to believe that the most important consideration in obtaining a job is to gain a sense of satisfaction and enjoyment from it. It should enable the individual to use all his abilities and faculties to the fullest extent. High pay is not seen as the most important consideration. The person who holds this view may be said to have an intrinsic attitude since he sees the work he is doing as having its own intrinsic worth. It is valuable in itself and not just

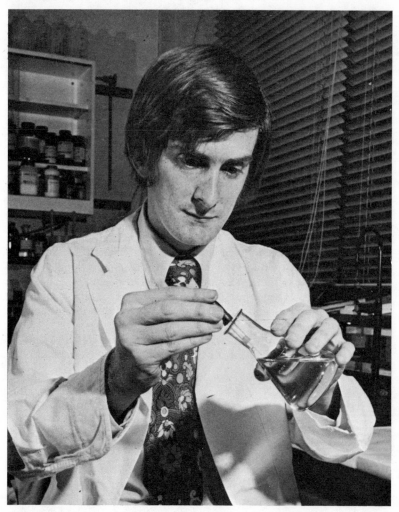

Laboratory research: the work offers more than monetary rewards

for the material rewards that it may offer.

3 *The Protestant ethic* Sociologists sometimes refer to another attitude which is held by some people. They may not gain great satisfaction from their work and may not see high pay as the most important consideration in choosing it; but they feel that work is morally and socially virtuous and that failure to work is immoral and degrading. It is only by working to the best of his abilities, however elevated or menial his job, that a person becomes a good and valuable member of society and a worthwhile citizen. This view reflects an acceptance of the Protestant ethic first established in the teachings of Luther and Calvin in the sixteenth century.

It is epitomized in sayings like 'God helps those who help themselves' and 'The devil makes work for idle hands'.

FACTORS THAT DETERMINE ATTITUDES TOWARDS WORK

One writer has said that 'The goals a person seeks are those he has absorbed from the groups of which he has been a member. He comes to act, think, perceive, and feel as his social group expect him to. He learns to accept values and to be the kind of person his society calls for. Specifically, he lives up to what is expected of persons in the status and roles he occupies. The individual learns to want and seek those things he is supposed to want according to the standards of his family, friends, and larger reference group.' (His reference group consists of those people around him with whom he compares himself since they seem to be similar types of people.) In this way individuals are conditioned by a wide variety of socializing agencies to accept particular doctrines, beliefs, and attitudes about the nature of work.

1 SOCIAL CLASS BACKGROUND

This is significant in helping to determine an individual's 'horizon of expectation', fixing for him his estimation of his own worth and level of ability. It may establish for him the kind of work he believes he ought to do or would be capable of doing, that is, the kind of work that a person of his social type and background should aim at. Some types of occupation may be seen to be unsuitable because they are associated with people of higher or lower social class than himself.

Examine the following table and consider the implications.

Social class of medical students, 1966

Class 1	Class 2	Class 3	Classes 4 and 5.
39.6%	36.2%	21.7%	2.5%

What is the reason that so few medical students came from the lowest end of the social scale in 1966, and why do more than 75% come from the two highest classes? The reason is not because those in classes 4 and 5 are necessarily less intelligent, but because very few would ever see themselves as potential members of a professional class, and because they would not receive the necessary encouragement either at home or in school to persuade them that they could become doctors just as easily as they could become motor mechanics if they obtained the right qualifications.

2 EDUCATION

One of the significant norms of social class 4 and 5 is that education has largely extrinsic worth. It is useful in that the individual is taught to read and write and acquire basic skills, but it is seen to have little significance after the age of 16. Whereas in order to obtain professional qualifications, which may involve years of study after the age of 16, it is necessary to see education as having some intrinsic worth — that there is enjoyment and value to be gained from studying for its own sake, and that it is a means of obtaining long-term goals. This is one of the dominant normative values of members of social classes 1 & 2. This helps to account for the educational success of children who come from this social class background. Lack of success in school or failure to obtain useful qualifications limits the choice of job. The individual must either enter unskilled work or take an occupation on a chance basis. Studies have shown that while compulsory school education has been steadily increasing, more than 50% of the school population continue to leave at the minimum age. In 1966 60% of all male school leavers went into unskilled and semi-skilled work and 35% went into an apprenticeship. The proportion going into unskilled work declines steeply as the age of leaving increases, but more children from the higher social classes stay on at school than do those from the lower groups.

3 THE PEER GROUP

The influence of the peer group is to reinforce the attitudes established in the home. Where an individual finds that all his friends and acquaintances are intent on leaving school at the earliest possible age, then he will almost certainly follow suit (unless his reference group is other than his immediate circle of friends, but this is unusual). Children whose parents gained little by way of qualification and status from their own education and who may wish for better things for them, nevertheless tend to fall short of the high ambitions their parents hold for them. Sons and daughters of unskilled parents may attain semi-skilled or even skilled status, but entry into the higher professional category is difficult and unusual. It has been found that for children who come from homes of unskilled workers and whose peer group consists largely of others from similar backgrounds, the general beliefs they hold even before starting work are that it will be unpleasant and restrictive, and will involve subjection to the control of others. The attitude handed down from one generation to the next is one of pessimism and resignation, which contrasts with the optimistic expectations of those in the higher social class categories.

4 CULTURAL AND LOCALIZED ECONOMIC FACTORS

Broad cultural factors and ideologies may help to shape an individual's attitude towards work. For example, in Japan the code of conduct demands: (a) subordination to superiors, (b) respect for elders, and (c) complete identification with the norms and values of the home, in which the roles and status of individuals are clearly defined. The consequence is that the attitude of the majority of Japanese workers towards their work and their employer is shaped by the prevailing code of conduct which they are taught to accept from an early age. In Britain such codes of behaviour are less strict and people may be less conscious of them. There is evidence of a certain degree of class and occupational solidarity. Some occupational

A car worker in Japan

groups would never consider strike action because it would contravene the accepted norms of their employment — 'people like us do not strike' — whereas other sections of the work force see strike action as a comparatively regular feature of working life.

Apart from the more general systems of belief that exist, there are also the more localized values which develop in particular areas or neighbourhoods. It has been found, for example, that in areas of high unemployment, which are often regions in which people feel a strong sense of roots, a powerful feeling of pessimism develops. The attitude grows that work is always going to be hard to find, it is advisable to take any job that is available, and all work is inevitably boring, but economically necessary.

5   THE WORK EXPERIENCE

Every individual has certain goals, aims, ambitions, and aspirations. These may vary according to background, personality, and education. If the goals are met in the work situation, then the worker will accept the authority of the employer with little question. (The man who seeks and attains promotion and responsibility is likely to be a contented worker.) The employee who finds intrinsic satisfaction has generally freely chosen his occupation, which is in some sense creative or meets his demands.

If, on the other hand, the goals of the individual are not met in the work situation, then the worker will be dissatisfied and will be in conflict with his employer. If he fails to obtain promotion or variety he will almost certainly lose interest in his work. It has been suggested that in some industries where workers are involved in boring and repetitive jobs strikes may become frequent since they are found to be enjoyable diversions from the depressing routine of the assembly line. The employee who finds only extrinsic satisfaction probably does not develop all of his abilities and aptitudes. High pay becomes an important means of justifying work that he does not enjoy. The worker loses his sense of individual worth and individuality. In some cases he becomes a 'slave to a machine', and in Marx's terms may be said to be alienated from his true nature, since his work serves only to dehumanize and debase him. It is a means of obtaining other ends — those of material goods. Extrinsic attitudes are likely to result where there has been little or no choice of occupation and the worker anticipates an unhappy work experience.

6   ATTITUDES TOWARDS WORK

The novelist Alan Sillitoe describes the experience of factory work in his novel *Saturday Night and Sunday Morning*:

The minute you stepped outside the factory gates you thought no more about your work. But the funniest thing was that neither did you think about work when you were standing at your machine. You began the day by cutting and drilling steel cylinders with care, but gradually your actions became automatic and you forgot all about the machine and the quick working of your arms and hands and the fact that you were cutting and boring and rough threading to within limits of only five thousandths of an inch. The noise of motor trolleys passing up and down the gangway and the excruciating din of flying and flapping belts slipped out of your consciousness after perhaps half an hour without affecting the quality of the work you were turning out, and you forgot your past conflicts with the gaffer and turned to thinking of pleasant events that had at some time happened to you, or things that you hoped would happen to you in the future. If your machine was working well – the motor smooth, stops tight, jigs good – and you sprung your actions into a favourable rhythm you became happy. You went off into pipe dreams for the rest of the day. And in the evening when admittedly you would be feeling as though your arms and legs had been stretched to breaking point on a torture rack, you stepped out into a cosy world of pubs and noisy tarts that would one day provide you with raw material for pipe dreams as you stood at your lathe.

A less literate but equally realistic view of the day-to-day work situation of manual workers is drawn by some apprentices who were asked to give some details of their work.

I hate getting up for work in a morning because it is so cold and I don't like getting out of bed. My old man gets me up about 6.30 and finally I get dressed about a quarter of an hour later. I leave for work at 7.30 and make my way to a bus stop. I arrive at work at ten to eight. I clock on and have a talk and a smoke. I go to my bench where my mate has already started. He works like a cat on hot bricks knocking the sides up. We make about three sides before dinner. We knock off for dinner about twelve and rush to the shop for chips and sandwiches. I only get half an hour for lunch because of the bonus. We carry on till it's tea break and then have a smoke. After that we start on the interiors and carry on working away till it's knocking off time. I quite like my job. It's hard work and I don't get back till gone six o'clock in the night. But it's varied and also I like to see what I have made being admired by others. Sometimes I feel quite proud and think – that's a part of me and it's there for good. I always wanted to work in wood because I was good at it at school. I hated writing lessons. Also there's good prospects and you can have a laugh and joke with your mates so long as you finish the job on time. In the night I watch TV then go to bed.
(*Apprentice caravan maker*)

In the early morning it's dark and perishing cold in winter. I hear my alarm – I get up, gemme boots on, get dressed, get breakfast and leave for work. When I get there I clocks on and talk to my mates about football usually. I takes off my coat and start work. First I go to stores to get sets for the men. It is noisy and not very warm in my shop (except in summer when it is too hot). Last week I got it in the neck for not getting the blades set right. It can be dangerous if you don't think about what you're doing. It's long hours but the pay is good. The worst thing is the noise and dirt. Also it can be very boring doing the same thing day in day out. But I suppose I will keep at it like the other men in the shop that have been there for ever since it started I shouldn't wonder. You haven't got much choice around here anyway. I really wish I had chosen something else when I left school – not that I chose this job really: there wasn't anything else going at the time. But anyway how do you know what you're good at? It's all luck. I don't suppose bus conductors or road sweepers like their jobs much, nor judges or nurses or people who work in offices. So I think I will stay where I am. You've got to do something to stop the boredom. (*Apprentice sheet metal worker*)

I think that I would go to work even if I didn't have to for the money. It's not so much because I like what I'm doing but more because I would feel guilty in a funny kind of way if I didn't. I think everyone ought to pull their weight and help the country. People on the dole are ruining this country of ours. (*Apprentice caterer*)

The disadvantage of our job is that we are doing the same kind of work every day of the year. Maybe that's because I've only recently started. But the other week I went snaggin (*sic*) for the first time. Its a very good advantage all right because you mend different furniture and learn about legs. We have no canteen, you have to bring your own flask — or you can have a fresh cup of tea done by a hot geyser — but the hot geyser is playing tricks at the moment — like squirting hot water on your boots which stains them white. My mate put fleshings (*sic*) in my tea which makes it taste horrible. I would prefer to be at work than be in school — the pay is better. I like working with my hands and I do quite a lot of woodwork at home for my hobby. So I think I have made a good choice. The first thing I ever made was a tea pot stand. Now I'm making kitchen units. I've come a long way in a short time. (*Apprentice carpenter*)

Consider how the examples provided in these extracts reflect the dominant attitudes towards work which sociologists have identified in British society.

Examples of those doing work that they do not enjoy, but from which they cannot see any means of escape, were given by David White in an article entitled 'Those Who Do The Butt-End Jobs' in *New Society*, 1973. He wrote: 'Those who lack qualifications and skills lack options. For the poorest sector the upshot is fear of unemployment, hard, dirty, and often night-time jobs. For those with little job choice the job tends to control the worker's time rather than the other way round. Overtime, shift work, and night work curtail people's rights to a full home or family life. One of the interviewees in a butt-end job, working in a Liverpool slaughterhouse helping to dispose of the unwanted parts of the slaughtered animals said, "Sure, I know I stink . . . it's a dirty job. But you get used to the smell after a bit. I've got so as I don't notice it. All my wife asks is that I have a bath when I get home." He had worked in the slaughterhouse for about eighteen months. He said, "It's not a job I'd choose if I had a choice . . . but there wasn't much else and this is an easy job to get into. The pay is better than I was getting at the post office." On average he earned £21 per week. This included overtime worked on Saturdays and Sundays. The best this man can hope for is eventual promotion to foreman. But he doesn't bother much about prospects. He merely assumes that he will be working in the same job in about five or ten years' time.'

The problem is intensified for such people if they have not only a poor educational background but also happen to come from a depressed area where there are high rates of unemployment and where a sense of despondency about job prospects may have developed. Liverpool, for example, had the largest percentage of unemployment in 1973 of any local authority area in the country – nearly 8%: over 48,000 people (of whom 37,000 were men) were out of work at the beginning of that year. The problem was seen to be so acute that the Education Committee asked the Government to designate the whole of the city as an Educational Priority Area, so that more finance would be forthcoming. A survey in 1972 found that the number of pupils going on to higher education in the city was 30% below the national average. Fewer than half the children in Liverpool were staying on at school beyond the minimum leaving age (compared with two thirds in Manchester). The Committee blamed the failure of the city to diversify its industries after the war, and so help raise the standards and aspirations of school leavers. The Report found that job satisfaction is low on Merseyside and poor working conditions have brought about a sense of grievance and militancy rather than satisfaction and ambition. New industries could have brought about greater interest and choice, but the industries that have been established have only increased the financial aspirations of workers, and have not introduced the demand for new skills. It was the lack of job choices that led to a lack of any wish to seek the mecca which is the reward of talent – but in the main people are satisfied with 'beer, cigarettes, and football'. The consequence is that teachers have difficulty in raising the aims and ambitions of pupils in city schools.

Why do not those who are unemployed, or are in jobs that they do not like, move to regions of the country where jobs are more plentiful and choices wider? There are a number of factors which may help to explain this phenomenon.

1   Those who have been unemployed for long periods tend to become more and more pessimistic about finding ways out of their difficulty. They may come to believe that they are not capable of finding permanent work.

2   They may have got into a rut and routine, and have come to accept their plight and believe that they are too old or too 'unintelligent' to train for a more worthwhile job. They come to rationalize the situation with a belief that 'given time things may get better'.

3   There may be a great lack of motivation especially among unskilled workers since they do not expect an income much greater than that obtained in their present situation. This will be particularly true where they hold a strong extrinsic attitude towards work: 'One may as well do a boring job here as anywhere else.'

4   They may not be sure that the level of pay and security offered else-

A course in bricklaying at a training centre run by the Department of Employment

where will be any higher than the present level obtained in social security benefits or pay.

5   Where the individual (or his wife) has long-standing roots in an area (especially where there is strong regional identification) a move to another part of the country becomes difficult. They may have developed stereo-types of what people 'in the south,' or 'in the north' are like, and believe that they will be radically different from themselves and their way of life. A move may also be more difficult for older people who have children in school and fear that a change may be detrimental to their progress. Women whose lives have become 'mum-centred' may be particularly un-happy to move when it means leaving close relatives and friends.

6   A move to the south of England is difficult for people coming from parts of the north of the country because house prices are much higher and accommodation of any kind will be difficult to obtain unless the income is relatively high.

7   People may lack information about the opportunities available in other areas. To encourage mobility of labour the Government offers travel

warrants for interviews, and if successful further travelling expenses for the worker, his wife, and family. There are also removal expenses, a housing allowance, and a £400 settling-in grant. But even where such information is available the job expectations and the horizons of such workers remain limited. The educational system may have failed to educate people to think in terms of retraining, an idea particularly difficult for those who have not succeeded in their full-time schooling in the first place. A study in Liverpool showed how in deprived areas the belief in the inevitability of periodic unemployment and of boring work becomes a normative attitude which permeates the consciousness and beliefs of the citizens of the area. Generally, for an unskilled or unemployed person to leave an area, the possibility of making such a change must depend on the extent to which the alternatives offer much greater attractions in terms of pay and prospects.

> There is no point in work
> Unless it absorbs you
> Like an absorbing game.
> If it doesn't absorb you
> It's never any fun.
> Don't do it.
>   *D. H. Lawrence*

Apprenticeship

Conditions of apprenticeship have changed considerably over the years. Compare the Indenture below, typical of those signed about 1900, with one of today.

This Indenture witnesseth that A —— son of B —— of the city of —— a wheelwright of his own free will and good liking and with the consent and approbation of the said B —— testified by his being a party to and executing these presents doth put himself Apprentice to —— of the city of —— Upholsterer and Cabinet Maker to learn the art and with him after the Manner of an Apprentice to serve after the day of the date thereof unto the full end and term of Seven years from thence next following to the fully complete and ended. During which term the said Apprentice his master shall faithfully serve, his secrets keep, his lawful commands everywhere gladly do. He shall do no damage to his said Master, not see to be done of others, but to his power shall tell or forthwith give warning to his said Master of the same. He shall not contract matrimony within the said term, not play at cards or dice tables or any other unlawful games, whereby his said Master may have any loss with his own goods or others. During the said term without licence of his said Master, he shall neither buy nor sell. He shall not haunt Taverns of Playhouses nor absent himself from his said Master's Service day or night unlawfully. But in all things as a faithfull Apprentice he shall behave himself towards his said Master and all during the

An apprentice in the 19th century: the 'printer's devil' cleaning up while the master printer is setting the type

said Term. And the said —— in consideration of such faithfull service will teach the said Apprentice in the Art of a Cabinet Maker which he useth by the best means that he can teach and instruct or cause to be taught and instructed, finding unto the said Apprentice sufficient meat, drink, lodging and all other necessaries during the said Term, or in lieu thereto shall pay unto the said father B —— for the use of the said Apprentice the sum of

> 3 shillings per week during the first year
> 4 shillings per week during the second year
> 5 shillings per week during the third year
> 6 shillings per week during the fourth year
> 7 shillings per week during the fifth year
> 8 shillings per week during the sixth year

and 9 shillings per week during the seventh year, and last of the said Term. But if the said Apprentice absents himself from the service of the said Master, such wages shall not be paid or payable and the said Father hereby agrees upon receipt of the said weekly sum to find and provide for the said Apprentice sufficient meat, drink, lodging, clothing and all other necessaries during the said Term.

Typical Modern Conditions of Apprenticeship

1   Present hours of work. Young people may not work more than nine hours in one day, or 48 hours a week.

2   Period of employment. Young persons may not work more than 11 hours in one day. They should not begin before 7 a.m. or work later than 8 p.m., or after 1 p.m. on Saturdays.

3   The spell of work. Young persons may not work for more than $4\frac{1}{2}$ hours without an interval of at least $\frac{1}{2}$ hour to follow, but if there is a break of 10 minutes, the work spell can be 5 hours.

4   Intervals: Everyone should take the same intervals except that the young worker may finish work earlier.

5   Overtime: Overtime is authorized only for pressure of work. Hours worked must not exceed 10 in one day. Overtime for *all* the factory must not exceed 6 in a week or 100 in a year, and must be spread over 25 weeks of the year if the maximum is reached. Exceptions of up to $\frac{1}{2}$ in one work spell exist for factories with special shifts. The overall total does not vary. All overtime by apprentices must be reported to factory inspectors.

6   Sunday work for apprentices is barred except for very unusual circumstances.

7   Holidays: apprentices are entitled, generally, to all Bank Holidays.

8   Apprentices may only work on shifts by permission, and they are very rarely allowed on night shifts.

9   A doctor's certificate approving the fitness of the apprentice is required for an employer.

10   No young person should be called upon to lift excessive weights.

Today's apprentice learning his trade

1   What are the main differences between the two indentures?
2   In what ways do the documents reflect some of the social changes that have occurred during the last 75 years?

Time and motion

Henry Ford invented the assembly line in 1910 and rapidly outpaced his rivals in production as a result. He was able to assemble a car on a moving conveyor belt by getting his men to add small parts to it as it moved past them. Farm boys with little education were disciplined to repeat simple tasks in order to produce the most complicated consumer product of the age – the Model T Ford motor car. This method of manufacture has become synonymous with modern industrial methods, especially in the motor industry.

The system has been described by many commentators: by Charlie Chaplin in the film *Modern Times* and by Upton Sinclair in his book *The Flivver King*, who wrote: 'Every worker had to be strained to the uppermost limit, everyone had to be giving his last ounce of energy . . . . It was that way everywhere, not merely at Ford's, but all through the cruel industry. Faster and faster until the hearts of men were seething with bitterness.' It was based on methods established by Frederick 'Speedy' Taylor, who had discovered that traditional methods of doing things in industry were inefficient, and that inefficiency costs money. He introduced new methods based on three principles:
1   The best men should be selected for the particular job.
2   They should be instructed in the most efficient methods and most economical movements to employ in their work.
3   They should be given incentives in the form of higher wages to work more productively.
Taylor carried out experiments and proved that increased efficiency was possible by these methods.

But there has developed a debate as to whether soul-destroying, boring, and endlessly repetitive work is justified in the name of economic efficiency. Many critics point to high rates of absenteeism, strikes, and high turnover of staff as evidence of the malaise resulting from such methods and the very nature of the work which the bulk of the labour force in an industrialized society undertakes.

Automation

Mechanization within a factory system introduced the necessity of the conveyor belt, but this is not the same as complete automation. Automation is a recent piece of terminology (1946) to describe production and control of output by machine with minimum human supervision. In an ideal case automation implies complete control over its own action from beginning to end. In this sense automation is most prominent in the kitchen — fully automated washing machines, refrigerators, cookers and central heating systems with thermostats, automatic tea machines, and the like.

The production and control of output by machines with little human intervention was developed in 1946 by Delmer S. Harder, who coined the term for a system he had devised for the Ford Motor Company to manufacture car engines. The system was entirely automatic. This was the first completely automated process to be utilized in large-scale industry. One engine was produced in less than 15 minutes, whereas before it took

Fully automated machining of cylinder heads in a car factory

more than 20 hours. In 1972 General Motors boasted the fastest and most automated assembly line in the world, producing 101.5 'Vegas' an hour for 20 hours a day. The production line requires a minimum of supervision and the machines are largely self-regulating. Their ability to regulate their own behaviour in order to obtain the optimum output and to take account of any changes that may occur in the conditions of production, is the major feature of automation in an industrial setting.

The question arises – is automation a blessing which will relieve the worker of boring, monotonous, and dangerously unpleasant work allowing him more leisure time and opportunities to show more responsibility for the automated processes? This is the optimistic view. Or is it a curse which will only increase dissatisfaction in a work situation which is already lacking in intrinsic satisfaction? This is the pessimistic view.

THE PESSIMISTIC VIEW OF AUTOMATION
There are those who believe that all individuals have the potential for expressing a wide range of talents and of developing their individuality but are forced through a variety of social circumstances into fields of work which do not permit the full development of their personal aptitudes. On this view automation in industry is seen as the further development of the impersonal and dehumanizing effects of the factory system. If the individual can obtain the fullest development of his personality and sense of worth only in a job which is more active than passive and in which there is an ability to exert control and responsibility, then it is believed that automation cannot facilitate such development. Button pressing and the supervising of fully automated processes can only limit and impoverish the daily work life of the individual.

THE OPTIMISTIC VIEW OF AUTOMATION
Those who are optimistic about the introduction of automation argue that the operator becomes freed from the dominance of the machine. One sociologist who is carrying out research in this area suggests that it does have advantages. The operator is no longer tied to one point on the shop floor, to one simple task, to the speed of the machine. In fact he obtains more responsibility than before since he must be alert to crisis and danger. He is an integral part of the management team, because his relationship with supervisors is characterized by shared information and responsibility. His findings to date support the optimistic view. Generally the men interviewed found the work interesting and satisfying (although they were largely men without formal educational qualifications and without transferable industrial skills). Those who did feel deprived of a sense of worth were mainly men who had previously worked in skilled manual jobs and those who had come in as school leavers with a few O levels. Their hopes of career advancement were not being satisfied and qualifications were not necessary for the job. They could well be working alongside someone from an industrial but unskilled background. However, for the

majority, their work in the highly automated petro-chemical industry appeared to be richer in intrinsic rewards than any other work they might have had.

Job satisfaction

> What a piece of work is a man
> How noble in reason
> How infinite in faculty
> In form and moving
> How express and admirable
> In action —
> How like an angel
> In apprehension —
> How like a god.
>
> *William Shakespeare*

The fact that so many workers are bored and disillusioned with their work is causing industrialists, economists, psychologists, and sociologists interested in the phenomenon to try to explain and overcome the problem.

'In 1972 more than 300 million days were lost through sickness in Britain, which was 13 times as many as were lost through all the strikes put together. The most common cause of absence from work included minor strains and sprains, neuroses, and nervous disorders. These have more than doubled since 1958. A recent report by the Office of Health Economics says: "Perhaps the most significant factor associated with sickness absence is job satisfaction. . . . The key to minimum of sickness absence, particularly short term absence, is in the hands of management." A Department of Employment survey showed that absenteeism among foremen (who are paid even if absent) is 4% whereas for the semi-skilled workers (who are not paid if absent) it is 25%.'

Employers are becoming more concerned to find ways of making work more worthwhile for their employees. A conference was held in London in October 1972 entitled 'Job Satisfaction and Productivity' arranged by the Industrial Co-partnership Association to examine the problems of the relations between worker and management and the worker and his work. It is noticeable that the terms used most frequently in such discussions are 'job satisfaction', 'job enrichment', and 'job enlargement'.

HOW CAN WORKING PEOPLE BE MOTIVATED?

Many industries are subject to lengthy strikes, disputes, and internal sabotage which disrupt production. There is much debate about whether programmes of job enrichment will overcome the problems of industry.
1 Those who believe that high pay is not a satisfactory way of inducing people to do unpleasant and boring work seek other alternatives. Some

employers are finding ways of reorganizing the traditional systems of work. Some firms have introduced a 'cell system' whereby small cells, or groups, of workers carry out a complete operation, working as a team at their own pace. The result is an increase in pay, in satisfaction, in speed of work, and in flexibility. The men may have to operate several different machines instead of only one as in the traditional system. The workers have been found to develop a greater sense of loyalty both to the firm and to each other; there is less absenteeism and a smaller turnover in skilled men. The major problem is that of redundancy – since fewer men may be required and only skilled operators are employed. It is also a costly procedure for the firm to make a change to this kind of system.

2   Job rotation schemes have been tried. Workers are trained to tackle a wide variety of jobs, rather than one repetitive job that requires little skill. The Volvo firm in Sweden has a system in which four men put in the front and back doors of a car, and every two hours in eight hour shifts they swop jobs. In June 1974 it inaugurated a new factory in Kalmar in which the assembly line has been abolished altogether. The factory, described as looking more like an art gallery, is hexagonal in shape and cost £10 million to build. The cars are assembled by 25 'work groups' operating as self-controlling units, and initially 30,000 cars a year will be produced with single-shift working.[1]

3   Implicit in such schemes are improved conditions of work. In the Volvo experiment all assembly men work by daylight rather than arti-ficial light. They work as integrated teams of 15–20 people rather than standing in anonymous rows unable to communicate with their work-mates. The groups choose their own leader and they distribute work among themselves according to their own wishes. The groups work in particular zones rather than on an assembly line. Most of the 'work groups' have their own amenities close to their working areas: changing and wash rooms, showers, saunas, pantries, etc. The philosophy behind the experiment is that in these improved conditions the machine will serve man rather than the opposite.

4   Worker participation has been advocated as a means of increasing interest and enthusiasm in work. It is a view which has long been argued by the Liberal Party in Britain. Some believe that workers from the shop floor should have seats in the boardroom with the directors in order to know at first hand the policies and aims of the firm; others suggest that workers should at least have the right to call directors to their meetings to explain developments within the firm. They also advocate the develop-ment of profit sharing schemes. The Labour party is also committed to a similar scheme, to provide for employee participation not only in profits but also in the decision making procedures of the company. This is a development which is gaining ground in Europe. The Saab motor company in Sweden encourages council meetings of workers to discuss problems,

[1] IBM has been operating a similar system since the autumn of 1973 in the typewriter assembly section of its plant in West Berlin.

A shop steward addresses a protest meeting. Will the result be a strike?

Alternative to the assembly line: the new Volvo factory at Kalmar, Sweden

elect group leaders, and raise questions for management. A scheme has been adopted by a firm in West Germany, the Süssmuth glassworks, in which the firm has become the property of the employees, who control management and investment decisions and distribute any profits as they think fit. At present the experiment is proving successful.

5   The four-day week has been introduced by some firms. Roundhay Metal Finishers in Yorkshire introduced it in 1965. The owner suggested that two hours should be added to the working day, which would then run from 7.55 to 6.25, with half an hour for lunch and no tea breaks, so that the employees need not work on Friday. For this firm the experiment has been a success. They have lost only two skilled men in the first eight years of the scheme, and there is a waiting list of men wanting to join. Absenteeism has been reduced, whereas wages and profits have increased. Productivity is up by 15%. From time to time the owner of the firm issues questionnaires to keep in touch with the attitudes of his employees. One of the recent questions asked, 'What would persuade you to leave your present job and go to work for a company working a five-day week?' Among the answers were, 'One million pounds', 'Nothing', 'Maybe double my salary'. Few of the men complain of boredom created by the three-day weekend. It is hoped that a 38 hour week can eventually be introduced. The managing director says, 'People don't go to work because they love the boss. They go to work to earn money. If a man has got to put a lot of hours in to earn a decent wage there is something wrong with the organization.'

In the United States more than 1,000 companies have introduced the four-day week. Experiments have also started in Holland, Germany, Japan, New Zealand, and Australia. A study in America into the experience of 27 firms which had adopted the method showed that the changeover from a five day week usually resulted in a more diligent and enthusiastic work force, less absenteeism, lower turnover of skilled staff, easier recruiting, and increased productivity. Production costs and overheads also dropped significantly. The critics of the four day week argue that —

1   They are sceptical of the long-term benefits. They predict that absenteeism, morale, and enthusiasm will gradually revert to the previous norm.
2   The customers of the companies that make the change may have difficulty in adapting to their work schedules. They suggest it is a system which can only work efficiently among small companies with minimal Trade Union representation. (The Unions are not altogether happy about their members working a ten-hour day, since they have long fought for an eight-hour working day.)
3   The change may affect the worker's traditional routine and day-to-day lives too drastically. Its success will depend on the ability of the worker to adapt. He must get up earlier, have fewer breaks, get home later, and be able to make good use of his added leisure time. It may cause difficulties between husbands and wives who are working different systems. The worker may also come to demand increases in wages more

regularly in order to pay for the additional leisure activities in which he will indulge on the extra day off that he gains.

However, those who favour an experiment of this kind believe that it is valuable in so far as it indicates a willingness on the part of management to come to terms with the basic needs of workers – a need to gain some sense of additional worth from their work. They believe that all attempts to enrich and enlarge the work experience are to be applauded. Such moves may be seen as the first constructive attempts to reach a better understanding and relationship between the management, who by and large enjoy their work, and the work force, who very often do not.

RESEARCH

Studies have shown that a full time housewife with no children will probably work a 40 to 60 hour week, a housewife with one child between 60 and 70 hours a week, one with two children between 70 and 80 hours each week. If these same women were employed outside the home they would probably spend in house work some 30, 40, and 50 hours a week in addition to hours spent in their non-domestic work.

The position of the modern housewife has been compared to that of the alienated industrial worker. Commenting on the four factors which are associated with alienation – powerlessness, meaninglessness, isolation, and self-estrangement (all of which are said to occur when productive work becomes an instrumental activity, subordinated to purely physical needs), Ann Oakley says, 'If housework is not an elaborated form of alienation – then what is?' She argues that modern technology leaves little room for 'art' in housework – little room for creativity and originality. Today's average housewife has lost her maternal function before middle age when her youngest child leaves for school; she then has two or three decades of active life left. Much of her work is repetitive, and she is isolated for considerable periods of the day in her own home, away even from the company of other housewives. Her status is low, and financial rewards for her work are non-existent. Some would say that the housewife of today is totally alienated – divorced more and more from her essential human nature. The increasing use and dependence on tranquillizers, anti-depressants, and sleeping pills, the increase in shop lifting, the prevalance of the 'battered baby syndrome' may be evidence of this fact.

She concludes that women in our society are oppressed, exploited, and alienated, and explains why the majority of women who are housewives apparently fail to realize their true predicament. 'The solution to the paradox lies in the socialization of women into the equation of femininity with domesticity. Through this socialization, which various forms of social control serve to maintain, housework becomes a part of themselves: not only of their lives but of their identities. They cannot conceive of housework as "work" in the sense that what their husbands do is "work". This conception is insidiously validated by society's refusal to place an economic value on housework and to assign any status to the housewife.'

RESEARCH: Dissatisfaction With Work, from *Adolescent Boys of East London*, by Peter Willmott

Boys' occupation and number of jobs since leaving school.

Number of jobs	Non-manual	Skilled manual	Semi-skilled and unskilled manual
Four or less	85%	83%	65%
Five or more	15%	17%	35%
Total %	100%	100%	100%
Number	45	95	37

Suggest some reasons to explain why the percentage in the unskilled and semi-skilled group who had undertaken five or more jobs is more than double that of the boys in the non-manual and skilled categories.

RESEARCH FINDINGS
The Worker in the Affluent Society, by F. Zweig.
This survey was designed to study the mutual impact of family life and industrial conditions on industrial workers. The research was carried out in two stages:
1 A pilot study of 161 interviews at a steel factory in Sheffield in 1958.
2 This was followed by a further 511 interviews at four other factories later in that year in different parts of the country.
The sample data are based on personal interviews, and were recorded immediately after informal interview conversations.

The sample consisted of hourly paid men on the production lines and a few weekly paid supervisors who were selected to cover all departments and all grades. Zweig interviewed all department heads and some foremen from each section of the plant; other interviewees were chosen at random. Foreign workers were excluded, since the survey was concerned only with the attitudes of the British worker.

The interviews were designed to elicit information about living standards, family relationships, leisure and social activities, attitudes to work, home, class, and degree of religious involvement. Further information was collected from departmental managers, personnel and training officers, housing officers, probation officers, marriage guidance workers, and those working in Labour Exchanges and welfare departments. Some wives were also interviewed. He tried to make the interviews as much like a conversation as possible to elicit the real thoughts of the interviewees rather than standard responses.

Zweig admitted 'the purely descriptive character of the study which imposed limitations'. He did not indicate his methods of selection of either the firms or the men he chose to interview. It is apparent that

170

With strikes and lay-offs continuing to be in the news, *Horizon* this week looks at the 'them and us' attitudes of bosses and workers and the new ideas of management training. Here David Gillard talks to an expert on the subject

Are you happy in your work? And does it matter if you aren't?

One cartoonist's view of the worker's lot: is this a suitable case for 'job enrichment'?

WHAT IS IT that makes us work? And – more important to British bosses – what is it that makes us work more productively? Is it money or something more elusive, like happiness?

Our working lives these days are the subject of much erudite academic study. Flocks of behavioural scientists – sociologists, social psychologists, occupational psychologists and social anthropologists – have descended on us to find out what makes us want to work or stop work, and have come up with complex and bewildering jargon, conflicting theses, and phrases like 'job enrichment.'

But these very theories, intended to enliven archaic management, keep workers happy and aid production, may be doing more harm than good.

David Robertson thinks so. He is head of publicity at the Industrial Society, an advisory and training body that works with both unions and management – their work is featured in Monday's **Horizon** programme, **For Love or Money?** He says: 'The enormous amount of complicated "motivational theories" have tended to make management dismiss this kind of new thinking. It seemed so obscure that nobody could understand what the hell it was all about.

'Really, the proposition is very simple. In order to work effectively people must get some sort of satisfaction from

their job.' And money *doesn't* mean everything because, on the whole, we don't get the most satisfaction from our pay packet. 'There are certainly people who are paid so badly that money is the most important factor,' he says. 'But in the majority of cases it is a combination of good pay and good conditions that keeps people happy.

'It is almost certainly true that the highest and most regular pay demands come from people who are doing rotten, boring jobs. The only way to ease their frustrations is to put in the pay claim. Within a short time the effect of the rise wears off. But the frustrations are still there. So they put in another pay claim.'

Experiments show that people are more motivated by changes which make their jobs more interesting than by pay rises.

'What's important,' says Mr Robertson, 'is that people in leadership positions know exactly what to do. Employees must be told whether they're doing well or badly, given some idea of what their targets are and made to feel that it *matters* that they are there.'

With brilliant leadership and 'enriched' jobs it may well be that worktime Utopia is on its way. But will Utopia mean equality of the sexes?

The fact is that, nowadays, men revolt against boring as-

sembly-line jobs. More strikes, militancy and discontent hit those industries where men do assembly-line work. Yet the majority of women seem quite content with this kind of tedious labour. Why?

Professor Stephen Cotgrove, Professor of Sociology at Bath University, sums it up: 'Work is important to men as a means of expressing themselves. Women have other means of what is called self-actualisation – in the home. Many see their work as an extension of their family life.'

David Robertson agrees, but he sees things changing: 'Most women work because they need the money for the home,' he says. 'When asked if they like their job many women will put a high value on the social aspect of their work – the chats they have with the rest of the girls on the assembly line.

'But this is because they are doing repetitive work – work from which they are not able to gain individual satisfaction. The tendency has always been to give women boring jobs.

'Only a few years ago a Government survey showed that only about one in six women received any training. The argument against training is that women leave to get married or have babies. Yet where companies have made efforts to enrich women's work, production has gone soaring up.'

From the Radio Times, 28.2.72

171

the companies were all large-scale, well organized, and in expanding industries in which the workers' rates of pay and overall earnings were above average.

The study can claim to be no more than a subjective impression of the social situation of a small body of workers in five particular factories, although the results are interesting within this context.

EXERCISES

1   In what ways do the following factors determine attitudes towards work? (a) Social class, (b) Education, (c) Peer group, (d) Social culture and local economic factors, (e) The work experience.

2   Outline the attitudes towards work expressed by: (a) D. H. Lawrence, (b) Alan Sillitoe, (c) Each of the apprentices on pages 155–156.

3   What is meant by 'job satisfaction', 'job enlargement' and 'job enrichment'? Why are new experimental methods being introduced into factories through out the world?

4   Explain how you would find out the dominant attitudes towards work on the part of various employees in a local factory. Give details of the hypothesis and methods of study.

ESSAY QUESTIONS:

1   Some areas have high unemployment rates whilst jobs are available in other parts of the country. What factors prevent unemployed people and those doing boring or unpleasant work from moving into areas where there is a wide variety of work to be had?

2   What are some of the major factors which determine a person's choice of work and his enjoyment or dissatisfaction with it?

3   What is meant by automation? What are the possible social benefits and disadvantages of the increasing use of automation?

4   Outline some of the methods that have been adopted to increase job satisfaction and explain why it has been thought necessary to undertake such experiments.

9 Leisure

The god of work must be cast down from his ancient throne, and the divinity of enjoyment put in its place. We must come to realize that leisure time, that time spent in pleasurable enjoyment, is the only kind of time that makes life worth living. All other time is tolerable only as it contributes to the richness and developmental context of our leisure. Henry Fairchild

Leisure should be regarded as the lighter, more enjoyable, phases of work rather than as freedom from required tasks. We should aim not at the increase of time free from all work, but at work which offers greater enjoyment, which involves a minimum of strain, of monotony, and of danger to our wellbeing. Otherwise we shall become a race of morons well fitted to enjoy the age of the labour-saving machine. Floyd Allport

Both of these writers seem to have a different view of the meaning and significance of the term 'leisure'. Fairchild sees leisure as being necessarily quite distinct from work and more important in so far as it is a means of developing and enriching the personality of the individual. Allport, on the other hand, seems to suggest that there should not be such hard and fast distinction between work and leisure, since work is fundamental to human nature; all that is necessary is to make work more enjoyable.

This debate illustrates the difficulty in using the term 'leisure'. We all seem to know what it means – and yet it is not easy to define precisely and therefore difficult for the sociologist to analyse. There is the added problem that it is used to cover such a wide variety of activities – many of which may have a strong 'work content': is the man, for example, who is digging his garden on a Saturday afternoon 'working' or indulging in a leisure activity? And what if he is digging the garden of a neighbour in his own time and is paid for doing so?

There are two basic views as to what constitutes 'leisure' – the subjective view is that leisure is 'time when I do what I want', or 'time when I rest'. This kind of definition is too loose and too wide to be of much value to the sociologist. A tea break would fall within the definition, but can this really be said to be a period of leisure time? Perhaps it is more usefully defined in an objective way: 'time free from the formal duties which a paid job imposes'. It is more useful still to itemize the particular factors which go to make up the concept of leisure. It implies:

173

Tea break on the building site

1   The antithesis of work. The paid worker knows when he is working and when he is enjoying his leisure. A tea break, being time for which he is paid, is thus more clearly seen as 'working time' rather than as 'leisure time'.

2   A minimum of obligation, freedom of choice, and of the amount of time spent on the occupation. The ability of the individuals to decide what they are going to do, when and how long they will spend doing it, is another important condition of leisure, as opposed to work, when the individual seldom has such choice to make. (The man who digs his neighbour's garden can stop and start when he likes, and can decide whether or not he wants to do the job in the first place. This would seem to place it more in the 'leisure' category than in the 'work'.) It eliminates the idea of imprisonment as a leisure activity.

3   There is likely to be an element of play involved in a leisure pursuit. The element of play helps to eliminate the idea of 'work', in which it is generally unacceptable.

4   An element of psychological satisfaction would be expected. The idea that one undertakes an activity because one will enjoy it for its own sake (unlike work, which is generally undertaken for the ends it provides), and will consequently feel better for having undertaken that activity.

5   There will be a minimum of social role play – so that the boss can mix informally with the workers and can step outside his normal work role; doctor and patient may play in the same football team without the normal sense of distance that necessarily separates them.

6   There is the added factor that the individual should be able to perceive his leisure as being different from his work: there are some

174

occupations in which it is difficult to make clear distinctions between their work and their leisure time since they may often merge imperceptibly: the artist, the social worker, the executive, the teacher, etc. are all difficult to assess in this respect, except in terms of what the individual reports and perceives to be the difference.

Work is a necessary consideration in order to make sense of leisure. The functions of leisure are to provide periods of rest, relaxation, and change which assist people to work more productively. Recreational activities are found in all human societies and would therefore seem to be a fundamental necessity to man. Such activities become particularly significant when the society reaches a high point of economic development in which more and more time becomes available for leisure pursuits, since it is not necessary to work continuously to ensure subsistence and survival. In general, one would expect to find that the more prosperous the society the more time is available for leisure.

Traditionally, leisure time has been associated with religious festivals. Celebrations of important events, times of birth, christening, marriage, and even death, were often times (as they still are) for religious ritual, and they provided an opportunity for recreation. Religious festivals are still very much associated with holidays. Leisure has also been long associated with the more privileged and wealthy social classes who

The procession at the feast of St Spyridion, Corfu

have more time to indulge in their own chosen activities than those in less fortunate financial situations. But the growth of technological innovation has created sufficient wealth and greater demand for increases in leisure time, for all social classes. In 1850 the working week was 80 hours, in 1930 it was about 50 hours, and in 1970 40 hours. An even shorter working week is predicted. However, it was not until 1938 that the Holidays With Pay Act entitled nearly 10 million people earning less than £250 per year to paid holidays for the first time. Subsequently, demand for increased leisure time and for improved facilities has grown.

There has been a very rapid increase in the popularity of participatory sports and also of the mass spectator sports – the latter caused by the fact that initially there were insufficient facilities in the major urban areas for sport to be played. Competitive games are a great attraction, and the number of spectators at football matches has increased dramatically since 1966 when England won the World Cup. Sportsmen are as much cult heroes as pop stars and film stars. Outdoor pursuits have been popularized by the products of the technological society in which we live. Comparatively cheap motoring and other forms of transport have enabled more people to undertake numerous activities which mobility has made possible.

Indoor activities are catered for on a similar scale. The mass media have revolutionized people's leisure pastimes. Musical evenings and intense after dinner conversation are growing more rare. Instead the cinema (although attendances have greatly declined since the war), television, dance halls, pubs, and clubs are all taking up more of people's time.

CATEGORIES OF LEISURE ACTIVITIES
There is no general agreement as to the most useful classification. Some writers suggest five main categories:
1 Those which aim at physical relaxation.
2 Those which serve to release pent-up energy.
3 Those which relieve monotony or boredom.
4 Those which gratify the senses (taste, sight, hearing, etc.)
5 Those which satisfy the intellect (study, visits to museums, etc.).

Others divide leisure activities into two broad groups: Active and Passive, and subdivide these into those which may be described as (a) relaxing (b) recreational, (c) obligatory, (d) educational.

Jerome Davis makes three simple groups:
1 Activities which are spontaneous (private recreation).
2 Those communally organized (sponsored by public agencies).
3 Those which are commercially motivated (provided by commercial enterprise). He sees this last group as the most popular, and asserts that commercialism tends to keep entertainment on a low artistic and moral level. He believes that non-commercial types of recreation need to be encouraged.

The amount of time devoted to any leisure activity and the type of

activity undertaken varies according to the social culture and the economic standards of the society. The main trends identified in western
industrial societies include:
1   The increasing development of commercial enterprises catering for the
leisure needs of the population.
2   The growth of facilities catering for needs on a non-commercial
basis – playing fields, national parks, and the like, which may involve
small charges, but do not have the overall aim of making profits at the
expense of the public's leisure.

Changes in leisure patterns since 1870

1   The increase in affluence and the mass production of goods has meant
that more people are in a position to undertake the leisure activities of
their choice, to join clubs, buy equipment, obtain transport, and so on.
The result is that leisure activities have become more diverse and varied
than ever. A greater proportion of income can be spent on recreational
needs once basic needs are satisfied.
2   The development of the mass media has radically changed leisure
patterns, so that there is less emphasis on people making their own
entertainment. More books, newspapers, and magazines are being sold
than ever and more books borrowed from libraries.
3   The commercialization of leisure has resulted in the growth of a
massive entertainments industry and the 'professionalization' of more
sports in which there was a tradition of unpaid amateurism. Footballers,
tennis players, and golfers have become some of the most highly paid
members of society.
4   Changes in attitude, including a more widespread belief in social
justice, have meant that people are less likely to have difficulty in joining
clubs. More provision is made for coaching and training. Workers enjoy
holidays with pay, so that two thirds of the population take holidays
away from home each year. At the same time the idea of a shorter working
week, which gives more time for leisure, is becoming more acceptable.
5   Changes in the educational system have provided greater opportunities
for travel and for becoming skilled in sports and other pastimes.

Factors affecting choice of leisure activities

AGE AND SEX
Clearly some activities are more likely to be engaged in than others
according to these factors – since they may require more physical stamina,
concentration, skill, or aptitude than another age group could manage;
and they may be more popular among one sex than the other because of
traditional associations – bingo and knitting are more popular among
women, vehicle maintenance and visits to pubs are more popular among
men, for example. These variables have proved useful ways of analysing
the patterns of leisure activities in Britain.

'Footballers, tennis players and golfers have become some of the most highly paid members of society' — Tony Jacklin drives off from the tee

As far as the teenagers are concerned, after school leaving, the economic independence gained by their wage packet and the desire to participate in the youth culture, which involves spending money, means that a high proportion of their leisure time is spent outside the home in the company of their friends. Studies confirm that all kinds of physical recreation, including dancing, are more popular than staying at home watching television. The cinema is one of the main attractions of young people in their leisure time, a higher proportion of the 16—25 age group attending regularly than any other.

With marriage, leisure patterns change. In a study by Abrams, he found that of those in the 25—34 age group who were questioned a quarter had not been out of the home for leisure purposes in the 7 days preceeding the interview. For them, do-it-yourself, home decoration, gardening, crafts, and hobbies became more significant as leisure activities.

For married women aged between 35 and 44, it has been found that the loosening of domestic ties, as children grow up and begin to leave home, does not necessarily mean an increase in leisure. About 40% of women in this age group are in employment or re-entering careers they may have temporarily abandoned.

The increase in home based activities becomes more marked in the older age group, television viewing becoming the most popular of all activities. Of those questioned in one study in the over 65 age group, 5% said they went to a cinema frequently, 15% visited a pub in the course of a week, and 40% said they took holidays away from home each year.

Interview parents, relatives, and friends of different age ranges. Compare the three main ways that you spend your leisure time with the ways in which they spend theirs. What were the most popular leisure activities twenty years ago? What were they fifty years ago?

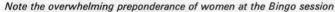

Note the overwhelming preponderance of women at the Bingo session

CLASS BACKGROUND

Some investigations have shown that membership of particular clubs and organizations is weighted more towards the middle class rather than the working class social background. It has been found, for example, that some clubs deliberately engineer their membership regulations to preserve their exclusiveness, by fixing high subscriptions and requiring nomination or recommendation and particular standards of play. (It may not be possible to join certain tennis clubs or golf clubs unless the applicant has attained a satisfactory standard.)

But it may be that the individual is deterred from joining a particular group or club or participating in an activity because he perceives it as containing members who belong to different social groups to himself, or that it seems to be undertaken by others with whom he does not identify. Theatre going, for example, may be perceived by those who go seldom as a middle aged, or middle class activity, and therefore unacceptable.

One of the important features of class membership is the fact that class groups develop class norms of behaviour. The more strongly an individual identifies with a group the stronger will be his acceptance of its norms. The degree to which social class background affects participation in particular activities will depend on:

1 The extent to which the individual sees such activity as acceptable to his own social circle. To break the class norms and join a polo club when the worker's friends spend their Saturday afternoon at a football match is to risk ridicule and ostracism.

2 The size of the group that he joins to pursue the activity. If it is a small group then social class background may not affect the choice, but rather degree of proficiency may be the important consideration. Two men from totally different social backgrounds may meet regularly to play tennis because their skills are evenly matched. But where the group is large, the members may either break down into class groups and have little contact with each other, or the club may have the reputation of 'exclusiveness' and deter many from membership.

3 Cost of equipment or membership. This may be a deterrent, even though the individual could afford the expense, if his background norms emphasize expenditure on necessities rather than luxuries.

4 The extent to which a person sees himself as being socially mobile. Those who see themselves as moving up the social scale may undertake those activities which they associate with the group with which they wish to integrate.

There are, of course, many leisure pursuits which are not correlated with social class background – cinema going, television ownership etc, although choice of film or programme watched may be affected by class membership.

OCCUPATION

This factor can be related to choice of leisure activity in so far as it may be influenced by the type of work a person does and his attitude towards it. That is to say, those in sedentary, office, occupations may be more likely to indulge in physical activities than those who are doing heavy manual work and who would identify such leisure activities too closely with the day-to-day work that they may not particularly enjoy.

The extent to which occupation affects leisure attitudes and choices seems to depend on the individual's own attitude towards his work and the degree to which he absorbs the norms prevalent in his occupational group.

Study the research findings on page 183 and explain how each occupation studied affects choice of leisure activity.

The costs of one leisure activity: Gambling

Gambling is becoming an increasingly popular pastime among the adult population. It is an industry which has developed rapidly since 1960. In that year Betting Shops were legalized, and by 1970 there were 15,000 of them, more than the total number of Post Offices. The turnover in gambling rose from comparatively little in 1960 to £1,000 million by 1965 to the figure of £2,135 million in 1972. This is an amount greater than that spent on education or invested in welfare facilities.

Studies suggest that one in three of the adult population gambles fairly frequently and 90% of the population will gamble at some time in their lives. About $2\frac{1}{2}$% (approximately one million people) are believed to be committed gamblers, many of whom are addicted to it as others are addicted to alcohol.

Two kinds of gambling can be distinguished:
1 Small stake gambling with the possibility of winning huge fortunes, typified in purchasing Premium Bonds or competing in the football pools. The risks are low and the actual process of gambling is hardly entered into.
2 The second, more insidious form, is gambling on risks where the stake is much higher and the reward lower. This would include gambling on horses, on dogs, and in casinos. It is in this category that one finds the habitual hard-core gamblers.

In a recent book, *Hazard and Reward*, Dr Newman says that gambling is becoming a social norm and that the non-gambler is 'the deviant oddity'. Non-gamblers fall into four groups: conscientious objectors; those who have some absorbity hobby; a group usually aged between 45−60 who have got in a rut; and 'detached youth', men married at an early age, who have a family and cannot afford to gamble. He estimates that as many as 20% of the men and 5% of the women he interviewed saw gambling as a significant feature in their lives and would be distressed if they were deprived of it. It has been suggested that those in jobs involving irregular hours of work and the handling of substantial quantities of loose cash are more likely to gamble than those in more restricted occupations, where they are not easily able to get to betting shops or race tracks. But it is also likely that where a worker finds that there is a norm of gambling amongst his immediate workmates and colleagues he will adopt it.

Bookmakers' stands at a point-to-point meeting

THE VOLUME OF GAMBLING

1 *Horse racing* There are more than 800 days of racing, covering 64 courses. 50,000 runners compete for £5 million in prizes. Amount bet on the results: £885,000,000, by about 4 million people.

2 *Greyhound Racing* Nine million people bet on the dogs. There are 148 tracks. The annual amount staked is £225,000,000.

3 *Boxing* Betting amounts to more than £50,000,000 a year.

4 *Casino gaming* This is controlled by the 1968 Gaming Act. There are 115 licensed casinos at which £750,000,000 is staked annually.

5 *Bingo* There are about 1,750 bingo halls which are attended by more than 8 million people, three quarters of whom are women. They gamble more than £100,000,000 each year.

6 *Gaming Machines* There are about 160,000 machines in the country, in which £30,000,000 is gambled.

7 *The Pools* More than £100,000,000 is staked each year. The first win of more than £600,000 occurred in 1973.

8 *Premium Bonds* The chances of winning £50,000 with any single bond in any one year are 800,000,000 to one against. The annual amount invested is £30,000,000.

The total volume of expenditure on gambling in Britain exceeds £2,135,000,000.

OTHER EXPENDITURE (1969)
Education   £2,000,000,000.
Annual consumer expenditure on meat, bacon etc.   £1,800,000,000.
Health Service   £1,500,000,000.
Annual consumer expenditure on bread, cereals etc   £830,000,000.
Annual consumer expenditure on electrical goods   £660,000,000.
Mental health provisions   £145,000,000.
Cinema   £61,000,000.

RESEARCH FINDINGS 1
The Influence of Occupation on Choice of Leisure Activity
S. R. Parker carried out a pilot study in 1963 consisting of interviews with two hundred men and women in ten occupations, half business and half service (mainly social work). The main hypothesis was that people in different occupations would vary not only in their degree of commitment to their present jobs, but also in the part that work played in their lives as measured by the encroachment of work on leisure time, the function of leisure for the individual, the extent of colleague friendships, and the preferred sphere of involvement (work, family or leisure). Of the ten occupations, three were selected for more intensive study: bank employees, child care officers, and youth employment officers.

Particular patterns emerged:

1 Bank employees were found to be the least involved in their work. They tended significantly more often than those in service occupations to experience lack of scope in their jobs, to see their jobs mainly as a means of earning a living, and to prefer to do another kind of work if financially free. They characteristically enjoyed their leisure because it was different from work, did not have much of their free time taken up by things connected with their work, and had their central life interest in the family sphere, with leisure second. They were not sufficiently engrossed in their work that they wanted to carry it over into their spare time, nor were they so damaged by it that they were overtly hostile to it. They were largely indifferent and unmarked by it in their leisure hours.

2 Child care officers showed a highly work-oriented pattern, and, together with youth employment officers, characteristically enjoyed leisure because it was satisfying in a way different from their work. They might have much of their free time taken up by things connected with their work, and have their central life interest in the family sphere with work second. They had a way of relating their work to their leisure: their work and leisure activities were often similar in content, with no sharp line of demarcation. They were involved in their work, and the main function of leisure for them was to develop their personalities.

By contrast, people like miners and deep water fishermen have been shown to have a pattern of opposition between work and leisure: their way of spending leisure is typically contrasted with the way they work. They sharply distinguish between what is work and what is leisure; their work is done chiefly to earn a living, and leisure functions for them as compensation for dangerous and unpleasant work.

The probability of an individual approximating to any one of these patterns will vary with the type of occupation and with the work situation or work values held in that occupation. On the basis of studies carried out so far, it seems clear, according to Parker, that the work–leisure relationship is more than a personal preference: it is conditioned by the various factors associated with the way people work. These findings may be useful in dealing with the social problem of the use of increasing leisure time which the growth of automation is likely to bring.

RESEARCH FINDINGS 2
Bulletin 27. Children at play. Department of Environment Report
Research on 15 modern housing estates indicates that a large proportion of children living on them may seldom get out of doors to play at all. The report suggests that children living on the tenth or twentieth floor in a high rise block were much less likely to be allowed out to play than those living on the second or third floor. The children that did go out to play did so in places close to their homes. But it was shown that never more than one fifth of the child's time was spent in specially provided play areas. The authors of the report argue that this shows clearly that the designers' primary concern should be to plan estates with the other four fifths of a child's outdoor leisure time in mind. In this respect, it is suggested, they should endeavour to provide the child with a wide range of experience and somewhere to meet friends well away from roads. But since roads will always be used for play there is a need for them to be made safer. Their findings indicate that it is highly probable that there are many who never, or rarely, use playgrounds or recreational play spaces if they are cut off by major roads. Play spaces are needed both in and out of doors.

The study also revealed that children preferred old-fashioned swings, sandpits, slides, and roundabouts to modern, architect designed shapes and mazes. It showed that there is a tendency for children from disturbed homes to do more housework and play less than other children. It is suggested that it is these children above all who need opportunities for forming relationships with other children and adults, and for them supervised play may be necessary. It is further recommended that since flat, garage roofs, like roads, are bound to be played on, then they should be made strong and safe enough to allow children to use them as play areas.

The overall conclusion reached from the 50,000 direct observations made of children at play and from the answers to the questionnaire completed by parents and children (as far as policy is concerned) is that planners should concentrate family homes near the ground, putting the childless couples and older people higher in the block where they will have more peace and quiet and better views; at present in the estates studied, the proportion of young children living near the ground in high rise schemes ranged from 33% to only 18%.

Percentage citing as chief leisure activity :

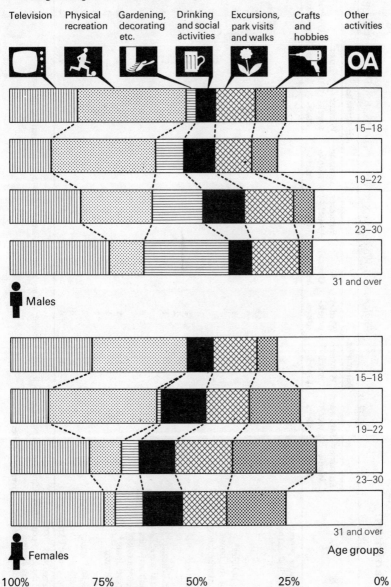

Relates only to the urban population of England and Wales including inner London.

Chief leisure activities: *England and Wales[1] September 1965 – March 1966 Percentages*

	All males					All females				
Percentage of leisure periods when activity cited as the chief pursuit:	Summer week-ends	Summer week-days	Winter week-ends	Winter week-days	Overall average	Summer week-ends	Summer week-days	Winter week-ends	Winter week-days	Overall average
Television	8	17	26	42	23	11	18	30	34	23
Reading	2	5	5	9	5	5	9	9	11	9
Crafts and hobbies[2]	3	3	5	5	4	9	17	15	24	17
Decorating and house/vehicle maintenance	6	8	10	7	8	1	1	2	1	1
Gardening	19	22	4	3	12	12	12	1	1	7
Social activities[3]	3	2	6	2	3	11	7	11	5	9
Drinking	3	4	3	2	3	1	1	2	1	1
Cinema and theatre	1	1	2	1	1	1	1	2	1	1
Non-physical games and misc. club activities	3	5	5	8	6	3	4	4	6	4
Physical recreation:										
(i) as participant[4]	16	10	12	5	11	6	4	6	2	4
(ii) as spectator	3	1	7	1	3	1	1	1	—	1
Excursions	18	4	5	1	7	19	5	4	1	7
Park visits and walks	8	7	3	2	5	9	8	2	2	5
Anything else	5	7	6	8	7	7	8	7	7	7
No answer or 'don't know'	2	4	3	4	3	4	4	5	4	4

Source: *Social Trends*, No 3. 1973.
[1]Figures relate to the urban population of England and Wales, excluding Inner London and are based on a sample of 2682 persons aged 18 and over.
[2]For women, mainly knitting.
[3]Visiting or entertaining friends and relatives, and parties.
[4]Includes dancing.

Television viewing

United Kingdom

	February					August				
	1968	1969	1970	1971	1972	1968	1969	1970	1971	1972
Average weekly hours viewed										
Age groups:										
5—14	19.4	21.1	21.9	20.7	21.0	14.8	16.4	17.0	18.8	20.1
15—19	15.6	16.3	16.7	16.6	16.6	12.0	13.3	13.4	13.9	14.7
20—29	15.6	15.8	16.6	17.0	18.3	11.2	13.4	13.9	14.0	14.3
30—49	17.4	17.8	18.4	18.4	18.4	11.4	12.8	13.2	14.2	13.7
50 and over	17.5	18.3	18.4	18.9	18.9	11.6	13.4	14.3	14.7	14.7
Social class of adults (15 and over):										
A	13.9	14.6	14.6	14.0	13.3	10.2	11.2	11.4	12.7	11.5
B	15.9	16.5	16.5	16.8	17.0	10.7	11.9	12.5	13.1	13.1
C	17.9	18.3	19.0	19.1	19.3	11.8	13.7	14.4	15.0	14.9
Overall average weekly hours viewed by all persons aged 5 and over	17.6	18.2	18.7	18.6	18.9	12.0	13.5	14.2	15.0	15.3
Television broadcast licences current at 31 March (millions):										
Monochrome	15.1	15.4	15.6	15.3	15.0					
Colour	—	0.1	0.3	0.6	8.0					

187

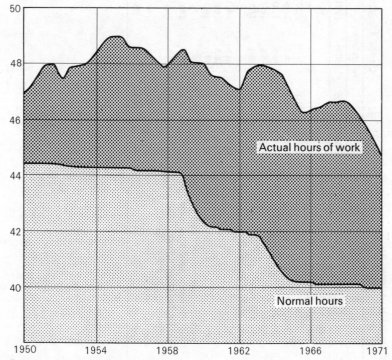

Annual paid holiday United Kingdom

Basic entitlement:

Three weeks and over

Between two and three weeks

Two weeks

1961   1971

Full-time adult male manual workers

Weekly hours of work United Kingdom

Actual hours of work

Normal hours

Full-time adult male manual workers

'Children preferred old-fashioned swings, sandpits, slides and roundabouts . . .'

EXERCISES

1   In what ways does the concept of leisure differ from that of work?

2   In what ways could schools educate for leisure?

3   Estimate the number of hours that you spend in a typical week on the following: (a) In school or college, (b) In travel to and from school or college, (c) In sleep, (d) In household chores (time not entirely your own), (e) Your leisure time.

4   Give examples of the probable leisure activities of the following: (a) Office boy or girl, (b) Pop star, (c) Miner, (d) Bank manager, (e) Factory worker engaged in repetitive work, (f) Teacher.

5   Study the table 'Chief Leisure Activities' on pages 186–187. Which are the three most popular activities among males and females on summer weekends, summer weekdays, winter weekends, and winter weekdays. Which are the three overall favourite activities?

6   Study the table showing television viewing habits. Show how these vary (a) by age, (b) by class, (c) by season.

7   What are some of the possible significant effects of the increasing holiday time available and the shortening of the working week as far as leisure is concerned?

ESSAY QUESTIONS

1 What do you understand by 'leisure'? What are some of the important factors which affect a person's choice of leisure activities?

2 'Occupation has a marked influence on leisure.' Discuss this statement with the use of examples.

3 One man is digging his garden; another is tending the flowers and shrubs in a large public park. Both are working hard, but only one of the two is enjoying his leisure time. Explain how this can be so, and what is the difference between work and leisure.

4 Outline the main factors that have affected patterns of leisure activities over the part 100 years and suggest the trends that we may expect in the future.

10 Crime and Delinquency

Crime and delinquency in Britain

The precise causes of crime are immensely varied. Criminologists, sociologists who study this area of social life, search for explanations of the deviant behaviour which occurs in order to try to understand the complex factors which give rise to such phenomena in society. In order to establish their theories they gather all the significant data relating to crime in society and see how far their hypotheses can be tested in light of the facts.

The following figures, taken from the Central Statistical Office's *Annual Abstract of Statistics* for 1972, combine indictable offences in England and Wales with similar figures in Northern Ireland and Scotland. The term 'indictable' refers to the seriousness of the offence. Some offences, like murder or assault, housebreaking, etc. are tried on indictment at the Crown Courts. Some lesser indictable offences can be tried in magistrates' courts or in higher courts. Indictable offences include larceny, fraud, breaking and entering, and sexual offences.

	1951	1961	1966	1968	1969	1970	1971
Offences known to the police (thousands)	616	926	1,363	1,457	1,665	1,748	1,858
Offences of violence (thousands)	8.2	19.2	30.3	36	42.5	44.5	51.3

The authors of *Social Trends* No. 3, 1972, point out the difficulties that are involved in interpreting criminal statistics.

The two most obvious dangers are perhaps: (1) ignoring the effects of changes in the reporting or recording of offences and (2) ignoring the effects of new legislation. For example, there is reason to believe that domestic brawls are more likely to be reported to the police now than before the war. A good example of the effect of new legislation is given by the change in definition of 'burglary' in England and Wales embodied in the new Theft Act 1968. Burglary before the Act and after the Act are differently defined and hence the statistics for the two cannot be directly compared.

In other words there may be hidden explanations to account for the figures and it would be wrong to interpret them on their face value. Over 95% of crimes known are offences against property. Offences of violence against the person fluctuate between two and three per cent of the total; these and sexual offences are never more than 5% of all recorded crime ... It is important to realise that almost all the increase in offences of violence against the person during the last decade has been in the less serious 'other' woundings ... Any statement about statistics of violence against the person would be incomplete without reference to the lack of uniformity among police forces in recording these and other indictable offences. The methods of recording crimes used by police forces have varied considerably over the years; consequently statistics of offences known to the police have to be treated cautiously. Over half the recorded offences are traffic offences, approximately 10% are theft, 5% burglary, 5% sex offences, and .001% are murders.

	1967	1968	1969	1970	1971
Total number of persons suspected of murder	124	135	146	154	156

The proportions of recorded and unrecorded crime are unknown. It may be that recorded crime is only the tip of the iceberg and we do not know the size of the submerged, unrecorded part. Whilst the known figures must be interpreted cautiously it may be that some of the increase can be accounted for by:

1 Improved methods of detection on the part of the police.
2 Increased willingness on the part of the public to report offences.
3 Changing social habits. Violence may be a less acceptable feature of social life now than in the past, so that it is not tolerated to the same degree and is more readily brought to the attention of the police.
4 More laws in operation to be broken. This is particularly true with regard to motoring and traffic offences.
5 The increasing proportion of offences committed by young people. In 1969 62% of offenders were under the age of 25 and 45% were under 21.

Some observers (often spokesmen for the police) blame the courts, penal reformers, and successive Home Secretaries for the apparently unrelenting rising tide of crime. In a report in 1969 the Chief of Constabulary, Sir Eric St Johnston, said, 'It is tempting to see in this rise some failure in those responsible for the maintenance of the police, but this would be to over-simplify the matter.' He went on to say that the increasing urbanization of society might have encouraged the expansion of criminal activities, but whatever the reason we could not escape the fact that a great proportion of the public was unfortunately becoming more dishonest each year. The greatest deterrent was the certainty of being detected, but that alone could not cure the rise in crime. An appreciable reduction would not be seen unless and until the commission of crime again became socially

unacceptable and a cause of concern to all law-abiding members of the community. He added that we could not afford to relax efforts to build a larger and a more efficient police force, the strength of which was 89,881 men in 1968.

Other commentators point to:

1 A lack of moral guidance in a permissive age, the breakdown of family and religious disciplines without any worthwhile code to replace them.

2 Overcrowding in prisons – men three to a cell – so that a criminal sub-culture becomes a permanent part of a prisoner's attitudes.

3 The increase of films portraying violence and criminal behaviour.

4 The increase in leisure time, for which many are unprepared and un-

able to utilize in a constructive rather than destructive way.

5   The effect of living in an affluent society in which people are encouraged to want and consume more.

6   The fact that there are more women at work and more 'latch key children' who lack supervision and wander the streets on returning home from school at four o'clock. (In fact there is no strong evidence to support this latter view, and there is some to the contrary, which indicates that such children show more independence and maturity than those whose mothers do not work; but other variables would need to be investigated, including the personality of the child, the district, the norms of the area, and strength of peer group attachment.)

They argue that there is an increasing sense of alienation and 'anomie' — rootlessness and lack of purpose, resulting from living in a crowded urban environment and doing uninteresting and unfulfilling work.

Delinquency

Juvenile delinquents are those young people aged between 10 and 17[1] who find themselves in court as a result of breaking the legal rules of society. A correlation has been shown to exist between the social class of delinquents and the frequencies of the offences that they commit. MacDonald showed that the variable of father's occupation was the one most closely associated with delinquency. Most of those in serious trouble come from households in the unskilled manual worker's group. There is evidence to show that there has always been a degree of deviant behaviour amongst the higher social groups, but poor socialization and unsettled home environment tend to produce the more socially deviant section of youth. There is also much evidence to show that the reconviction rate of boys discharged from Borstal is increasing steadily since 1955. Between 1966 and 1969 the figure was 52%. This suggests that present methods of training are failing with a considerable proportion of boys. In 1972 there were 7,000 boys and 300 girls in Borstals.

Sociologists are interested to see whether there are particular patterns of deviancy which occur between particular types of young people and whether there are theories which can be formulated to explain the facts that they uncover. The sociologist Mays suggests that working class offenders have characteristics which differ from those in the middle class. They tend to be more impulsive and their offences often crudely carried out. They are frequently repetitive and become the more chronic thieves and housebreakers. The use of force is common, and offences are often directed against other people's property and possessions. Middle class offenders are more careful in selecting the kind of offence that is hard to pin down. They are more likely to commit crimes of fraud, false pretences, and confidence tricks. They are more skilled in choosing the best moment to carry out the crime and may be less often detected. The result is that the middle class

[1]The age of criminal responsibility is being raised in stages to 14.

criminal does not provide such a good model to children since he is likely to break the law in ways which are not available to them. This may be another explanation of why there are more delinquents in the working class sector.

SOME THEORIES TO ACCOUNT FOR DELINQUENCY:

1 *The Ecological Theory of Shaw and McKay*

Shaw and McKay tried to uncover a relationship between the social geography of a city and the situation of the juvenile delinquent's home. They based their theory on the idea that a city can be broken down into a number of area zones, formed by a series of inner circles, each zone representing an area inhabited by a different social segment: a business sector, a residential sector, etc. They found an underlying pattern of deviant behaviour associated with each of the main zones of the city. They established that there was a clear increase in frequency of offence the closer they moved to the city centre.

They used the records of delinquents, court cases, and police files to confirm their hypothesis. Their study of Chicago revealed the fact that there were more young delinquents in the socially deprived areas than in any others. They found the highest rates in the 'central zones of transition' which contained the ghettos housing the poor, the immigrants, and others at the lowest end of the social scale. Here an average of 20% of boys aged between 10 and 17 would be arrested each year. These they termed the 'delinquency saturated' zones.

They found that the norm of delinquency and social deviance seemed to imprint itself on the area, so that although new families came and went the rates of delinquency remained much the same, showing that the norms of the area were assimilated and transmitted to each new wave of inhabitants. The community itself seemed unable or unwilling to eradicate the problem and re-establish a new set of socially responsible norms. But this theory of the city and its zones of delinquency has not held good for all large urban areas and does not explain patterns of behaviour in British cities since there has been a different system of growth and development.

Suggest some of the differences that one would expect to find in the growth patterns of British cities. In which sections would you predict that the highest rates of delinquency would be found? Why do few people live in the centres of British cities? Where are the large housing estates situated?

2 *The Status Frustration Theory of Albert Cohen*

Cohen's research indicates that some forms of delinquency can be explained in terms of the failure of certain sections of young people, particularly the lower working class youth, to attain the goals and values which are dominant in British society. Middle class children have little difficulty in obtaining the relevant qualifications and prestige to succeed in life. But working class youth becomes acutely frustrated to find that the attainment of such goals is beyond its reach. The result is a sense of rejection of conventional values and morality. This is shown in hostility and anti-social activity. Middle class culture is denigrated and ridiculed. The attitudes they hold would include the views that theatre going is for the middle aged and middle class — and poets are effeminate young men who waste their time spouting verse to daffodils! — whereas aggression and toughness are highly valued as personal qualities. Delinquent acts become emotional outlets for those sections of young people who experience acute status frustration and are labelled social failures from the time they start school to the moment of leaving with very little to show for more than ten years of full time education.

The dining hall of an 'open' Borstal

3 *The Delinquency Sub-culture Theory of Miller*

Miller argues that delinquency and deviant behaviour result not so much from a sense of frustration at a failure to attain the goals of society, but much more by chance. His research suggests that the life styles and patterns of values which govern the behaviour of the lower class section of youth cause them to fall into trouble as much by chance as anything else. The concept of trouble is a natural part of day-to-day life which any one living in that sector of social life is likely to encounter, since life is full of unavoidable hazards. He argues that such young people often find themselves in court not because of any intentional and premeditated act. He sees trouble as 'an inevitable part of life in a slum environment, a topic frequently on people's lips, one of the everyday hazards of life'. Some of the dominant norms which govern their behaviour include conflict for conflict's sake, bravado, the use of alcohol, and an amoral attitude towards sex.

Closely associated with this view is that of Matza, who notices how delinquents use a great deal of rationalization with regard to their acts. They defend them by saying 'But everybody does it' or 'They wouldn't miss them'. It becomes a matter of luck whether an offence is committed and whether they are caught. The lack of a clear structure within the world of the potential delinquent to inform him of the rightness of wrongness of his acts means that when he breaks the law it may not be intentional or even seen to be illegal. In this sense he is in a state of 'drift' — on the fringe of an appearance in the juvenile court.

4 *The Vacuum Theory of Short and Strodbeck*

Short and Strodbeck's view is that delinquency arises as a result of a kind of vacuum in the lives of young people who lack any structured way for attaining the values considered essential by those in the higher social strata. Whereas the middle class youth is being guided by parents and teachers into their appropriate roles and occupations, which involve them in much academic study and a sense of responsibility, the less privileged sector of youth fill their time with activities which have no significance or connection with the world of work and citizenship. These pursuits may include search for entertainment, dances, fights, and delinquent acts, the kind of behaviour which causes them to be labelled as delinquent and results in the view of Stanley Cohen in their becoming the 'folk devils' of our time. They are set apart from the remainder of orthodox society and often perform the kind of acts which fulfil the expectations held of them. In this sense their deviance is the product of having a great deal of empty time which they do not fill in any constructive way, while others more successful than themselves spend their time in productive work towards prescribed goals.

5 *The Defective Personality Theory of Yablonsky*

Yablonsky's study shows that in conditions of poverty and congested urban life it is often those boys with defective personalities who make most use of the gang. They form its central core and they may often be severely disturbed psychopaths who lack the ability to show any emotional response to their victims. In this view much of the violence and deviance that occurs results largely from the psychological problems of the gang leader.

In the gang the street boy feels himself important. Nowhere else does he seem to matter. Not at home (if he has what can be called a home). Not at school where he can barely read, where there is nothing he can do well enough to give him even a faint glow of achievement. Not in the job, where the boss makes him feel inadequate and inferior. But with his comrades in his gang he is important. He is needed. He is wanted. He has a place. His gang is his life. As it grows in reputation so he grows in reputation. . . . Chico is a typical gang member:

He can hardly read. He doesn't speak English well. He is seldom at home. The only place he feels that he belongs is with the Cobras. He drinks every day. His pride is that no one has as much heart as he has. He will do anything to show this. Actually, Chico is suicidal. He doesn't care what happens to him. Not after a few drinks.

Gangs led by people life Chico are led into suicidal encounters with larger and more powerful street enemies . . . and will embark on ventures which bring on fatal encounters with the police.

A certain vicious East Harlem gang has suffered an annihilating crisis each year for the past five. The gang's leadership is provided from one large, disorderly family. When one brother leads the gang into a debacle (involving a gun battle with police, a fatal knifing or some other major crime) the next oldest boy succeeds to gang leadership and starts out again with a group of slightly younger boys.

Hugh Johnson of the New York City Youth Board has spent ten years in close observation of street gangs. He believes their leadership follows a fairly definite cycle. In the first stage there is quite normal adolescent leadership with few pathological tendencies. As conflict sharpens, the gangs push forward a new type of leader — the deeply disturbed, homicidal individual. Such youngsters usually come to a quick inglorious end and drag the gang down with them.

CONCLUSIONS

It is clear that there is no single cause of deviant behaviour. Many investigations by different sociologists have shown that there are many plausible theories to explain delinquent activity. The views of Miller and Matza are widely followed as explanations of a general type in Britain when they suggest that a high proportion of delinquents drift into trouble as a normal pattern of life. The roots of deviant behaviour have long been recognized and have been discussed by observers since the early studies of poverty were made at the turn of the century. They include defective family relationships inside the home (the absence of a father figure is often significant), poor local environment, defective discipline (either too severe or too lax), and specific personality problems resulting in emotional instability.

Studies show that there is a delinquency-prone section of the population — the disadvantaged lower class youth, who are labelled as school failures, often attending overcrowded schools with poor facilities and unable to attain the prestigious goals for which middle class children are groomed from an early age. Consequently an alternative pattern of life style develops. Working class children have a different set of attitudes and values, they have less pressure on them to pursue educational goals. They have more time on their hands and less training in how to use it effectively. Group membership implies adherence to the norms of their peers, of which conflict with the law may often be a prime requisite.

Recent research suggests that boys seem to be more vulnerable than girls, psychologically. It has been found that there is a strong association between large family size and delinquency, low verbal ability, and poor reading skills. This was present in all social classes. But society is in a constant process of change and all explanations are subject to further research and investigation. Social policies change according to the facts revealed by investigators, and new attempts are made to overcome the problems and assist those in danger of becoming hardened criminals.

THE CHILDREN AND YOUNG PERSONS ACT 1969

This Act was designed to bring about a major change in the role of juvenile courts and of the relationship of police, social workers, and teachers with regard to the delinquent. The aim was to prevent the deprived and delin-

quent children of today from becoming the unstable citizens of tomorrow. The two main techniques introduced to achieve the aims were:
1 Helping parents of deprived children, providing effective support, and keeping them out of the courts.
2 Providing through the juvenile courts an extended range of provisions which were more flexible in meeting the needs of each individual child.

The Act puts more onus on the social worker to help children in trouble. It also puts the age of criminal responsibility up to 14. Rather than prosecute all young people it becomes possible to substitute a 'care order' — where it can be shown that the young person is in need of care and control, has been neglected, and is guilty of an offence other than homicide. Now no constable or authorized person may bring a child or young person before the Juvenile Court without consulting the relevant Children's Department. The Children's Department must inquire into the case, and the local authority must provide the court with full details of the child. There are special facilities for those children who have not been before the courts before, and there will be help in remedying a difficult family situation. The social workers will become more responsible for deciding the kind of treatment a child or young person should receive. The Act also provides for a system of community homes to be established.

RESEARCH FINDINGS 1
Street Corner Society, by W. F. Whyte
Whyte was given a three year research scholarship to study the social structure of a slum community. In the initial stages he had decided to employ ten interviewers for the duration of the work, in such specialized fields as economics (living standards, employment, etc.) politics (relations with the police, etc.), religion, education, and social activities, but he dismissed the idea as too ambitious. Instead he decided to build up any necessary staff as the survey progressed.

He made numerous attempts to gain acceptance into the slum community, and eventually did so when a social worker introduced him to the local gang leader. He gradually became accepted as 'one of the gang', which assisted him in obtaining information by way of participant observation. He joined in all the gang's activities, even to the extent of committing crime with them, and this caused him to begin to lose his objectivity as a reporter of events.

Although he set out to study gang and group relations within the community, his study was centred on a select few of the group. He found that a relationship existed between the gang structure and social performance and mental health. The core of the group was centred very much around those who were otherwise lacking in any kind of social status, and were therefore striving to assert their influence in a situation from which they could gain identity and prestige.

Apart from the significant details of the life styles, attitudes, and values of a gang, the study is also useful in revealing the great problems that exist in attempting a major piece of research on the basis of participant observation. Once he had become integrated into the gang and had accepted its norms and modes of behaviour, Whyte was no longer a scientifically detached researcher but a subjective member of the group, whose reports were likely to be coloured by this fact.

More recently a similar attempt has been made by James Patrick and described in his book *A Glasgow Street Gang Observed*. His conclusion was that the gang had little internal cohesion of its own and that it existed essentially 'to oppose others and to provide coveted status for its members and especially its leaders'.

RESEARCH FINDINGS 2

Dr Alistair Gordon examined 60 male patients who were attending a London drug clinic and who had begun to take drugs before they were 21. Only six were referred to the clinic by probation officers or the courts. Ninety-two percent of the patients held at least one conviction. Fifty percent had a court conviction before they took to drugs (which they started, on average, at the age of 15 years and 9 months). All types of offences were represented, including larceny, fraud, and motoring offences. The pattern of their crimes remained the same after they has started on drugs, with one exception, and that was offences of violence. Whereas only 17% of the boys has been convicted of a crime of violence before taking drugs, 40% were so convicted after they had started to use drugs. Dr Gordon found that this link between drugs and violence was more marked for hard drugs than for soft drugs. One in eight of the boys who eventually took heroin had been involved in violent crimes before starting on drugs, afterwards more than one in two were so involved.

Concluding his survey, Dr Gordon comments that these figures do not in themselves provide evidence that drugs cause violent behaviour (say, through some kind of chemical action); on the other hand there was no evidence either that they diminish violence through the tranquillizing effect that some of these drugs are said to have.

The Home Office is carrying out similar research in several other London clinics to see whether these results can be confirmed.

Percentage of crimes committed by under 17 year-olds

		1969	1970	1971
All offences	Boys	24.6%	23.7%	22.4%
	Girls	18.9%	18.3%	15.3%
Violence	Boys	10.5%	11.8%	13.1%
against the person	Girls	16.7%	15.8%	20.7%

EXERCISES

1 Why are sociologists interested in studying crime and delinquency in society?

2   How many known offences were there in 1951, 1961, and 1971?

3   What factors might account for the increase?

4   What are the problems in interpreting criminal statistics?

5   Outline the main theories that explain delinquency. Select one and suggest how it could be tested.

6   What is the object of the Children and Young Persons Act 1969?

ESSAY QUESTIONS
1   To what extent does the environment that a delinquent lives in affect his behaviour? Give examples to illustrate your answer.

2   To what extent do sociological theories contribute to an understanding of deviant behaviour?

3   What are the causes of the increase in crime and violence in Britain in the last thirty years?

4   There is no single theory to explain delinquent behaviour: why not?

11 Religion

The interest of the sociologist

Sociologists wish to make an analysis of religious behaviour in society in order to see what are the functions and significance of religion, and the trends and changes that have taken place over particular periods of time. They are interested in the effect that specific forms of doctrine may have on the behaviour of members of the different denominations and sects, and the differences that exist between them. They wish to make clear statements about the causes and effects of behaviour which are related to religious involvement.

Ronald Robertson in *The Sociology of Religion* says:

> One of the most intriguing intellectual phenomena of the mid-twentieth century is the widespread interest in religion at a time when there is also extensive agreement that religious belief, as traditionally understood, has markedly declined in its intrinsic significance for most members of modern societies. More fundamentally, however, intellectual interest in religious beliefs and institutions appears to be a part of a generalised concern with problems of meaning and purpose in social life, the foundations of ethics, morals and values, and so on.

What is religion?

Precise definitions are difficult, and the conceptions that people hold about religion vary widely. Some make a distinction between the person who has a clear understanding of the difference between what is 'sacred' and what is 'secular' or 'profane'. The religious individual is the one with a sense of the spiritual and whose behaviour is in accord with this view. The non-religious person makes no distinction between sacred and secular; he believes only in natural causes and discounts the possibility of divine intervention. He sees man as being in total control of his own destiny.

Often a definition of religion attempts to stress the existence of a divine force or spirit at the heart of religious belief—but Buddhism, which is regarded as a major religion of the world, does not teach the existence of a superhuman power, but rather encourages meditation and self-help in its followers. Some observers argue that all men have some form of religion, although not necessarily of the orthodox kind, that recognizes a specific doctrine, Church and set of beliefs. On this view religion is the response that the individual makes to the day-to-day problems that face him, the philosophy that guides his behaviour and his attitudes. It is sometimes described as a 'materialistic religion', since it provides a set of beliefs which are derived from the individual's human needs. It may be said of a person that 'money is his religion', implying that all his energies are directed at attempting to make more and more money for himself. This forms the basis of his 'belief system' about the way life should be conducted, and determines his attitudes and his behaviour. In the same way others may have a total faith in science or political creeds as providing the path to salvation. Communism, for example, points to the attainment of a heaven on earth if particular principles are followed. Marx becomes the Messiah and his books the sacred writings, akin in importance to the Bible for Christians. Rituals equivalent to those of the Church would include the party meetings, the singing of party songs, marches, demonstrations, and the sense of comradeship which any group identity affords.

However, such a definition is clearly very wide and so all-embracing that almost any 'passion' could be termed a religion. The football fanatic might be said to hold that sport is his religion: the ritual of the game each

'The sense of uplifting happiness when the team wins'

Saturday, the 'god-like' stars whom he 'worships', the emotion, the chanting, the sense of uplifting happiness when the team wins — it is possible to find analogies at almost every level. But there are those who argue that these have become the substitutes for religion for a great number of people in the secular age in which we live. Whether or not one accepts this, it does illustrate the difficulty of making clear and universal definitions of a term like 'religion'.

Theories of religion

Some of the definitions used by theologians and sociologists include those of Tillich who said, 'Religion is that which concerns us ultimately'; the American Yinger said, 'Religion is a system of beliefs by which people struggle with the ultimate problems of life.' Durkheim, one of the most important of the early sociologists, said, 'A religion is a unified system of beliefs and practices relative to sacred things, that is to say things set apart and forbidden — beliefs and practices which unite into one single moral community called a Church all those who adhere to them.'

Durkheim based his theory of religion on the view that it promoted group unity and cohesion. He noted one basic function in all religious activity, and that was the regular meeting of large groups of people unified by a common purpose and sense of brotherhood and friendship. He argued that it was as a result of this sense of community that the individual became more closely integrated into the social group, which is a basic human need. In this way he suggests that the symbols of religion are also symbolic of society, and the rituals and the worship become the unconscious worship of society and the social group. He argues from this that religion helps to support and reinforce the social system and maintain order in society.

Max Weber saw the principle task of the sociologist as understanding social behaviour, and the study of religion as being concerned with the effect that belief in the supernatural has on such behaviour. He was interested in religion as a source of social change since it is one of the most significant cultural forces in society. He said that religious behaviour is that which is affected by a belief in something behind or beyond external appearances and specific events. His study of the historical development of societies showed that all the major breaks with tradition had come from prophets, who are thereby the instigators of change in the society. He pointed out that since about the eighth century B.C. the western religious tradition has included a 'prophetic element' of social criticism. The western religions of Judaism and Christianity are unique in this respect, and the nature of religion rooted in criticism of the social order may explain why socialism and modern reform movements originated in the west rather than in the east where there is no such tradition.

It was Weber who developed the theory that the ethics of Calvin and Luther, in contrast to previous religious teachings, were largely responsible for the growth of the spirit of capitalism in the west: they justified business life by showing that poverty is not meritorious, but rather it is a duty to choose the most profitable occupation available. In this way they allied money making and religious piety. Hard work becomes a natural way of serving God and obtaining spiritual salvation.

Marx and Engels believed that religion was 'the fantastic reflection in men's minds of those external forces which control their daily lives, a reflection in which the terrestial forces assume the form of supernatural forces'. They believed that its roots stemmed from the earliest stages of human development to assist primitive man in his helpless condition. In a modern class society, they argued, the masses are oppressed and their exploiters foster religious beliefs to persuade them that their sufferings on earth will be rewarded in heaven. Hence religion becomes in their terms 'the opiate of the people', a drug to hide reality from them. They believed that by taking the means of production into their own hands the proletariat would free themselves from bondage and the religious reflection would vanish. Their belief that they had a complete explanation of the functions of religion in society is now considered by most sociologists to be too general and all embracing.

The evolution of religion

In simple societies religion is more akin to what would be called magic or superstition in a complex technological society. The aim is generally to influence events in the short term, to gain protection from enemies and other hazards, to change the course of ill luck, to help crops grow, etc. The rituals are used at times of social or individual crisis – at birth, in ill health, war, and so on. Magical prescriptions are used to ensure success at such times and to imbue newly constructed objects or newly sown crops with good fortune. In this sense economic organization is closely associated with religious behaviour, as are family life, education, and the initiation of children into adulthood, all of which may be marked by religious ritual and ceremony.

Over long periods of time religious activities become more sophisticated, and as the society evolves into a more complex and industrialized one the underlying philosophical implications are elaborated and made more coherent. The religious specialists, the priests, theologians, and administrators are given specific roles in society, becoming responsible for all official rituals and ceremonies associated with the ruling *élite* as well as the education and care of their followers. Archbishops and bishops are invested with political power and wars are fought in the name of religion.

The Church may become significant in a society apart from its function as a source of spiritual knowledge. It operates schools, provides social activities and clubs for its members, distributes financial aid, and becomes a centre of social life for its adherents. All societies display some form of orthodox religious life, suggesting that it is of fundamental importance

Uganda: the ceremony of blessing the cattle takes the form of a mimic battle

to human civilization. Attempts in Eastern Europe to eradicate organized religion have not entirely succeeded, even though they have had the support of legal sanctions.

Religious trends in modern societies

In modern urban societies religion is less concerned with the world of magic and the unknown and more with the moral life of man. Religion plays a smaller part in day-to-day life, and religious ritual does not accompany many of the activities that are performed, as it would in a simple society. Church and State have become separated in most European societies, but less so in the Middle East, where, for example, Judaism is an integral part of Israeli life, as is the Islamic religion in many Arabic countries. Also religion plays a smaller part in the educational process in a modern society, whereas it has exerted great power and influence in the past. The State has taken over responsibility. The influence of religion also declines in relation to its significance for art, music, and literature, for which it often acted as patron in earlier times. The philanthropic function of the Church remains a comparatively important one, since the State can never meet all the needs of its disadvantaged citizens. This

207

transfer of function from Church to State and other non-religious bodies occurs as a society becomes more highly industrialized and is termed secularization. However, there is much debate as to the degree to which a modern urban society like Britain is less religious than in previous times.

IS THE INFLUENCE OF RELIGION DECLINING?

It is very difficult to measure how religious people actually are. There is little doubt that church attendance is diminishing. A religious census in 1851 revealed an average weekly attendance of 40% of the population. It also showed that the larger the town the smaller was the attendance. It is currently estimated that average weekly attendance in the 1970s is between 10% and 15%. However, when questioned about their religious beliefs a much higher percentage express some degree of belief in aspects of religion.

In 1957 a Gallup Poll survey in Britain found that 78% of the over 20s and 62% of the under 20s believed in God, while between 5% and 6% said there was no God. Fifty-four percent of the over 20s believed in a life after death. Eighty-five percent thought it was unnecessary to go to church to be a Christian. Forty-six percent thought that the Church should re-marry all divorcees. In 1964 Gallup found that one in five of the population were fairly regular church goers.

Statistics with regard to infant baptisms, confirmations, and Sunday school teachers

Year	Infant baptisms	Confirmations	Sunday school teachers
1885	623 per 1,000 live births	371 per 1,000	196,000
1910	689 per 1,000 live births	356 per 1,000	206,000
1940	641 per 1,000 live births	251 per 1,000	127,000
1962	531 per 1,000 live births	315 per 1,000	85,000

There are two main points of view. The sociologist Bryan Wilson puts the pessimistic case. He argues that statistics show an overall decline in religious belief. He suggests that the Church is being used more as a kind of social welfare department offering consolation and encouragement to its adherents by means of the ceremonies associated with the 'rites of passage' — at birth, adolescence, marriage, and death. He says that the Church follows rather than leads in social developments; that it changes its doctrines according to the way in which the moral wind is blowing — especially over such issues as birth control, abortion, divorce, etc. He believes that the clergy have lost status and no longer have a valid role in the twentieth century. They are becoming increasingly irrelevant to the modern world.

He sees the weakening influences as:

1   The growth of scientific rationalism, the search for explanations which

can be shown to be scientifically valid. This has an impact on the intellectuals who begin to defect from the Church.

2 The influence of new books and writers who attack religious attitudes and who have a wide following. The same may be true of other 'stars' and 'heroes' who provide a model of behaviour for young people in particular.

3 The weakening of family relationships in an urban society whereby the family may lose influence over the behaviour of its young members, who are more influenced by their peers, friends, and workmates.

The optimistic case is put by David Martin. He argues that decline in church attendance is not the only way of measuring the degree of religious belief in a society. He suggests that there are other ways of considering religious activity and its significance for people. There are the factors of Church membership (a sense of belonging to a particular Church without actually attending regularly), the sense of identification with a religious group, and personal devotion – the extent to which people pray privately, visit churches, read religious books and take religious papers, etc.

He believes that the degree to which people identify with a religious body is as good a way of measuring religious belief as any. On this basis the numbers identifying with the Church of England amount to approximately two thirds of the population, with the Roman Catholic Church

British kings and queens are crowned in Westminster Abbey. During part of the ceremonies the monarch is escorted by the Bishop of Durham and the Bishop of Bath and Wells

about two in ten, and with the Free Churches about one in ten. He says that attendance figures are not as bleak as Wilson believes they are. He has found that approximately 15% attend every Sunday, 25% every other Sunday, 30% each month, 40% every three months, and 45% once a year.

He believes that all individuals have a strong sense of religion which is evidenced by the numbers who express some belief or acceptance of aspects of orthodox religion and by the large numbers who are superstitious or who express belief in what he describes as 'subterranean theologies' — that is, the stars, luck, political parties, and so on. He points out that religion is still taught in schools and the ideas of Church and religion are still important in the lives of a great proportion of the population as a moral force and the basis of their ethical code. Religion is still linked with many national festivities and it legitimizes many social institutions — the monarch is crowned in a cathedral, marriages are solemnized by religious service, even the end of the television service is marked by prayer and early morning radio broadcasts by a 'thought for the day'.

He notes the great variety of beliefs to which people adhere: studies have shown that 9 out of 10 people believe in God; 2 out of 3 venerate Jesus; 1 in 3 say prayers; 1 in 6 believe in hell; 4 out of 5 consult a horoscope; 50% go to fortune tellers. There remains an overriding belief in the sanctity of hard work and the Protestant ethic it implies. There is a growth in the number of sects and cults. He says that all this stems from the same source. They all have a deep religious origin. Many young people seem to be on a religious quest, not always of the orthodox kind, but nevertheless spiritual in its nature.

It is facts such as these that lead Martin to argue that religion is not in decline. Orthodox religion is not maintaining high attendance rates, but, he says, people are no less religious. Indeed, he is optimistic that the reverse is true — that people are becoming more religiously inclined, although they may be expressing their needs in different ways.

Church membership England and Wales 1956 in 1000s

Baptist Union	324	Note:
Brethren	146	The criteria for membership differ between the
Church of Wales (and Welsh Independents)	324	denominations. For
Church of England	2,923	example, the Roman
Congregational Union	220	Catholic Church includes
Methodist	744	members of the R.C.
Presbyterian	224	population of all ages.
Society of Friends (Quakers)	21	
Roman Catholic	3,170	
Others	119	

The functions of religion

FOR THE INDIVIDUAL

1　Religion provides the answers to questions regarding the nature and purpose of man and the universe.

2   It may help to satisfy his emotional needs — man needs support and reassurance in times of crisis and difficulty.
3   It provides moral code by which he can guide his conduct.
4   It provides a sense of community and identity and of group membership.
5   Prayer and sacrifice offer a release from tension and aggression that might otherwise endanger the group.

FOR SOCIETY
1   The answers that a particular religion offers to the ultimate questions which face man help to provide a sense of community and integration within the social group. Religion provides a sense of brotherhood and belonging. It is important as a means of obtaining social stability. (Where there are two or more dominant religions in the society it may also become a source of conflict.) The ceremonials and rituals of the religion help to unify the group, since they provide a common bond.
2   Religion functions as an important agency of social control. It lays down a generally accepted code of behaviour which invests certain activities with a sacred quality and makes them acceptable, and others, which are considered anti-social, with the notion of 'sin'. Supernatural sanctions back up the norms and mores of the society providing it with a greater sense of stability and cohesion. For example, it adds depth to the meaning of marriage and the family in western society and helps to conserve them by providing a holy and sacramental quality. (The Roman Catholic Church deters its members from divorce on the grounds that it would nullify this sacred aspect.)
3   Religion in society may affect economic behaviour — the Protestant ethic, it is suggested, gave rise to the spirit of capitalism in the west, and the element of social criticism in Christianity may have given rise to the Socialist movement and other movements for social reform.

RESEARCH FINDINGS 1
In 1969/70 George Greening undertook a study to see whether an element in British society is becoming more permissive in its attitudes towards sex, violence, use of drugs and whether there is a parallel decline in the strength of religious attitudes. He questioned 760 students in technical colleges throughout the country (together with a small sample of 60 students from universities). Of the total sample 75% had attended secondary modern schools and were in classes 3, 4, and 5 of the Registrar General's categories. He found that 17% of his sample attended church regularly although 60% claimed a belief in God and in the value of prayer. Religious education in school seemed to make little impact on their beliefs, except to harden their attitudes against religion.
   His conclusions were that permissiveness is strongly characterized in their attitudes towards adultery, gambling, abortion, divorce, and prostitution, which received comparatively high rates of approval. This

conclusion is supported by Home Office statistics on delinquency and crime which show increases of nearly six times since 1945. The females who were questioned were notably more religious than the males. Those who showed high degrees of religious belief appeared to be more compassionate and charitable in their attitudes towards others, and they were less promiscuous and permissive. The factors affecting the degree of religious belief in the individual seemed to be age, sex, educational background, social class, and occupation. Nevertheless, more than 42% of the youth questioned still paid lip service at least to basic Christian ideals. More than 90% agreed that people should show respect for their parents and that it is wrong to steal or murder, and they showed a good knowledge of the Ten Commandments. Other answers revealed a high degree of idealism in the young people questioned in this interesting study.

RESEARCH FINDINGS 2

A study by R. J. Rees in 1967 examined the religious attitudes of undergraduates in Oxford, Cambridge, and the University College of North Wales in Bangor.

Belief in God	%
Practising Church member	28
Belief in Christ (but uncommitted to a Church)	11
Tolerant agnostic	28
Atheist	13

Churchgoing	%
Regularly	32
Sometimes	20
Never	48

Private prayer	Total %	Arts students %	Science students %
Regularly	18	27	17
Sometimes	34	18	41
Never	48	55	42

Belief in life after death	%
Eternal life after death for those who believe in Christ and punishment for those who do not	10
Eternal life for those who believe in God and seek to do his will	14
Almost certainly some form of personal survival after death	22
Some form of survival after death very unlikely	30
Belief in a future life merely wishful thinking	24

Belief in the Bible as historical fact	% of sample
Crucifixion	88
St Paul's shipwreck	73
Resurrection	36
Ascension	25
Water into wine	17
Expulsion from Eden	4

The survey also confirms that traditional beliefs are stronger than may be supposed. Scientists do not seem to be less religious than arts students, although they pray less regularly. There remains a good deal of interest in religion among young people and a belief in its value as the source of social morality.

EXERCISES

1   Why are sociologists interested in studying religion in society?

2   Why is it difficult to provide a simple definition of religion?

3   How did the following explain religion? (a) Yinger, (b) Marx, (c) Durkheim, (d) Weber.

4   What is the difference between religion, magic, and superstition?

5   Some people argue that religion is declining in modern society. What is the problem in defending this point of view? How could it be tested?

6   What does 'secularization' mean?

7   Wilson believes that religous power is declining. What is the basis of his argument?

8   Martin holds the view that religion is as strong as ever. What is the basis of his optimistic view?

9   Compare the typical students investigated by Greening and Rees.

ESSAY QUESTIONS

1   What influence does religion have on social behaviour? Is there evidence to suggest that the influence of religion is declining in Britain?

2   What are the functions of religion in society?

3   Outline the main theories of religion in sociology. What is meant by 'substitute religions'?

4   Account for the changes in attitude towards organized religion since 1851 when more than 40% of the population attended a church on a regular weekly basis.

This infra-red photograph shows part of the vast conurbation that houses Sydney's 2.7 million inhabitants

12 Urbanization

Urbanization means the growth of densely populated cities and their satellite suburbs which are the source of many exciting innovations in social development. They provide new forms and wider choice of entertainment, employment opportunities, housing, and welfare schemes. They may also be the source of many disruptive factors in social life; the noise and speed of life is increased, there are congestion, strain, and higher living costs.

It has been suggested that the characteristics defining the city include:
1   The size of the community is greatly increased compared with rural towns and villages.
2   A system of taxation is introduced which results in surplus capital. This can be used for public works and improvement schemes which in turn attract more immigrants.
3   There emerge specialists in administration, trade, and other important areas of daily life, and this facilitates social stability and growth.
4   There is the growth of a privileged *élite*, who hold power, and an organized bureaucracy (the specialized government administrators). In some societies, such as ancient China, power may have been obtained by virtue of a man's literacy in a generally illiterate age, or by a man's soldierly qualities. How do administrators gain their power in Britain?
5   The art of writing and the use of mathematics develop since it becomes important to maintain records and accounts of business transactions. Facilities for improving these abilities in the city population gradually develop.
6   Initially the power of the dominant religion is great and it influences and patronizes the art of the time. In contemporary industrialized urban cities the power and influence of the Church is declining.
7   The beginnings of exact and predictive sciences occur in cities. As these become more elaborate and wide ranging the value of religion declines and secularization occurs.
8   The early cities became centres of trade and commerce and localized power as a result of efficient organization and surplus production.

215

The interest of the sociologist

Sociologists study urban development to see whether there are patterns of behaviour and development common to all cities, and, if there are differences, what they are and why they should exist. It has been found, for example, that in American cities patterns of delinquency and crime are fairly similar. The central areas, being the poorest and oldest, tend to produce more delinquents than any other. In Britain the reverse tends to be true. Few people live in central areas from which the city developed because these have become the business sections. Redevelopment causes people to be moved to estates in outlying areas, which may become the problem centres. Sociologists may also wish to know what accounts for the growth of urban areas and the characteristics and atmosphere that they display. They investigate the problems associated with urban life and the effects of redevelopment on people who may have roots in particular areas. They are searching to uncover definite facts about urbanization in order to understand all aspects of social life more fully.

Factors which affect urban development

The evolution of technology and of necessary social institutions formed the basis for the growth of cities as centres of great social and technical change. The exact time when the city first originated is not known but it is a comparatively recent development. The expansion of cities in Britain has been most rapid following the innovations of the Industrial Revolution.

The major factors affecting the mushrooming of the great cities include:

1 The geographical features of the area – the degree to which the climate, local resources, and environment can assist man's development of the region. It has been suggested that one of the reasons why Britain became the first industrialized nation was the favourable climate.

2 The degree to which local resources can be utilized and so enable a technology to develop.

3 The extent to which the society incorporates social institutions which facilitate urban development – an emphasis on literacy, an organized administration, a dominant religion with accepted moral codes and a sense of stability and accepted leadership.

It is difficult to make precise comparisons between different countries to see which are the most urbanized, since there is no common definition of the term 'urbanization'. In the United States the line between rural and urban is drawn at a population of 2,500, in Iceland it is 300, and in Holland 20,000. There is a strangely high degree of apparent urbanization in countries like Australia and Argentina which are not noted for extensive industrialization. This is explained by the geographical factors. Many of the major cities in these thinly populated countries are situated on the coast which makes them well placed for international trade. On the basis of the percentage of population living in places with more than 10,000 inhabitants, Britain and Holland are amongst the most highly urbanized countries in the world, with more than 70% of their population in this category. The least urbanized countries, using this criterion, include Turkey, Yugoslavia, Portugal, and India, with less than 20% of their populations in the category.

The consequences of urbanization

It would not necessarily be correct to equate all that is bad or unpleasant in modern life with urbanization and all that is good and ideal with a rural existence. Agricultural workers' wages are amongst the lowest in the country, and many isolated homes lack modern amenities that town dwellers take for granted. Both have their advantages and disadvantages. Some of the consequences of urbanization can be identified in a general way, although sociologists who specialize in urban development would wish to obtain very specific details of each.

1   There is a decrease in the number of primary relationships (that is, close interfamily relationships), since it becomes more and more difficult for people to know many members of the locality personally. (Unlike life in a small rural community.) Secondary relationships become more dominant, in that people are on less familiar terms and often may not know their immediate neighbours.

2   The nuclear family becomes more usual and the extended family less in evidence, since in an industrial society the close-knit family unit breaks down as family members move away in search of employment which large cities offer.

3   The population becomes more diverse, to include others from different regions and other countries. Responsibilities are delegated more widely, and class differences between citizens also become more distinct.

4   There is an increase in the number and type of social problems including poverty, overcrowding, crime, suicide, alcoholism, and other forms of deviance.

5   There is an increase in the number of specialized agencies of welfare, education, training, and entertainment.

6   In a city the place of work becomes more widely separated from the place of living, and daily travel, often involving long distances, becomes necessary. Efficient forms of transport and communication are developed.

It has been said that the rise of urbanism and the subsequent rise of secularism are the two major hallmarks of our era. Cities and the types of community that develop in them differ according to particular factors:

1   The kind of economic activity that goes on in them. Some areas develop as centres of trade and industry, others are business or commercial centres, others again may be pleasure resorts. The major cities in a society will almost certainly be a combination of all these types. The kind of social life and atmosphere common to a city or a particular part of it is influenced by factors other than its size.

Motor traffic in Cannon Street, London

2   The historical background. Some cities have a long history of multi-racial and multi-class content, like London and Birmingham. Others are associated with rural life and developed as market towns offering little incentives to aliens as a place of residence or work – cities like Gloucester or Hereford. Others, life York and Canterbury, grew up as centres of religious activity. There are cities which are noted for their specialized fields of work – Hull for its fishing industry and Sheffield for steel. Although some diversification has subsequently taken place, nevertheless the historical background is significant in affecting the overall culture of the city, making for different attitudes, atmosphere, and social characteristics in day-to-day life.

Social problems associated with urban life

1   There is more crime committed in cities than in rural areas. This is especially true of crimes against property. For crimes of violence against the person there is not so much difference.
2   Death rate tends to be lower in rural areas despite the fact that welfare facilities may not be so good. Sickness rates are higher in urban areas. There are higher admissions to mental hospitals. This does not prove that cities are more conducive to mental illness. It is possible that those who go to live in cities are more likely to have an unstable personality and are consequently more likely to become mentally ill.
3   The Buchanan Report 1963 accepted that traffic noise is now the predominant noise nuisance in towns, and that it is becoming more prejudicial to the general enjoyment of town life, destructive of the amenities of dwellings on a wide scale, and interfering with efficiency in offices and other business premises.

The Report went on to say that fumes and smell are a further unpleasant byproduct of the motor vehicle, both as pollutants of the air and hazards to health. The motor vehicle is in direct competition with environmental requirements; there are the visual intrusions of the motor car, the clutter of signs, and the destruction of historical and architectural scenes.

4 When an area of a city becomes unfashionable or declines in standards it often becomes the home of the poor and those who can not afford the more fashionable residential areas. Over generations such areas may become centres of delinquency, and crime develops as a deviant subculture.

5 To meet the strains of growing and changing, large urban areas require large sums of money to increase facilities. Levels of taxation increase to cater for the new demands and to resolve the social problems which arise. Since 1870 with the introduction of Education Acts, Public Health Acts, Local Government Acts, National Insurance Acts, Children's Acts, etc., governments have tried to come to terms with and overcome the problems that manifest themselves where large groups of people live in close contact. All the needs must be answered if society is to be stable and harmonious. The need for jobs, amenities, safety, and education must be met promptly and efficiently.

Man is adjusting slowly to the urban way of life, and there is evidence

There are no cars to endanger children in this shopping precinct in Stevenage New Town

to show that the urban community is subject to constant change. In America a new term to describe the way in which the city begins to engulf and absorb its satellite suburbs has been coined. It is 'megalopolis'. It is in such areas that supermarkets have become 'hypermarkets'. In Britain there is a trend for those who can afford it to have not only two cars but also two homes – one a weekend retreat in the country as an escape from the confines of city life. More new towns are being built which include an 'industrial estate' well away from residential areas. Many cities are re-designing their centres to give pedestrians precedence. Streets are blocked off from traffic and made into shopping precincts. In Nottingham a free bus service was introduced in 1973 to take shoppers into the centre of a largely car-free city. Planners are becoming more aware of the problems of urban life and are seeking ways of offering citizens a well-planned city environment in the future.

RESEARCH FINDINGS

The Evolution of a Community, by Peter Willmott.

Willmott wished to obtain information regarding the way in which an estate in Dagenham was developing, having regard to the varied back-grounds of the people who had moved there. In the course of his investiga-tion he interviewed councillors and officials of the London County Council to obtain their views on problems and difficulties which might have arisen. His team of researchers observed the day-to-day life of residents in the streets, in parks, pubs, cafés, and shops. Most of the information comes from interviews with people in their own homes. These were carried out in 1958–9, and Willmott returned in 1961 to interview 30 families and some teachers, civil servants, and councillors for further impressions.

There were three main samples in the first survey.

1 *General sample* This was chosen to reflect the population of the estate as a whole. Names were chosen at random from the electoral register of those parts of Dagenham, Ilford, and Barking which made up the estate. The registers were those published in 1958 and contained 66,393 names from which 1,090 were selected.

Names drawn	1,090
Not contacted (death etc.)	97
Refusals	116
Number interviewed	877

The number who could not be contacted (about 9%) and the number of refusals (12%) appeared to be a normal proportion for a survey of this kind. The interviews were carried out by 15 interviewers working from a head-quarters in Dagenham Borough Council Library. The interviews were formal and standardized, and the questions straighforward and factual: e.g., age, job, length of residence, etc.

2 *Marriage sample* This consisted of 143 married subjects living at home

with their husbands or wives, who had two or more children under 15. Some of these were chosen for further interviews on a random basis until there was a final group of 50. The interviews varied from 40 minutes to over 2 hours, and some who were specially co-operative were recalled three or four times. These interviews were carried out by Willmott and one colleague.

There was a schedule of questions to provide a framework – on, for example, why they lived in that area, what they thought of work in the house, their children's education, their neighbours, politics, social class, and so on. They followed any sidetracks raised by the respondents. Half of the sample had two children, a quarter had three, and the other quarter four or more. The husbands in this sample were generally more skilled than those in the general sample.

3 *Tenants sample*. Another sub-section of the general sample was drawn. Those interviewed under this section were tenants or the wives of tenants who had come to live on the estate before 1930. There were 150 of these, chosen at random to make up a sample of 20 (two more were chosen later to cover refusals.) The interviews were again informal, covering the same topics as the second sample, together with questions on how often they saw their in-laws, their children, etc.

The result is a detailed and fascinating picture of the way in which the community was evolving and adapting to the ongoing changes in the environment. It is a valuable insight for those who are concerned with the preparation and implementation of social policy, and for those interested in the process of urbanization and its consequences for those living in urban areas.

EXERCISES
1 What does urbanization mean?

2 What are the important characteristics of the city?

3 Why are sociologists interested in studying urban development?

4 What are the main factors that affect urban development?

5 What are some of the important consequences of urbanization?

6 Explain how you would investigate some of the problems of urban development.

7 What are the advantages and disadvantages of urban life and rural life?

ESSAY QUESTIONS
1 What factors have contributed to urban development in Britain since 1850?

2 Discuss some of the major social problems that have arisen as a result of the development of urbanization since 1870.

3 Date   % of population living in urban areas
   1850   50%
   1901   75%
   1939   80%
   1961   90%
Discuss the consequences of urban development.

13 Population

The specialized study of population is known as 'demography'. Reliable evidence about the growth and composition of population in Britain has existed since 1801, when the first census was taken. Censuses have occurred every 10 years since, with the exception of 1941. Information is collected by the office of the Registrar General who is responsible for the publication of data.

In order for a government to prepare its policies with regard to the social welfare of its citizens it is necessary to have accurate data and estimations of future trends, prepared by demographers and sociologists, with regard to changes in population distribution and growth. It is important to be able to break down the population into various categories in order to see how its composition is changing over periods of time. It may then be possible for government departments and other interested agencies to draw up plans and policies to cater for the ongoing changes as they begin to affect the economic and social structure of the society.

The interest of the sociologist

Studies of changes in the structure and composition of the population are relevant to sociology because they are based on facts about what has actually happened, so that statistical methods can be applied to forecast future trends. The data which are collected are relevant in terms of social policy, and with regard to the pressure on scarce resources: land, housing, finance, etc. Changes in population density are also significant for other aspects of the social structure: education, employment, welfare.

Population growth

There are three main factors affecting population growth:
1   Birth rate (fertility rate): the ratio of total live births to the total population, usually expressed in 'births per 1000 of the total population'.
2   Death rate (mortality rate): the ratio of total deaths to the total population. Usually expressed in 'deaths per 1000 of the total population'.

3 Migration (immigration/emigration). This factor tends to be of minimal importance in Britain. From 1871 to 1931 Britain lost population through migration. Between 1951 and 1961 there was a net increase of 389,000. In recent years there has been a net loss of 31,000.

Where birth rate is higher than death rate the population will increase. For many centuries, until the middle of the eighteenth, both birth rate and death rate were high, and the population grew only slowly. In the eighteenth and nineteenth centuries death rate dropped rapidly while birth rate remained high. Hence population grew very rapidly.

	1700 (est.)	1801	1871	1901	1911	1921	1931	1951	1961	1971
Birth rate	36	36	35	28	24	23	16	15	17	16
Death rate	35	30	20	17	14	12	12	12	12	11

(Source: *Social Trends*, No. 3)

REASONS FOR THE DECLINE IN BIRTH RATE AND FAMILY SIZE SINCE 1870

1 New and cheaper methods of birth control have been developed.
2 The popularization of family planning methods was initiated by a court case involving Charles Bradlaugh M.P. and Annie Bessant, who were prosecuted for publishing a book advocating family limitation in the 1870s.
3 After 1870 children became more of an economic liability rather than an asset because
(a) Education had become compulsory.
(b) The employment of young children was gradually eliminated by legislation and the development of Trade Union power.
(c) Standards of child care were improving. It was no longer necessary to have a large family in order to ensure the survival of a few children.
4 The economic depression of the 1870s, 1880s, and 1920s and 1930s accentuated the problems of supporting a large family: poverty and the fear of unemployment may have encouraged reductions in family size.
5 People wished to improve their status in the community, and in order to do this it may be necessary to increase one's material possessions, which may involve restricting the size of the family.
6 The emancipation of women meant that increasing numbers of women wanted to go on working after marriage, and to have too large a family may mean an interruption of career.
7 Social norms and fashion have changed: in the nineteenth century large families were fashionable, especially among the wealthiest sector. In the first half of the twentieth century this section of society began to have smaller families, a trend followed by the rest of society.
8 The increase in secularization and the decline in religious authority has resulted in changes in attitude which have enabled new legislation to be passed with regard to abortion, birth control, etc. In 1972 a survey showed that 64% of the electorate believed that the government should

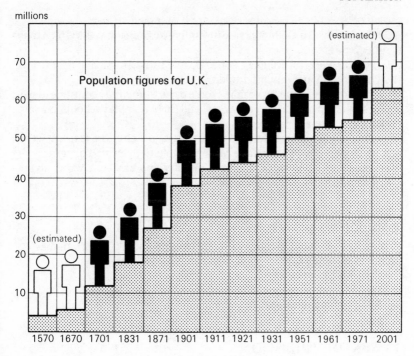

millions

Population figures for U.K.

(estimated)

(estimated)

1570 1670 1701 1831 1871 1901 1911 1921 1931 1951 1961 1971 2001

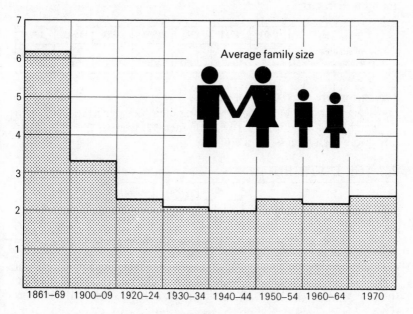

Average family size

1861–69 1900–09 1920–24 1930–34 1940–44 1950–54 1960–64 1970

provide a free birth control service for all men and women.

There has been a slight increase in family size in recent years which may be due in part to:

(a)   An increase in affluence: once people satisfy their material wants they may then have larger families.

(b)   Improved welfare provisions: some occupations may continue to pay salaries to mothers during pregnancy, and thereafter play schools, nursery schools, etc., are available.

(c)   An increase in the numbers of marriages just after the last war. (The economic depression may have caused people to defer marriages.)

(d)   Change in fashion and norms (royalty and aristocracy are having larger families, which may set a trend).

Population patterns

Patterns of population growth, composition and distribution may be analysed in terms of:

1   Distribution of sexes.
2   Distribution of age groups.
3   Regional distribution.
4   Occupation.

1   SEX DISTRIBUTION

The population is now equally divided between the sexes. There are slightly more women than men, although generally about 5% more boys are born than girls.

	1901	1911	1921	1931	1951	1961	1971
Ratio of males per 1000 females:	937	937	915	920	934	941	947

Two factors are responsible for this:

(a)   There is a higher death rate among men. Life expectation for men is 69 and for women it is 74. (By 2001: men 72, women 79.)

(b)   More men than women emigrate.

2   AGE DISTRIBUTION

	1901	1921	1951	1971	1981
School age or under (0—14)	32%	28%	22%	24%	23%
Working age (15—65)	61%	64%	63%	60%	60%
Retirement (60/65 +)	7%	8%	15%	16%	17%

In a pre-industrial society the average age is typically low because of high mortality rates and low expectations of life. Present trends indicate that the average age is getting higher; there is an increase in the proportion of the population who are in the retired group, which means that an increasing number of elderly dependents will be supported in the future by a declining proportion of economically productive people. Governments in the future will have to provide more in the way of pensions and welfare facilities for this section and prepare for a declining number of young people entering the work force.

3 REGIONAL DISTRIBUTION

Since the industrial revolution Britain has changed from being a country in which the greater part of the population lived in rural areas to one in which the majority are in urban areas.

1851 the urban population equalled the rural population for the first time.

1901 75% lived in urban areas.

1939 80% lived in urban areas.

1961 52% lived in towns with populations greater than 50,000
40% lived in the six major conurbations.

Statistics relating to urban and rural populations are to some extent difficult to state with precision, since there is some difficulty in defining the terms. The official statistics are based on the administrative division of the country into boroughs and urban and rural districts.

If a line were drawn from Hull to Chester dividing the country into two approximately equal halves, it is estimated that about 20 million live in the north and 32 million in the south. The greatest concentration of population is in the Greater London conurbation. In the past 10 years the population has increased most rapidly in the South-east, the Midlands, and the North-west.

4 OCCUPATION

As a nation becomes more prosperous the proportion of the workforce engaged in primary production (agriculture and extractive industries) declines; the proportion engaged in secondary industries (manufacturing) at first rises and then begins slowly to decline, and the proportion engaged in tertiary industries (distribution, professions, and services) increases. The total manpower on Britain is approximately 26 million – 16 million are men and 10 million women. Ninety percent of the working population are employed for a wage or salary. About 2 million people are either employers or self-employed.

Possible effects of a rapid increase in population

1 PRESSURE FOR ACCOMMODATION

In 1967 there were about 15,700,000 dwellings in England and Wales, and of those 1,836,000 were estimated to be unfit for habitation (from *Economic Trends*, No. 175).

Tenure:	50.8% were owner occupied.
	27.1% were rented from the local authority or new town corporation.
	21.4% were rented privately.
	0.7% were awaiting demolition.
Age:	38.4% were built before 1919.
	27.1% were built between 1919 and 1944.
	34.5% were built between 1944 and 1968.
Amenities:	18.6% lacked an internal water closet.
	13.4% lacked a fixed bath.
	19.4% lacked a wash basin.
	18.0% had no hot water.
Slum clearance:	Houses demolished in England and Wales since 1945:

1945–54	90,000
1955–59	200,000
1960–64	300,000
1965–68	270,000

Note: In 1969 the Government announced a housing shortage of 18,000. Whereas Shelter (which fights the cause of the homeless) said it was greater than three million. They also said that 400,000 people are living in conditions of 'extreme overcrowding', while 1.6 million were overcrowded by census standards.

Changing tenure of households 1947–67

	1947	1962	1967
Owner occupiers	26%	43%	51%
Council tenants	13%	21%	27%
Other tenants	61%	36%	22%

These facts and figures indicate that Britain has a housing problem which is constantly changing as standards change. The trend since the war has been to encourage the growth of council housing and private ownership. There has been a decline in letting. But all the time the number of households (i.e. those who require an independent home) is increasing. But the building rate is very slow – about 2% per annum. Possible solutions include the renovation of old buildings rather than demolition. If landlords are becoming scarce other investors may have to be encouraged. A better knowledge of who is in need could be obtained so that long-term policies could be planned. Those who are in greatest need include the elderly, the young married couples, immigrants and low wage earners; it may be that for them new and cheaper forms of housing could be developed.

2 PRESSURE FOR EMPLOYMENT

There would be pressure for employment which might be difficult to meet. The first Poor Laws formulated the need to 'set the poor to work', but the causes of unemployment have only begun to be understood in this century, and many new economic policies have been introduced in an attempt to deal with it.

3 PRESSURE ON THE EDUCATION SERVICES

In 1972 there were: 161 Colleges of Education, training 100,000 teachers
28 University Education Departments
5 Departments of Education in Polytechnics.

In 1957/58 28,000 teachers were being trained. Nevertheless, there remains a shortage. In 1969 there were 360,000 teachers in schools, and it is anticipated that there will be 420,000 by 1975. More than 40,000 more would be needed to reduce classes below an average figure of 40. It has been found that more than 500,000 schools have no hot water; 670,000 children are in overcrowded classes; 780,000 children are classified as educationally subnormal, although there are many others who require specialized treatment but are unable to obtain it because insufficient facilities. In 1965 only 372 teachers were released for special training. It is estimated that 1% of the school population is illiterate, and 25% of school leavers are semi-literate.

4 PRESSURE ON MEDICAL SERVICES AND OTHER SOCIAL FACILITIES.

G.P.s in England and Wales 1967.

In 1967 there were 21,305 G.P.s in England and Wales working in 10,143 practices.

Doctors and population in Great Britain 1911–1995

	Popn. (mill.)	No. of doctors active	Doctors per mill. of popn.
1911	42	26,000 (needed)	654
1931	46	33,000	745
1951	50	48,000	987
1965	54	62,000	1,181
1975	56	68,100	1,207
		78,000 (needed)	
1995	66	119,800 (needed)	1,801

Medical and social services: *Health staffs 1967, England and Wales*

Nursing and Midwifery	Full time	188,000
	Part time	79,000
Health visitors	Full time	1,000
	Part time	6,500
Home nurses	Full time	6,000
	Part time	4,500
Home helps	Full time	3,000
	Part time	64,000

In 1958 there were 2,521 hospitals.
In 1964 there were 132,895 patients resident in mental illness hospitals in England and Wales.
In 1967 there were approximately 12,000 social workers.

Reigate, Surrey, in 1910

The same street on a Saturday afternoon in 1974

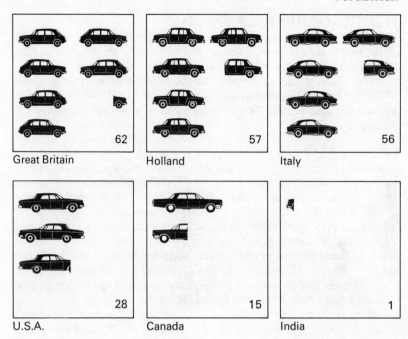

(above) *Vehicles per mile of road 1972*

(below) *Motor cars in Britain 1904—2000 (predicted)*

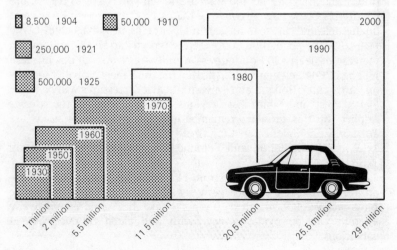

5 ENVIRONMENTAL PROBLEMS

There would be environmental problems resulting from the increased use of the motor car. At present Britain has more vehicles per mile of road than any other country in the world.

If the trends shown in the graph on the previous page continue, there will be a total of 38 million vehicles, including lorries, buses, etc. by 2010. By then we shall be near the saturation figure of roughly one car for every two people.

6 POVERTY

It is likely that poverty would increase. A survey made in 1966 calculated that nearly 500,000 families, containing 1,500,000 children, were either living on Supplementary Benefit or had incomes below Supplementary Benefit level. But poverty is more than a matter of low income. Poor housing, a poor physical environment, poor education, lack of cultural stimulation, and poor health all help to contribute to the same daily difficulties and dreariness of life style. Such deprivations and handicaps are interlinked so that problems are multiplied for particular families.

Does Britain need a population policy? Some facts and opinions were put forward in an article by Gerald Leach. He wrote:

Britain is sitting on an ominously ticking population bomb. The ticks may be slow but they warn us of a doubling of our numbers to 112 million in little more than a century. Few people doubt that the bomb must be defused or our environment and hopes for a decent life will be squeezed intolerably. Yet there has only been one debate set down in the House of Commons on Population since before 1939. But the first and most basic problem is how any elected government can ever decide when it must act to curb population growth, and then what the authorities can do in terms of legislation. Governments are elected to manage things and they are far too insecure to tell voters not to have more children, so they have to convince themselves that growth is the great unalterable and can be managed. But is our growth manageable? In the year 2000 the population of the U.K. is expected to be 64.0 million (an increase of nearly 20% on today's 56 million). Nearly all this increase will be in England and Wales, already the third most crowded country on earth (after Holland and Taiwan). Heaviest pressures will be in the North West and South East regions. Consider some of the stresses implied by this growth – remembering that most social needs are already badly under-catered for already.

1 The car population and demand for countryside recreation are expected to triple.

2. The under 15's will jump from 11.5 million to nearly 15 million – an average increase of 2000 per week. Two 650-child schools must be built each week for the next 30 years to take these children before any attempt can be made to deal with antiquated or overcrowded conditions.

3   The extra 10 million population will need houses equivalent to building 30 Nottinghams.

4   Urbanisation and industrialisation are expected to bury an area equivalent to Cornwall and Devon under concrete and asphalt.

5   Farm yields must rise by 80% if we are to continue growing half our own food.

6   Each of us in Britain consumes in a lifetime 10 to 20 times as much, of the earth's finite resources as the average Indian, and pollutes on a similarly vast scale. By this measure our population is more of a global disaster than India's 500 million. To say the least it is unwise to assume that this imbalance can continue indefinitely.

Any delay is dangerous. A gentle touch on the brakes now to reduce births will take 25 or 30 years before its impact is really felt. The longer we delay the more likely it is that when we do act it will be in panic, with harsher curbs that will produce more drastic changes – much like a skid when one stamps on the brakes rather too late.

But why act at all? Growth is slowing down from 27 per 1000 in 1901, to about 18 per 1000 in 1971. But this is still a long way from the rate of 14 that would give exact replacement; in other words zero population growth in the long run. And as the Register General's latest projections warn, this still gives a picture of substantial growth. In terms of family size exact replacement has to be 2.1 children per family. It is unlikely that anything short of tough policies or a huge swing in fashion will pare families down to this figure. Instead current projections suggest that family size will remain around the 2.4 mark. Brides under 20 tend to have larger families than those between 20–29. Thus young brides are a major target for population control. One solution would be to launch a massive effort to improve birth control and cut down on the thousands of unwanted or unplanned children. Illegitimate births account for 1 in 12 of all births (67,000 babies in England and Wales in 1969). There is also a high divorce rate among shot gun marriages. A recent survey by Dr. Anne Cartwright found that for their most recent birth 15% of all mothers were 'sorry it ever happened'. Where the birth was the third baby in the family 19% were sorry, for the fourth 25% and the fifth 39% and for later births 50%. But if none of these unwanted children had not been born it would not make much difference to average family size – it would not drop below 2.27 from its present 2.4. To achieve zero growth parents will have to be persuaded not to have children they want. But how? This is one of the dilemmas of population control. The more radical wing – Kingsley Davis, for example, insists that only tough measures will work. The main aim, he suggests, is to smash the image that the family has rights to have as many children as they want. A whole range of measures has been proposed – from the extreme of sterilisation after a certain number of children (a measure which would be impossible to enforce) to legislation to increase the legal age of marriage, or substantial fees for marriage licences, grants for first marriage, when both partners are over a certain age, tax benefits for the single, or parents of small families, withdrawal of family allowances after so many children (with safeguards for the poorest families). But most moderate experts are doubtful as to how well such measures would work. Incentives or disincentives would have substantial to have any impact. And there are always loopholes. Nineteenth century laws to clamp down on early marriages in Switzerland were avoided by a huge rise in illegitimacy. In fact there is little evidence to show that patterns of marriage and family building have been altered by anything but very major changes in the whole social climate. Improved family planning programmes may help and there may also have to be a more liberal attitude towards abortion and sex education in schools. There will have to be a steady shift of opinion that a small family or even childlessness is no stigma. Basically what we have to do is to have one child less between every 3 families – which doesn't seem much to ask as a step to avoid a lot of unpleasantness in the not so distant future.

AN ARTICLE FROM THE *DAILY TELEGRAPH*, 29 JULY 1971

POPULATION STUDY – OFFICE REJECTED IN WHITE PAPER

The Government has rejected for the time being at least, a recommendation by the Select Committee on Science and Technology that a permanent 'special office' should be established to advise the Prime Minister how to deal with the problem of Britain's rapid population growth. A White Paper explained 'The Government does not, at this juncture, consider that the addition of a new piece of permanent official machinery would necessarily be the most appropriate way of tackling the problem. The question of whether or not the government should have a population policy or policies is complex and controversial. But a team of specialists would be set up immediately which would carry careful and dispassionate analysis in depth.' It will be chaired by Professor C. R. Ross, already a member of a team which advises the cabinet on long-term problems. Behind the Government's manoeuvring is the unpleasant fact that the present average net increase in the British population is 0.7% per year. This may not seem a very high growth rate and it compares favourably with an average annual growth rate of 2% for the whole world. But populations of tremendous density are forecast if the 0.7 per cent growth rate is allowed to continue. Britain's present population of 55.7 million would become 60 million by 1980, 64 million by 1990, and 69 million by 2000. It is doubtful if Britain could accommodate a population of 980 million, with an average of 10,000 people occupying every square mile but the 0.7 per cent rate leads to this terrifying figure for the year 2500. Any compulsory limitation of families is highly unlikely. The government is expected to decide on an 'optimum population level' and then use birth control propaganda to try to achieve it. (*Observations by the Government on a report from the Select Committee on Science and Technology*. Command Number 4748 H.M.S.O.)

Static population is foreseen in the U.S.A. A recent report in that country stated: 'A distinct possibility of nil population growth this century is predicted. Child-bearing is declining at a record rate. In 1970 there were 15% fewer children under 5 years of age than in 1970. This is the first decrease since the depression and the greatest since 1850.' The report predicts that the huge 'war baby' generation may not produce children as abundantly as had been expected (because of changing attitudes towards family size and developments in contraception and availability of abortion). The report says the effects of this trend are apparent in the declining sales by the toy industry, and it believes that manufacturers of records, clothes, etc., will be affected. Russia's birth rate is also thought to be declining. The birth rate in Moscow is down to 11 per 1000 (the overall rate in the U.S.S.R. is 18). One child families are common in the cities due to the high percentage of working women. Also abortions are free and legal in Russia. But a call has been made to increase the birth rate.

RESEARCH

The population of the United Kingdom may reach 65,900,000 by 2012. This prediction is made in *Population Projections, Number 3. 1972–2012* published by the Office of Population Censuses and Surveys. This represents an 18% growth on the 1972 figure of 55,900,000.

Other factors which emerge from the research of demographers is that the work force is expected to increase from 33,400,000 to 40,700,000. It is assumed that the net balance of migration would be outwards in the future.

Women are expected to outnumber men over the next 40 years. Marriage rates have increased compared to past years. In the 20 to 64 age range, the proportion of women married is expected to rise from 78.5% in 1972 to 82.4% in 2011. An increase in births is expected in the mid-seventies.

EXERCISES

1 What are the arguments for and against a population policy?

2 Show how the population has increased since 1801. What are the explanations?

3 Suggest the ways by which you could find out how attitudes have changed towards family size since 1900.

4 In what ways does public opinion influence family size? What is the significance of social class norms?

5 Draw graphs to show the proportion of the population in the following age groups: 0–16, 17–40, 41–65, 66+ in 1870, 1900, 1930, 1970. (see *Whitaker's Almanack* for details.)

ESSAY QUESTIONS

1   The population of Britain is about 56 million. Describe some of the important differences it would make if the population rose to 80 million in a comparatively short time.

2   Birth rates/death rates of Great Britain 1871—1970.

	Birth rate	Death rate (per 1000)	Population size
1871	35	20	27 m
1901	28	17	37 m
1950	16	12	50 m
1970	16	11	55 m

(a)   Explain what is meant by birth rate and death rate.
(b)   Why has the population continued to rise although birth rate has fallen?
(c)   How would you account for the fall in birth rate since 1871?

3   What are the sociological explanations of the causes of the increase in population during the last 100 years? What are some of the major problems that have arisen as a result?

14 Political Systems and Political Parties

Democracy and Dictatorship

Democracy: The word comes from the Greek — *demos* meaning 'people' and *kratos* meaning 'power'. It is generally said to mean government freely chosen by and responsible to the governed. The power of choosing who shall govern them is in the hands of the people of the society. It involves decisions by majority vote, but the rights of minorities are protected as far as possible. The underlying principles which democracy implies are tolerance, criticism without fear, the responsibility of the people who hold power to those who have elected them, free speech, equal rights, and the ability of an opposition to put forward alternative policies which may enable them to become elected to power at a later date. Democracy also involves parliamentary government, in which policies are debated and compromises are made where they can be shown to be weak or unlikely to succeed. In ancient Greece, which was divided into small city states, direct democracy was possible. Meetings could be called which all citizens could attend and all could voice their own opinions so that it could be certain that all policies were in the interests of the majority. In a modern, complex, industrial society, with large populations widely dispersed throughout the country, indirect democracy is in operation. Individuals are elected to represent particular areas, called 'constituencies'. Members of Parliament and local councillors are elected to work on their behalf. If they fail in their duties in any respect they can be replaced at a future time by the electoral process.

The theory underlying democratic government is that it attempts to combine the beliefs in equality, liberty, and independence, by establishing that power is held by those whom the people elect in free elections. Its significance lies in the fact that it determines and controls the way that power is held. The systems of government in Britain, United States, and France, for example, are all democratic.

Dictatorship: This system of Government is rule by an individual, a group, or a class. It is most generally used to imply that absolute power and control is held by one man which he has obtained by undemocratic means — by a *coup d'état* or as a result of revolution (power subsequently being passed on within a small circle of policy makers without reference to the will of the people). The revolution which brings the dictator to

Athens: the Acropolis

A demonstration in Petrograd (Leningrad) during the Russian Revolution

238

power often occurs with the support of the armed forces, since they have access to weapons, and the new ruler is himself often an officer with command of a section of the troops.

In the case of dictatorship or 'totalitarian' rule there is little chance of obtaining an alternative ruler or government since dictators do not permit the existence of opposition. They may later try to legitimize their rule by providing a system of elections, but they and their supporters seldom lose them. In Russia in 1917 Lenin seized power in the name of the workers and the Tzar and his family were eradicated. In 1922 Mussolini assumed power in Italy, and in 1933 Hitler took control of Germany. Franco came to power in Spain in 1936 and assumed dictatorial powers. There have been numerous similar seizures of power and rule by non-democratic means in Africa and South America throughout the period since 1945.

The characteristics of dictatorship include:

1   The forcible suppression of all other parties and opposition of any kind.
2   The breakdown of any previous liberal, democratic form of government (although sometimes one dictator replaces another by force of arms, or counter-coup).
3   The withdrawal of basic freedoms — including freedom of speech, the press, movement around the country, public meetings, etc.
4   The dictator usually comes to power with the support of a particularly powerful section of the society.

All dictators tend to be ruthless in the achievement of their ends, and the most successful tend to be good orators and have strong, charismatic personalities.

Socialism and Communism

This is a theory of social organization which affects both the political and economic systems of a society. The facilities for the production of goods are in the hands of the community; they are nationalized and are said to be under social control. Individuals cannot own factories or shops or employ others to work for them, nor can they have unearned income from investments, stocks, or shares. The object is to prevent an unequal distribution of wealth by ensuring that all citizens have equal opportunity to develop their talents and abilities without fear of exploitation. The underlying theory is that by changing the environment so that no one is disadvantaged it is possible to change social attitudes from those of competition to those of co-operation. It was seen by Marx as a major stage in the development towards the communist utopia and he predicted that it would follow the collapse of capitalism. The theory of communism, summarized in the phrase 'from each according to his means, to each according to his needs', can be traced back to early Christian principles and to theoretical systems discussed by Plato and others. Marx is the writer most widely associated with the more recent discussions of the ideas of communism. It is an advanced stage of socialism. Theoretically, there can be no class distinction within such societies since it is intended that there should be total equality. According to Marxian theory the workers, hitherto exploited under the capitalist system, are able to overcome their alienation and regain their true sense of worth. The State no longer requires administrators and 'withers away', and the utopia is attained.

Capitalism

This term describes the economic system of a society in which capital or machinery for the production of wealth is controlled by private enterprise. Any individual can invest his money as a shareholder in a company, and so obtain interest and dividends from profits. He can, if he wishes, buy a factory or shop or other business, employ others to operate it on his behalf and keep the profits. Capitalism is usually used in contrast to the term socialism in which there is little or no private enterprise, since all profits go to the State for redistribution. The advocates of capitalism as an economic system point to the advantages that competition brings, as an incentive to make companies more efficient and productive. Capitalism is largely a product of industrialization, which gave rise to the factory system and the competitive race for wider markets.

Fascism

This system of government is associated with the regimes of Mussolini (1922—43) in Italy, and Hitler (1933—45) in Germany. It is based on an authoritarian philosophy which upholds the absolute power of the ruler and the ruling *élite*. Fascism lays down specific codes of morality, law, and social behaviour which must be upheld at all times under pain of severe legal sanction. The State is said to be 'corporately organized' — meaning that the Parliament is elected not by constituencies as in the democratic system of Britain, but by local corporations which have been officially recognized by the ruling *élite* and which thereby buttress their power. (It would be, for example, like the Trade Unions electing the Labour Party into perpetual power with no alternative government.) There is no opposition and no party politics under fascist rule. Fascism is strongly anti-communist (although it shares certain organizational factors with communism). The State is all-important, and a strong leader is necessary to direct society along the path chosen by the rulers. But fascism does not believe in equality among the people — it holds that there should always be a ruling *élite* and a hard-working, but less able and less intelligent working sector. Neither does it believe in the concept of the State withering away. The ruling *élite* are seen as the necessary leaders since they are believed to be best fitted to govern. It advocates in its philosophy violent nationalism, belief in the fatherland, and the purity of the national race. Aliens and others not acceptable to the regime are persecuted as were the Jews, negroes, and others under Hitler's anti-Semitic policy. National expansion is obtained by mobilizing society for war, and the nation and the leader are glorified. In modern times, the governments of South Africa and Spain contain many of the elements of fascism.

Political parties in Britain

The efficient organization of Parliamentary business and the existence of an effective government in Britain depend on the existence of organized political parties, one of which, as the result of free and secretly balloted elections, provides the government of the day. The Prime Minister emerges from elections within his party and he is responsible for selecting his cabinet. The minority parties, with fewer elected members, form the opposition, and, as such, the competing teams for election at a future

Hitler and Mussolini

date. A government can remain in office for no longer than five years, after which further elections must be held. If a member dies or resigns a by-election is held in the constituency to elect his successor, who may come from any of the contending parties. The efficient working of this system depends on certain assumptions. All the parties must accept the rules of the Constitution, which govern procedure and the behaviour of party members. There must be a high degree of tolerance between the parties regarding their conduct. MacKenzie, who studies political behaviour, says that these assumptions are largely taken for granted in Britain. In the course of the last 30 years neither of the major parties has threatened at any point to disrupt the parliamentary system in order to impose its own policies or prevent its opponents from implementing theirs. He says the agreement on fundamentals is today very nearly as great as it has ever been in the modern history of British politics.

THE LIBERAL PARTY

This was the Whig, or Country, Party until the new name was officially adopted in the 1860s by Gladstone. Its principles were those of reform and social change. It advocated policies of 'laissez-faire' and free trade, that is, trade and other commercial enterprises should be as free as possible of government interference and control. During the 46 years between 1868 and 1914 the Liberals were in power for 23 years in all. In the later years of the period the Liberals began to lose working class support to the new Labour Party. Under Lloyd George from 1906 to 1914 the Liberal Government undertook many significant and major reforms: e.g., the Unemployed Workmen's Act, the Children's Act (the State accepted obligation to provide for the young in default of parental care), the Old Age Pensions Act, which first introduced a pension of five shillings (25p) a week, the Labour Exchange Act, and the National Insurance Act, all of which laid the basis of the Welfare State provisions which were implemented in 1948. After 1918 the Liberals never again held office. Consequently, the power of the leader of the Liberal Party is not great now, since the number of seats held by the Party is less than 15. In recent years the Liberals have advocated entry into the Common Market, emphasized their dislike of strong central control and encouraged home rule for Scotland and Wales.

THE CONSERVATIVE PARTY

This is derived from the Tory, or Court, Party (which opposed the Whigs). In the eighteenth century it included mainly the small landowners and the clergy in its support. In the nineteenth century the Conservative Party strongly favoured by the great landowners and those who had deep traditional roots in the wealthiest sector, as opposed to the new merchant sector who favoured the Liberal principles of free trade. The principles of the Party, which are basically those of 'conserving' the *status quo* — keeping the best of the past, whilst allowing for slow change in the future —

W. E. Gladstone

Benjamin Disraeli

were firmly established by its leader, Disraeli, in 1872. He said, 'The Tory Party has three great objectives ... to maintain the institutions of the country, to uphold the Empire of England, and to elevate the conditions of the people.' In 1948 the Maxwell Fyfe Committee was called into existence to review the Conservative Party structure. The committee stipulated that 'the leader of the Party has exclusive responsibility for the formulation of party policy. He may consult whom he wishes, he may pay attention to the resolutions passed by various organs of the party, but he remains the main fountain and interpreter of policy.' The report went on, 'The Disrealian principles are as valid today as when they were first propounded.'

In the twentieth century the party has been in office under Balfour (1902—06), Bonar Law and Baldwin (1922—29), in the National and Coalition Governments under Baldwin, Chamberlain, and Churchill 1935—45. Later conservative Prime Ministers have been Churchill, Eden, Macmillan, Home, and Heath. Conservatism today stands for the maintenance of existing political and economic systems, for gradual reform, free enterprise, and the conservation of traditional institutions, including the Monarchy, the House of Lords, and Public and Grammar schools.

THE LABOUR PARTY

The first step towards an organized party was taken in 1900, when the Trade Union Congress formed the Labour Representation Committee, which became known as the Labour Party in 1906. The first Labour member of Parliament was Keir Hardie, who was elected in 1892. The financial backing for the Party comes mainly from the Trade Unions via the 'political levy', a small amount of individual members' subscriptions which is paid into the Party funds. In 1922 the Labour Party displaced the Liberals as the second major British party. It formed its first government under Ramsay MacDonald, but it lasted only a few months. In 1929 a second minority Labour Government was formed, but it fell in 1931 and was replaced by a coalition. After the Second World War the Labour Party won a decisive majority under Attlee and remained in power until 1951. During that time it introduced the National Health Service, and nationalized coal, steel, electricity, gas, and some transportation services. In 1964 the Party returned to power, led by Harold Wilson with a small majority. It increased its majority in 1966, but was defeated by the Conservatives in the election of 1970. It was returned to power in February 1974 and again in October of the same year, but without a majority in the Commons.

It was not until 1918 that the Labour Party provided itself with a broad definition of its objectives and a specific set of policies which became the basis for its electoral programmes thereafter. On 26 February 1918 a Labour Party conference adopted a new constitution. Until that time the fundamental objective had been 'to organize and maintain in Parliament and the country a political Labour party'. In 1918 a definitive socialist aim was incorporated, to 'secure for the producers by hand or by brain the

Keir Hardie

full fruits of their industry, and the most equitable distribution thereof that may be possible, upon the basis of the common ownership of the means of production, and the best obtainable system of popular administration and control of each industry and service'.

It has been suggested by some observers that the British Labour Party has been unusual, historically, because it has accepted the traditional rules of British democracy, and has not adopted extreme socialist theories which have led in some countries to conflict and a total breakdown in the machinery of government. There are also some who believe that true socialism will never be achieved within the structure of the 'capitalist' British society. This is the source of much of the debate within the Labour Party on whether or not Britain should have joined the Common Market. Some believe that it is a 'rich man's club' and pushes the possibility of socialism further into the distance, whilst others in the Labour Party believe that the increased wealth which ought to result from membership will enable more money to be spent on funding the important social welfare policies which they believe the Party should implement. There are those who argue that British socialism will regard its main task as fulfilled when the State has control of the major productive units and wealth and income are more equitably distributed.

Pressure groups

'The complexity of modern Government has exaggerated its remoteness from the electorate. This has encouraged the growth of pressure group activity in an attempt to exert direct influence on politicians and to cut through routine but slow procedures.' (Grace Jones, *The Political Structure.*)

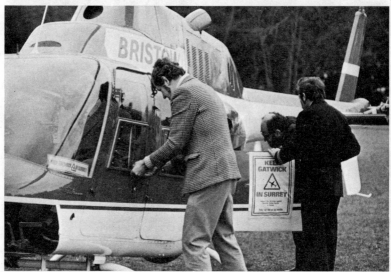

Action by a 'defensive' pressure group

246

WHAT ARE PRESSURE GROUPS?

They are formed by a number of people who have common interests and who feel strongly that changes ought to be made in policies or attitudes which affect their interests. They aim to exert influence on people who hold power, or on public opinion, and they seek to obtain information about future developments. They form because individuals believe that unless they work as a group they are relatively powerless, whereas a number of people together may have success. Some groups aim to supplement existing programmes and policies which are seen to have deficiences until official Government agencies can take over their work. There are examples of particular charities and other voluntary organizations in this area.

TYPES OF PRESSURE GROUPS

There are two main categories:
(1) Promotional groups which are formed to champion a particular cause, and (2) Defensive or protective groups which are formed to defend the interests of their members.

Examples of typical pressure groups:

Defensive	Promotional
'Hands off . . . Wing, Maplin Sands'	Campaign for Comprehensive schools
Trade Unions	Women's Liberation
National Council for Civil Liberties	Anti-apartheid movement
Aims of Industry	Campaign for Nuclear Disarmament
R.A.C. and A.A.	Child Poverty Action Group

THE FUNCTIONS OF PRESSURE GROUPS

1   To promote or defend the interests of their members.
2   To educate and inform public opinion and to try to change the policies of ministers and those in positions of power.
3   To keep governments informed of trends in the country and the strength of public opinion.
4   To assist political parties in their aims by championing on their behalf particular causes which represent an integral part of overall policy. The Monday Club, in the Conservative party, for example, seeks to publicize and promote the more conservative principles of the party, whereas PEST — Pressure for Economic and Social Toryism — endeavours to promote more liberal policies within the party.

THE SOURCE OF PRESSURE GROUP POWER

1   Some groups exert power because they are well organized and have a large, well disciplined, and cohesive membership. The Trade Unions are such examples. The majority of members are prepared to undergo many difficulties for prolonged periods in order to attain their ends.
2   Others exert power because of their prestige and status in society.

The views of senior Churchmen are respected because of their acknowledged standing in society.

3　Power may be exerted because the group includes some well-known personalities. The C.N.D. movement was led by Bertrand Russell, the philosopher; a group expressing concern for the rapid growth of population and advocating the more widespread use of family planning methods is led by Michael Parkinson, a television personality.

4　A group whose members work in important industries will be more powerful than whose members are in luxury occupations. Miners, for example, are more powerful and more successful in obtaining their demands than shop assistants or hairdressers.

5　Some pressure groups are particularly wealthy and can advertise more widely and obtain greater publicity, even though their membership may be smaller.

Generally, however, a small group of dedicated members is more likely to succeed in achieving the ends for which they are fighting than a vast but inactive membership.

MEMBERSHIP OF PRESSURE GROUPS
There is a wide variation of membership according to the type of pressure group. Defensive groups tend to have a mass membership – especially those formed on the basis of occupation, like Trade Unions. The larger the size of membership the more power such groups have, in general. Subscriptions tend to be low in order to encourage membership. Promotional

Gas workers queue up at the House of Commons to lobby their MPs

groups tend to rely more on the status of their membership than on vast numbers. A comparatively small number of reputable members can exert a great deal of power – especially where they have access to the decision makers, as a pressure group within a political party may have. Aims of Industry consists largely of directors and executives of industry whose prestige carries a great deal of weight in negotiations and discussions. Their subscriptions are likely to be high and membership more exclusive.

Pressure groups are not the same as political parties: despite their similarities there are major differences. (It has been said that the political parties are themselves a coalition of diverse pressure groups.) But they do not seek to obtain total power as a result of their activities. Pressure groups do not work to form a government based exclusively on the policies they advocate. They do not take part in elections except to support a particular policy of a party. They may not endorse the entire manifesto. The Monday Club, for example, would certainly not approve of all the Conservative Government's policies. They also tend to have a great many non-political functions. They may run social activities almost like a club and quite apart from their intended purposes.

Pressure groups are important in a democratic society as a means of ensuring that individuals who would otherwise feel powerless to express their feelings and obtain changes in policy can influence decision makers.

Voting behaviour in Britain

'The study of voting behaviour and the study of the behaviour of the campaigners are both important in understanding politics.' (Richard Rose, *Influencing Voters.*)

'Political opinions and actions are largely the result of habit based on irrational assumption.' (Wallas, *Human Nature in Politics*, 1908.)

'Voting behaviour cannot be explained by purely rational criteria or by neat formulae and it is beset by contradictions.' (Grace Jones, *The Political Structure.*)

THE INTEREST OF THE SOCIOLOGIST

These quotations may help to explain why sociologists study voting behaviour. They wish to know what are the factors that affect the way in which people vote. To what extent do the factors of social class, age, and knowledge of political matters affect the choice of party? Why do some people fail to vote although the struggle to obtain voting rights has been a long and hard-fought one throughout British history? Under what conditions does a government become unacceptable and susceptible to revolutionary action to establish a new one? To what extent and by what means can the individual who is dissatisfied by a particular policy change it?

Sociologists study voting behaviour as an aspect of political life and to help them to gain a better understanding of the political system itself and its significance for people in the society. Contradictions have certainly been discovered, and the sociologist is interested to try to resolve them. Why do many people in the working class sector of society vote for the Conservative Party, which traditionally would not seem to be in their best interests? Why is the turnout in General Elections high and in local elections generally low? Why are the abstainer and the floating voter significant at election times?

It is questions such as these that sociologists try to resolve when they study this aspect of political behaviour.

The interest in politics in Britain

Politics is concerned with the way in which power is distributed in a society, with decisions about ways of governing the society, and the organization of its social and economic life. But interest in debate concerning such factors is generally low in Britain. Some studies have shown that as few as 15% of the adult population are concerned in any detail with political affairs. There is similarly low membership of political parties and in the numbers of politically active members of the population. When asked to give a simple explanation of the basic phiosophies underlying 'Conservativism', 'Socialism', or 'Liberalism', few can give coherent or accurate answers. There is a great indifference to politics among the young, the working class sector, and women, perhaps because only women over the age of 30 became entitled to vote in 1918, and those over 21 not

until 1928. The Young Conservatives are the most successful of the politically motivated youth groups, claiming more than 80% of the interested youth as its members, although it may be that many of the members have joined not so much out of political beliefs but more for the social life the organization offers. Studies which ask respondents to name their M.P. show that the percentage who can do so is small, even where the Member has been occupying the seat for a great many years.

These are several possible reasons to explain this lack of interest. It may be that people have a growing sense of the inability to make their voice heard and opinions felt, and that Parliament is like a steamroller that moves slowly but relentlessly forward regardless of the wishes of the individual. (Pressure group activity is often successful in obtaining changes in policy, however. Public opinion caused the Government to think again about the site of London's third airport and to abandon Stanstead and Wing in favour of Maplin Sands.) There is the factor of the effect of 'saturation coverage' of political events by the mass media, which leads to a sense of boredom and lack of interest in political activity. There is the sense of distrust and disillusion resulting from disclosures of political scandals. The Profumo affair, the Lambton/Jellico affair, the Lonrho affair, the Poulson case, and in America the Watergate scandal – all involved major political figures who were shown to be either dishonest or disreputable in their dealings.

Some studies show that many people feel that it does not matter which party is in power since they see little difference between the parties – they all seem to keep the ship of state afloat and steer it more or less in the same direction.

ABSTAINERS

Abstainers are those who fail or refuse to vote at an election. In Britain turnout at a general election is consistently high. It is estimated that approximately 10% of the electorate consciously abstain. Another 10% fail to vote for other reasons – forgetfulness, or because the electoral register is out of date by the time of the election and the voter has moved or has died, or because of a total lack of interest.

It has been found that abstaining from voting is most common among women, young voters and the elderly, and the least well informed of the electorate. But the abstainers are important in elections because the outcome between the parties is generally very close, and by obtaining the votes of previously uncommitted voters who might otherwise have abstained the election outcome may be changed. This is particularly important in areas where a seat is 'marginal', with only a few hundred votes separating the parties. These abstainers, together with the 'floating voters', those who are uncommitted to either party and vote at the last minute according to the circumstances of the day, are known as the 'target voters', since they have become the target of canvassers, party political broadcasts, and last-minute campaigns.

Votes cast at General Elections 1951—1966

	1951	1955	1959	1964	1966
Labour	13,949,105	12,405,246	12,195,765	12,205,581	13,064,951
Conservative and Associate	13,718,069	13,311,938	13,750,965	11,980,783	11,418,433
Liberal	730,552	722,395	1,661,262	3,101,103	2,327,533
Irish Nationalist	94,587	152,310	63,915	101,628	
Communist	19,640	33,144	30,897	44,576	62,112
Welsh Nationalist	10,920	45,119	77,571	68,517	61,071
Scottish Nationalist	7,290	12,112	21,738	63,053	128,474
Others	66,523	78,490	61,225	90,908	201,032
Total	28,506,686	26,760,754	27,863,338	27,656,149	27,263,606

FACTORS AFFECTING VOTING BEHAVIOUR

In Britain there is a longstanding stability with regard to party loyalty. There are 630 M.P.s, and the number of marginal seats that may change hands on a fairly regular basis is between 25 and 35. The remainder are 'safe seats'. The majority of voters are committed to a particular party, as can be seen from the table showing the number of votes cast at general elections since 1951. They do not switch allegiance on the basis of party record. The factors that affect the way in which people cast their votes include:

1   Stereotypes: Each party has a core of voters, and according to the extent to which individuals identify with the image of the party, their votes may be cast accordingly. If an individual has a simplified image in his mind of what a particular party stands for and of what the typical supporter of that party is like, then he may vote for that party if he sees himself as fitting into that category of party supporter. In other words, it may be the image rather than the issues at stake which determines the way some people vote.

2   Social class and family background: These help to create the individual's impression of the type of person he is and how people like himself are expected to behave in all kinds of social situations. Where a person is strongly socialized into the normative patterns of his family group and class he is likely to cast his vote in the same way as his parents. The political parties in Britain have become closely associated with class groups owing to their historical development. The Labour Party was founded by the Trade Union Congress in 1900 in order to ensure a parliamentary voice for their particular policies and attitudes. The roots of the Conservative Party are in the wealthy middle and upper class sector of society, with the support of the traditional establishment, the Church, and the aristocracy. Consequently the images of the two parties have become allied to particular class groups and expectations in the electorate. The Conservative Party has become identified with the interests of business

253

and industry, with skill in foreign and colonial policy, free enterprise, and experienced leadership from the aristocracy and the professional class. The Labour Party has become identified with concern for the disadvantaged, social justice, and radical change and as the supporter of the rights of the poorest sector in society and the non-professional groups. But research has shown that about one third of working class voters support the Conservative Party. This has been explained in terms of deference – a belief in the voter that Conservatives are better leaders because they represent the more highly educated section of society. There is also the fact that such voters may see themselves as middle class people, because they have relatively high incomes and have attained many of the middle class trappings of high social and economic status. But Lockwood and Goldthorpe found in their study that although they may have believed themselves to be middle class, in fact they did not hold the middle class attitudes and there was little social intermixing between executives and workers, even though they lived on the same housing estates.

3   Religion: This is not such a significant factor in Britain as in some other countries, but it has been shown that the traditional association between the Conservative Party and the Church of England remains to some extent; and there is a tendency for more Roman Catholics to vote for the Labour party.

4   Age and sex: Youth is not significantly more radical than the older generation. Over two thirds of young voters vote in the same way as their parents. The Conservative vote is predominantly middle aged and female. Men tend to vote more radically than women at all ages and in all classes.

5   The mass media: Research shows that the mass media do not appear to have a great influence in changing attitudes. They do help to inform and educate, but serve largely to reinforce existing views.

The cumulative effect of all these factors is reinforced still further by the influence of friends and associates both at work and in clubs and social situations. In adult life group membership and identification becomes an important source of influence. In youth the peer group is significant. These influences guide people in their thinking about themselves and others, and they establish and reinforce patterns of normative behaviour which affect the choices and actions of the individual.

RESEARCH
Political Change in Britain, by Butler & Stokes

The book identifies the long and short term influences on the way people vote. The largest single consideration is class. More people than ever seem to be voting on class lines, although with less intensity of feeling about 'us' and 'them'. Next as a significant influence has been found to be the political nature of the home environment in which the individual grows up. Where the household are fervent Conservatives or Socialists it is highly likely that first votes will be cast by young voters in the same way.

The authors introduce the concept of 'differential fertility' and 'selective death' into their book. At present the oldest generation is predominantly Conservative, so that deaths in that generation are working against the Conservative Party. Meanwhile, many more people are being born into Labour homes than used to be the case. To support this view, the authors analyse the swing between the 1959 and the 1964 elections which shows the extent to which the changes in the balance of the population affected the result.

The Decline of Working Class Politics, by Hindess
Hindess attempts to explain why more and more of the working class sector of society are becoming increasingly less interested in party politics. Previous studies have shown that as many as two thirds of working class voters traditionally vote Labour, a large section vote Tory, and the remainder abstain. He examines the reasons for the growing abstentions. He locates a circle of decline in political activity in the more working class areas of cities, which results in a shift in power towards the more middle class areas. 'This in turn leads to a further decline in the more working class areas. This process, whereby political power at the city level becomes concentrated in the middle class areas, results in the appearance of a substantial degree of agreement between the different parties and in the political isolation of substantial sections of the population.' He argues that the relationship between class and voting behaviour seems to be breaking down, and produces evidence from election results and opinion polls conducted since 1966. Working class people seem to be losing the belief that political action can achieve change.

EXERCISES
1   Explain the meaning and characteristics of (*a*) democracy and (*b*) dictatorship.

2   Outline the historical background of (*a*) the Liberal Party, (*b*) the Conservative Party, (*c*) the Labour Party.

3   Explain the underlying philosophies of the three Parties.

4   Explain (*a*) Socialism, (*b*) Capitalism, (*c*) Communism, (*d*) Fascism.

5   Suggest a cause for which you might organize a pressure group. How would you organize it to ensure success?

6   There seems to be a lack of interest in politics in Britain. Why might this be so?

7   It is argued that if all voters voted on class lines the Labour Party would not have lost an election this century. Why is this so?

ESSAY QUESTIONS

1   What are the factors that affect the way in which people vote in Britain?

2   Abstainers and floating voters have become known as 'target voters'. Why is this so?

3   What are pressure groups? How do they recruit their members and what is the source of their power?

4   Outline the main types of political system that have operated in Europe since 1900. Contrast the system that has operated in Britain. What are the strengths and weaknesses of the various systems?

Definitions of Sociological Terms

ALIENATION — The loss of the individual's sense of worth and self-esteem. The associated factors are those of powerlessness, meaninglessness, isolation, and self-estrangement. Usually applies to the worker involved in impersonal and dehumanizing work.

ANOMIE — A loss of function or role; confusion of values and identity in society. Related to patterns of suicide and mental disorder in modern society.

ANTHROPOLOGY — A social science concerned with the comparative study of the evolution of man, his culture and social life. Often undertaken by way of field study of simple societies.

ATTITUDE — The learned response made by an individual towards an object or situation. There is an emotional and a reasoned aspect. The standpoint taken on an issue enables the individual to respond to other related situations in a consistent way.

AUTOMATION — Production and control by machine with minimum of human supervision.

BELIEF — An idea about what is true and right for the individual. Beliefs and attitudes form the structure of a person's perception of the world and his role standing and actions in it.

BIRTH RATE — The ratio of total live births to the total population, which is usually expressed in births per thousand of the population.

BLUE COLLAR WORKERS — Manual workers of all types, particularly in a factory situation.

CAPITALISM — An economic system in which the means of production is in the hands of private individuals who are free to employ labour and

257

	accumulate profits. It is possible to obtain unearned income through investments in property, land, etc.
CASTE	Society is divided into social groups, membership of which determines occupation, status, place of residence, etc. Membership is based on heredity, and movement between groups is not possible. In this sense caste society is said to be closed.
CHANGE (social)	There may be alterations to a part of the social system through reform or to the entire system by way of revolution. There may be changes in attitude, fashion, or ways of behaving as a result of innovations by opinion leaders who establish new trends.
CLASS (social)	The classification of the population into broad groups, which are ranked in socially superior and inferior positions, on the basis of objective criteria (generally, occupation, attitudes, life style). Movement between groups is possible.
CONCEPTS	Ideas concerning the attributes of a specific category to be analysed (e.g., the concept of social class involves a consideration of power and status in order to understand its full implications).
CONFORMITY	Behaviour which is acceptable to the group or society as a whole.
CONURBATION	A large area of dense urban settlement including city and suburbs.
CORRELATION	The connection or interrelationship between two measurable variables, so that a change in one is connected with a change in the other (e.g., class background and rate of delinquency).
CRIME	Any act prohibited by law; any serious offence against people or property.
CULTURE (social)	All those accepted ways of behaving and of organization in a society which are transmitted from one generation to the next.
DEATH RATE	The ratio of total deaths to the total population — usually expressed in deaths per thousand of the population.
DELINQUENT	Juvenile law breaker (aged 14—17).
DEMOCRACY	Government freely chosen by and responsible to the governed.

DEVIANT	Failing to conform to the norms of the group or of society at large.
DICTATORSHIP	Government by a single person, class, or group whose authority is total and allows no organized opposition.
DIFFERENTIATION (social)	Categorizing the population according to particular criteria, age, sex, race, class, etc.
EDUCATION	The constant ongoing process wherby information, knowledge, and skills are transmitted in a formal and informal way to individuals to fit them for life in the society.
ELITE	A small group holding particular power and privilege over others.
EMPIRICAL	Proof based on experiment or observation.
EXTRINSIC	Of value, outside and extraneous (e.g. the extrinsic value of work may be monetary reward).
FAMILY	A group of closely related people, consisting of parents, children, and other kin members. A universal social institution.
FOLKWAYS	Traditionally accepted ways of behaving; organized or repetitive forms of behaviour (e.g., shaking hands).
FUNCTION	The purposes and consequences of an item within the social framework (the function of marriage may be said to be to legalize and formalize a relationship and to provide for increased social stability).
FUNCTIONALISM	The analysis of social phenomena in terms of the functions they serve. The entire social system is seen as an interrelated unit in which every part has a specific function, so that a change in one part will cause a change in another.
GROUP (social)	Two or more persons linked in a common purpose, behaviour, or interest.
HIERARCHY	Ranking in order of superiority according to some criteria.
HYPOTHESIS	A guess or tentative statement of belief to explain an occurrence which can then be tested for verification.
IDEAL TYPE	A concept consisting of all the characteristic elements of the social feature being analysed. It is helpful to be able to compare the reality that is being observed with the idealized concept of the same feature.

IDEOLOGY | A belief system which governs the behaviour and attitudes of the group which hold the values, since they are accepted as being correct and true. (Beliefs in democracy, communism, religion, etc. may be said to be examples of ideologies.)

INDUSTRIAL SOCIETY | Characterized by technological inovation, machine power, the factory system, and a developed economic and monetary system.

INSTITUTION | A socially approved or accepted custom or organization which establishes relevant patterns of behaviour (e.g., marriage, religion, education, etc.).

INSTRUMENTAL | Being the means by which other things are obtained.

INTERACTION | The relationship through language and gesture between two or more people.

INTRINSIC | Containing something of value within itself; having inherent merit or value.

LEISURE | Time free from the formal duties which paid work imposes.

MAGIC | The ability to manipulate forces over which there is normally no human power, by use of spells, potions, incantations, etc. Magic seeks to compel the powers of nature to obey man.

MARRIAGE | A social institution which formerly legalizes the relationship between the parties and provides certain rights and duties which facilitate the functioning of family life.

MASS MEDIA | All those methods of communication which make it possible to communicate with large numbers of people at the same time: the press, broadcasting, cinema, etc.

METHOD (of sociology) | The approaches of the sociologist by which he acquires information, tests hypotheses, and makes analytical studies of social features. Researchers make use of question-naires, surveys, official statistics, observation, etc.

MOBILITY (social) | The ability to move up or down through class or status groups.

MONOGAMY | One man is married to one woman.

MORES | Highly valued or esteemed norms (e.g., marriage).

NORMS | Patterns of accepted behaviour in a group or

in a society to which members are expected to conform.

OBJECTIVITY — The ability of the investigator to make observations and reports without allowing them to be coloured by the attitudes and personal beliefs of the researcher.

ORGANIZATION (social) — The relationships between individuals and institutions in society which make for stability, and which are based on accepted normative patterns of behaviour.

PEER GROUP — Others of similar age and social background with whom a person mixes in a social context.

POLITICAL PARTIES — Organized groups concerned with the way in which the society should be governed and power distributed.

POLYANDRY — A type of polygamous marriage in which one woman may be married to several men at the same time.

POLYGYNY — A type of polygamous marriage in which one man may be married to several women at the same time.

POVERTY — A relative term but used in general to mean having insufficient income to meet the bare necessities of life. For the purpose of welfare benefits there is an official poverty line which varies according to individual circumstances, income, size of family, outgoings, etc.

POWER — The ability to implement policies and influence the behaviour of others.

PREJUDICE — To prejudge an issue, having already formed opinions and attitudes, often without recourse to facts and evidence.

PRESSURE GROUPS — Organized groups with common interests working to obtain information from those whose policies they wish to influence. They tend to have specific areas of interest (unlike the broadly based political parties) and often disband once their objective has been achieved. They may be divided into Promotional Groups and Defensive Groups.

PRESTIGE — A high degree of social standing within a group or in society on the basis of some ability or achievement which carries respect and recognition from others.

PRIMARY GROUP	Those intimate relations and friends with whom a person mixes on a face-to-face and personal basis.
PROFESSIONAL GROUPS	Members of Class 1 in the Registrar General's scale, being those in the 'professions'. They include doctors, lawyers, professors, and other highly qualified individuals. Their occupation is recognized as one requiring academic qualifications and subject to control by an organizing body with wide powers and authority (e.g., the Law Society).
RATIONAL	Through reason; logical argument or behaviour.
REFERENCE GROUP	The group with which a person compares his own standing, behaviour, and levels of pay, and which he may use to help define his attitudes and values.
RELIGION	A system of beliefs, emotional attitudes, and practices by means of which an individual or group of people attempts to cope with and come to terms with the problems of life.
RITUAL	Customs having symbolic significance and usually signalling important events.
ROLE	Behaviour patterns prescribed by occupation or position in society or by the expectations held by others.
SANCTION	A penalty aimed at discouraging certain types of behaviour.
SCIENCE	The quest for knowledge and understanding according to logical and methodologically sound principles.
SCIENTIFIC METHOD	The principles by which the scientist operates: the identification of a problem; hypothesis by way of explanation; experiment to test the hypothesis; analysis of results; retesting results; reporting findings and conclusions; the establishment of a theory to verify or disprove the hypothesis which explains the phenomena.
SECULAR SOCIETY	A society whose values are rational and scientific and have limited reference to the sacred or spiritual.
SELF ACTUALIZATION	To realize a sense of worth and potential and to obtain fulfilment and satisfaction from an endeavour, work, etc.

SOCIAL BEHAVIOUR	Behaviour which is affected by another person or group.
SOCIAL CONTROL	The formal and informal methods by which a society exerts control over its members. They include: family, education, religion, legal sanctions, and the power of public opinion. Those who deviate from the social norms risk ridicule and ostracism or legal punishment.
SOCIALIZATION	The process by which an individual becomes integrated into a group by adopting its norms and values, so that he obtains a sense of identity and role within the group and is accepted as a member.
SOCIAL SCIENCES	Those disciplines which study human beings and their social organization in a scientific way. They include sociology, psychology, economics, and anthropology.
SOCIAL STABILITY	Change occurs slowly and through accepted means, so that society remains in a state of equilibrium and order.
SOCIETY	Consists of individuals, groups, and institutions and their relationships to each other — resulting in an organized social life.
SOCIOLOGY	The scientific study and analysis of society, social behaviour, and organization. A scientific approach is adopted in order to test hypotheses and establish theories to predict and explain social phenomena.
STATUS	The degree of prestige and deference held by an individual in different groups to which he may belong. A person can have many statuses (captain of a football team, owner of an expensive car, etc.). Each status position is expressed in terms of a role, an expected pattern of behaviour. Status obtained through skill and endeavour is said to be 'achieved'; status acquired by virtue of birth, family background, etc. is said to be 'ascribed'.
STEREOTYPE	The tendency to take particular characteristics in an individual (nationality, features, etc.) and assume that they are totally representative of his character and nature. Although it is inaccurate and oversimplified

it is a strongly held belief because it is probably shared by the individual's reference group.

STRATIFICATION
Ranking in society according to certain social differences such as power, wealth, privilege. Systems of stratification include class, caste, and slavery.

STRUCTURE (social)
The interrelated parts of a society which form a framework for social organization.

SUBCULTURE
The culture of a specific sector of society which differs in certain ways from the culture of the rest of society (e.g., criminal subculture).

TABOO
The prohibition of certain actions punishable by the group or community.

THEORY
An attempt to provide a predictive and systematic explanation of an event which is open to test and retest.

URBANIZATION
Refers to the growth of cities, the increase in scale of a society, and the culture of city dwellers.

VARIABLES
Social features which vary: age, sex, class, race, etc.

VOTING BEHAVIOUR
The facts with regard to the way in which people cast their votes and the influences which affect such decisions.

WHITE COLLAR WORKERS
Clerical and other indoor, office workers whose work is largely non-managerial and non-manual.

WORK
The disciplined activity, which in modern complex societies provides the means of livelihood, and which subjects the worker to certain regulations by which he is contractually bound.

YOUTH CULTURE
Particular behaviour patterns common to the youthful section of society and different from those of the older generation.

Resources and Books for Reference

Resources

It is useful to illustrate aspects of the topics studied in the course with films, filmstrips, project kits, and other audio-visual aids. Magazines and specialized publications are also available. Some of the sources of such material are listed below together with some examples of the resources provided.

Concord Films, 201 Felixstow Road, Ipswich.
A non-profit making organization with a wide variety of films available (including some recent television productions). An illustrated booklet containing their list is published, price 25p. Some of their films include:

The Block — a B.B.C. film showing the effects of poor housing and poor social environment on the people living in a tenement in London.
75 minutes. £6.00.
Not in Our Class, Dear. A study of class divisions in Britain.
30 minutes. £2.00.

Concordia Films, Concordia House, 117–123 Golden Lane, London EC1Y 0TL.
Poverty film strip, with 5 inch tape. £1.75.

Educational Audio Visual Ltd, 30 Drayton Park, London N5 1PB.

Common Ground Filmstrips, published by the Longman Group Ltd, Pinnacles, Harlow, Essex.
A wide variety, including *Social Changes* (in two parts) and *A History of Justice*.

Educational Productions Ltd, East Ardsley, Wakefield, Yorkshire.
Comparative Religion (four religions are studied, and an audiovisual tape is available), *Tradition and Change*, and *Meet your Neighbour*.

Sunday Times (*film strips*): Times Newspapers, 200 Grays Inn Road, London WC1X 8EZ.
Religion and the Permissive Society, Mass Communications, Marriage, The Welfare State.

Social Education, published by Macmillan on behalf of the North-West
Regional Curriculum Development Project.
Macmillan Educational, Houndsmills, Basingstoke, Hampshire.
The kits provide material for discussion and research on relevant topics
and include filmstrips and tapes. Titles include:
Towards Tomorrow and *The British*. £14.25 each.

New Society Magazine, 128 Long Acre, London WC1V 7BA. Useful articles
on current social developments. There is a group purchase scheme by
which the magazine can be obtained at half the normal price where ten
or more copies are ordered.

The National Council of Social Service,
26 Bedford Square, London WC1B 3HU.
This organization issues a wide range of publications on various aspects
of the social services, many of which can be used as specific class texts,
projects, and background material. A publication catalogue is available
on request.

Activity Factsheets, published by Thomas Nelson and Sons Ltd, 36 Park
Street, London W1Y 4DE.
Valuable as a source of factual data and in stimulating class discussion
and debate.

Books for Reference

There are a great number of books available which cover all areas of
sociology, some very detailed and intended for higher study. However,
it is important that the student who is starting sociology should become
familiar with the names of sociologists and their books and articles. It
is necessary to do as much reading as possible around the topics of study
and an attempt should be made, therefore, to read some specific studies.
Here are some suggestions.

Berger, Peter L., *Invitation to Sociology* (Penguin, 1970)
Worsley, Peter, *Introducing Sociology* (Penguin, 1970)
Ogburn, William F., *A Handbook of Sociology* (Routledge and Kegan Paul,
    1960)
Butterworth, Eric, and David Weir, *The Sociolgy of Modern Britain* (Fontana,
    1970).
Farmer, Mary, *The Family* (Longman, 1970)
Dominian, Jacob, *Marital Breakdown* (Penguin, 1968)
Fletcher, Ronald, *Family and Marriage in Britain* (Penguin, 1969)
Willmott, Peter, and Michael Young, *Family and Kinship in East London*
    (Penguin, 1969)

Willmott, Peter, and Michael Young, *Family and Class in a London Suburb* (New English Library, 1971)

Parkin, Frank, *Class, Inequality and Social Order* (1972, out of print)

Douglas, J. W. B., *The Home and the School* (Panther, 1969)

King, Ronald A., *Education* (Longman, 1969)

Jackson, Brian, and D. Marsden, *Education and the Working Class* (Penguin, 1969)

Townsend, Peter, and D. Wedderburn, *The Aged in the Welfare State* (Bell, 1965)

Rodgers, B., *The Battle against Poverty* (Routledge and Kegan Paul, 1969)

Abel-Smith, Brian, and Peter Townsend, *The Poor and the Poorest* (Bell, 1965)

Halloran, J. D., *The Mass Media* (Longman, 1974)

Parker, Stanley, *The Future of Work and Leisure* (1972, out of print)

Mays, John Barron, *Crime and its Treatment* (Longman, 1970)

Yinger, J. Milton, *Sociology Looks at Religion* (Collier-Macmillan, 1963)

Pahl, Raymond Edward, *Patterns of Urban Life* (Longman, 1970)

Rose, Richard, *Studies in British Politics* (Macmillan, 1969)

Jones, Grace Anstice, *The Political Structure* (Longman, 1969)

Wright, Christopher, *The Working Class* (Batsford, 1972)

Reader, W. J., *The Middle Class* (Batsford, 1972)

Lane, Peter, *The Upper Class* (Batsford, 1972)

Kelsall, R., *Population* (Longman, 1972)

Index